Teaching through
Self~instruction

Teaching through Self-instruction

A Practical Handbook for Course Developers

Derek Rowntree
Professor of Educational Development
The Open University

 NP

**Kogan Page, London/Nichols Publishing
Company, New York**

Author's Note:

You will notice that this book has not been set in type.
Instead, it has been reproduced by offset litho using
the author's original typescript as "camera ready copy".
We did this for two reasons:

1. To set in type a book as large as this would have
    been very costly, and you would have had to pay a
    perhaps prohibitive price for your copy.

2. Equally important, we hope the production quality
    will reassure you that you don't need high-tech
    printing technology to produce self-instructional
    materials and that perfectly adequate results can
    be obtained using a typewriter and the kinds of
    low-cost methods of reproduction available to most
    educational and training establishments.

First published in Great Britain in 1986 by Kogan Page Ltd
120 Pentonville Road, London N1 9JN
Reprinted 1988

British Library Cataloguing in Publication Data

Rowntree, Derek
    Teaching through self-instruction: a practical
    handbook for course developers.
    1. Individualized instruction
    I. Title
    371.3'944   LB1031

    ISBN 1-85091-148-7

Library of Congress Cataloging-in-Publication Data

Rowntree, Derek.
    Teaching through self-instruction.

    1. Distance education.   2. Self-culture.   I. Title.
    LC5800.R68   1986   371.4   86-5163
    ISBN 0-89397-250-9

Printed and bound in Great Britain by
Biddles Ltd, Guildford and King's Lynn

CONTENTS

Chapter 1: Getting to Grips With Self-instruction 9

Two Basic Distinctions 10
What Can You Expect from this Book ? 13

Chapter 2: Organizing for Course Development 19

Who is to Produce the Course ? 19
Co-ordinating Group Activity 23
Could You Adapt an Existing Course ? 30
Course Maintenance 32

**Chapter 3: Planning Your Teaching -- Learners
and Content** 35

A Framework for Planning 35
Who Will be the Learners ? 39
What Aims and Objectives ? 43
Deciding on Content 48

**Chapter 4: Planning Your Teaching -- Sequence
and Methods** 61

Sequencing the Learning 61
Choosing Your Teaching Media 72
Assessment and Evaluation 76
A Lesson Specification 79

Chapter 5: Writing a Self-instructional Lesson 81

Teaching Through Self-instruction 81
Why Not Use Existing Materials ? 87
Sample Pages from Self-instructional Texts 91

Chapter 6: Promoting Active Learning 119

Teaching Through Activities 120
How to Develop Activities 126

Chapter 7: Structuring Your Lesson   137

    Remember Your Outline   137
    Teaching Concepts and Principles   138
    Two Basic Teaching Strategies   148
    Variety of Stimulus   152

Chapter 8: Easing Your Reader's Access   163

    Access Devices   163
    Before the Lesson   164
    During the Lesson   168
    After the Lesson   176

Chapter 9: Teaching With Pictures   181

    Getting Away from Solid Prose   181
    Why Use Pictures ?   190
    Guidelines for Using Pictures   198

Chapter 10: Making Your Lesson Readable   207

    The Conversational Style   207
    Writing Plainly   211
    Measuring Readability   229

Chapter 11: Introducing Other Media   233.

    Practical Work   234
    Audio Material   242
    Video Material   250
    Media Notes   257
    Computer Teaching   261
    Human Media   266
    Final Media Checklist   272

Chapter 12: The Physical Format of Your Lessons   275

    Packaging Your Lessons   275
    Four Methods of Text Production   278
    Layout   281
    Typography   289

Chapter 13: Assessing Your Learners   301

    The Nature of Assessment   301
    The Purposes of Assessment   302
    What to Assess ?   304
    Methods of Assessment   305
    How to Use Assessment Results   321

Chapter 14: Evaluating Your Lessons   333

    What is Evaluation ?   333
    Critical Commenting   334
    Developmental Testing   338
    Continuous Monitoring   350
    Using Evaluation Data   356
    Final Checklist for Lesson Evaluation   359

Chapter 15: Starting, Keeping Going, and
                Finishing Off   361

    Starting to Write   361
    Editing Your First Rough Draft   363
    Typing Your Draft   365
    Getting Copyright Permissions   368
    Correcting Your Proofs   373
    Towards a Final Draft   378

Index   379

1. GETTING TO GRIPS WITH SELF-INSTRUCTION

Self-instructional teaching seems to be cropping up everywhere these days. Keen-eyed connoisseurs of the absurd will have noticed that even the infant hero of the film *Superman* was kept sensibly occupied by a distance learning course throughout his intergalactic journey from Krypton to Smallsville.

Who uses S-I ?

And, in the real world, correspondence colleges continue to flourish; more and more schools, colleges and universities are requiring students to do some of their learning from specially-prepared teaching materials (and some, like Britain's Open University, have thousands of students working from self-instruction only); and much professional, military and industrial training is now accomplished through pre-packaged courses.

The spreading of S-I

I assume you are reading this book because you are interested in teaching through self-instruction. Teachers and trainers are becoming increasingly involved with self-instruction -- not least because it enables them to reach learners they would otherwise be unable to reach, but also because it offers benefits that are not obtainable from classroom instruction. These teachers and trainers may know self-instruction by any of a variety of pet names, like:

The many names of S-I

o distance education
o packaged learning
o Keller Plan
o open learning
o flexistudy
o independent/individualized learning
o Postlethwaite system
o home study
o supported self study
o computer based training/computer aided instruction

o   directed private study
o   programmed instruction/learning
o   correspondence education
o   learning by appointment
o   resource-based learning...and so on.

I don't intend to go into detail about each of these forms
of self-instruction. You will know which one you are
likely to be involved with -- perhaps it even goes by yet

*This book
concerns
all S-I*

another name in your institution. And what I have to say
in this book is relevant to any kind of self-instruction.

TWO BASIC DISTINCTIONS

Although I do not intend to describe every variety of
self-instruction, there are a couple of basic distinctions
I must make clear:

Distance v On-site Self-instruction

Some forms of self-instruction cater for learners who are

*Forms of
distance
learning*

learning "at a distance". That is to say, the learners
will not be in regular contact with the teachers who
design the courses. Indeed they may have little or no
face-to-face contact with any teachers at all -- or even
with other learners. "Correspondence education" is
typical of this form, and so is much "open learning".

*S-I courses
"on site"*

Other forms of self-instruction are used on the
premises of the institution that is sponsoring the course
-- e.g. in a college laboratory, a civil service office,
or the staff room in a retail store. With such "on-site"
self-instruction, learners may still see little or
nothing of the teachers who produced the course. But at
least they may be able to meet one another, and perhaps
someone more experienced who can guide their studies. In
this category we may encounter, for example, "learning
by appointment", Keller Plan and Postlethwaite courses,
and a wide variety of package-based training schemes.

Reliance on pre-recorded teaching

Whether "on-site" or "at a distance", learners working with self-instruction have one important thing in common. Because they have much less contact with a teacher than "normal" learners do, they rely very heavily on **specially prepared teaching materials**. That is, the teaching will have been largely pre-planned, pre-recorded, and pre-packaged. It will be presented in instructional texts, audiotapes, videotapes, assignment exercises, and so on.

Self-instruction v "Conventional" Instruction

With normal or "conventional" instruction, learners meet together regularly in classes, and much of their learning is done face-to-face with a teacher. Although they may also spend a considerable amount of time learning on their own (more perhaps than they spend in class), this will usually involve them in using materials that **already** exist -- e.g. books and journals. That is, their private study materials will not have been created especially for them, with **their** particular course needs in mind. Furthermore,

Learning from existing materials

v

Materials designed to teach

their teachers may make little or no attempt to structure that side of their studies.

Self-instruction, on the other hand, depends on materials specially written -- or at least specially selected and modified -- with particular course objectives in mind. Furthermore, they will be structured in such a way that learners can do most, if not all, their learning from the materials alone. The materials must carry out all the functions a teacher would carry out in the conventional situation -- guiding, motivating, intriguing, expounding, explaining, provoking, reminding, asking questions, discussing alternative answers, appraising each learner's progress, giving appropriate remedial or enrichment help...and so on.

A self-instructional system may, of course, encourage learners to make occasional contact with a tutor. It may

even **demand** that they do so. But the contact will be
slight, compared with that in conventional instruction.

Only slight
contact
with tutors
teachers...

For instance, learners working at a distance may have no
contact other than by mailing occasional assignments to
a teacher and getting the teacher's written comments
some time later. Of course, they may also be expected
to speak to the teacher on the telephone from time to
time. They may even be expected to meet teachers for a
seminar or tutorial occasionally, or even for a weekend

in distance
learning:

workshop or residential summer school.

Similarly, on-site learners may find that a series of
self-instructional sessions is topped and tailed by a
group meeting with a teacher. They may also be expected

in S-I
on-site:

to complete regular progress tests that are checked
(perhaps in their presence) by a teacher or by a more
advanced learner acting as "proctor". Even one-to-one
remedial tuition may be available for learners who are
having untoward difficulties in coping with the
self-instructional materials.

Apart from teachers and materials, learners can learn

Learning from
one another...

a great deal from one another. This will be especially
the case in professional training and in aesthetic or
social areas -- e.g. in sales training, literary criticism,
or child-rearing. Here, learners benefit from the
realization that other people's values and beliefs and
experiences lead them to see things differently. But

may not be
possible for
S-I learners

face-to-face interaction with their peers may not be
readily available to learners working with
self-instruction -- especially when they are learning
at a distance, perhaps dispersed over a wide geographical

Can materials
compensate ?

area. So self-instructional materials may need to
compensate for lack of contact with other learners as
well as with teachers.

Finally, it is worth remarking that even a largely

Mixed courses

"conventional" course or teaching system may incorporate
some self-instruction. Thus, the learners may take one

or two courses in packaged form, while the bulk of their
courses are conventional. Similarly, even within an
otherwise conventional course, the teacher may have
prepared or obtained self-instructional materials to help

Using S-I
selectively

learners with some of the topics that are difficult to
teach to a group -- perhaps because different learners
master different bits of them at different speeds, or
because they require demonstrations that not everyone in
the group would be able to see at the same time.

```
****************************************************
*                                                *
*   SELF-INSTRUCTION MAY BE AN ALTERNATIVE        *
*                                                *
*   TO OTHER FORMS OF TEACHING.                   *
*                                                *
*   BUT IT CAN BE COMBINED WITH THEM.             *
*                                                *
****************************************************
```

WHAT CAN YOU EXPECT FROM THIS BOOK ?

Before we get into the details of developing
self-instructional materials, I'd better let you know
what I'm trying to do in this book. I'll say a few words
about what I'm assuming your interests might be, about what

Where are
we going ?

my own background is, and about the aims and objectives of
this book and how you might wish to use it.

Who Are You ?

I assume you are someone who needs **practical** advice on
teaching with self-instruction. You may be, for example:

Who are my
readers ?

  - a school-teacher, helping students learn from
    specialist materials that were largely produced,
    perhaps, by other teachers;

  - a college or university lecturer, introducing
    self-instruction on campus or developing a
    distance or open learning scheme;

  - a trainer or instructor in business or the civil
    service, producing training packages for the benefit

of trainees who cannot easily be brought
together to form a class; or

- an author or editor, preparing self-instructional
materials for a publisher or correspondence colleege.

The ideas I discuss in this book should be of value to
people in any of the above groups -- and maybe in others
I have not thought about. Throughout the book, I shall
use the word **"teacher"** to stand for teacher/lecturer/coach/
tutor/trainer/instructor/author, etc. -- just as I shall
use **"learner"** to stand for any kind of student, trainee,
or reader in search of systematic enlightenment.

"Teachers"
& "learners"

I assume that you are an experienced teacher. This
book is not an introduction to teaching as such. It is
a guide to applying what you know of teaching to a new
enterprise. All the same, if you are to make your
teaching "public" in the form of self-instructional
materials, you may find yourself agonizing over aspects
of teaching and learning that you have never needed to
pay much attention to before.

Rethinking
teaching and
learning

Who Am I ?

I have been working in self-instruction for more than
25 years -- writing materials myself, running training
workshops for intending writers, editing or rewriting
the work of other writers, and helping teachers rethink
their courses in terms of distance learning and other
forms of self-instruction.

A quarter
century
of S-I !

Throughout the 1960s, I was concerned with programmed
learning. I wrote programmes, and helped others to
write them, in a wide variety of topics, some for use
in schools and colleges, some in industrial or
professional training. My first book (*Basically Branching,*
1966) was actually a forerunner to this one, being a guide
to writing programmed learning materials.

Programmed
learning

*The
educational
technology
approach...*

Towards the end of the 1960s, like many of my colleagues at the time, I realized that the principles of programmed learning might have wider applications in helping people learn. I put them to use, and extended them, in developing the new approach that became known (rather unfortunately, I think) as "educational technology".

*in the
Open
University*

Since 1970, I have been pursuing that approach in Britain's Open University -- the world-famous pioneer in distance learning in post-secondary education. Here I have been concerned with understanding the processes of teaching and learning through self-instruction in order to develop effective materials and systems myself, and help others to do so. The teaching I have been involved with ranges from year-long courses in literature, history

*Courses of
all sorts
and sizes*

or psychology for undergraduates to short packs and courses (15-100 hours of learning time) for family doctors, managers, and social workers.

I have taught in secondary school, teacher-training college, polytechnic and university, and have been a consultant on training to many industrial or public service organizations (from family planning, through

*Variety of
situation...*

coal mining to the Civil Service). So my ideas about self-instruction relate to a wide variety of learning situations. Similarly, my experience with a wide range

*and of
subjects*

of subject-matter has assured me that I can give useful advice to a teacher planning self-instruction, whatever his or her chosen topic.

The Aims and Objectives of this Book

The overall aims of this book are to help you gain sufficient confidence to start producing self-instructional

*How might
you gain ?*

materials and to help improve your ability to teach with such materials.

More specifically, in terms of objectives, I hope you will begin to work towards improvement in the following areas:

Our objectives
in this book

o   Formulating aims and objectives for whatever
    materiala you plan to produce.

o   Identifying the skills, knowledge and attitudes
    that learners will possess before starting upon
    your materials.

o   Being realistic about the constraints within which
    you and your learners must work.

o   Choosing the subject content of your materials
    and deciding how it might best be sequenced to
    help the learners learn.

o   Selecting appropriate teaching media and deciding
    how they may be effectively combined.

o   Using the media effectively to produce
    self-instructional teaching from which the learners
    do learn.

o   Designing assessment tests or situations that will
    give a fair indication of what your learners have
    learned.

o   Evaluating your materials by critical analysis and
    by trying them out on learners.

o   Improving your materials (and the system within
    which they are used) in the light of evaluation.

Seeking your
own answers

No standard
solutions

This book is meant to raise questions -- questions you
will recognize as so important that you must seek out
answers that are right for you in your situation.   In
other words, I am trying to provide a stimulus to your
thinking and decision-making -- which is likely to
continue developing over a period of several months, or
even years.   I am not offering a set of hand-me-down,
ready-made, all-purpose solutions.   There are none.

How to Use this Book

One thing we do know about distance learning materials is
that we can't rely on learners paying too much attention
to suggestions we make under a heading like the one
above. Different people use the same material differently.

*My chapter
order is not
sacrosanct*

All I want to do here is assure you that there is no
need for you to read the chapters in the order in which
I've presented them. Of course, I think that order is
reasonably logical, and many readers will be content to
start at the beginning and work their way through to the
end. But I have taken care to write the later chapters
in such a way that you'll be able to follow them even if
you have not worked through earlier ones.

*Decide your
own sequence*

So, have a quick skim through the book to see what is
dealt with where. (Note particularly the sample pages of
self-instructional material in Chapter 5.) Then, if you
don't feel like following my sequence, feel free to
plunge into whichever chapters or sections deal with the
issues that concern you most at present. The other
chapters can wait until you're ready for them.

*Using the
book with
other people*

The book may also be used as the basis for a series of
workshops, under the guidance of someone more experienced
in producing self-instructional materials. Or it may
serve simply as the common reference point for a group of
colleagues learning the art of self-instruction together
by discussing common problems and commenting on one
another's work. Either way, learn what you can from
other people's approaches -- but don't expect any of
them to be entirely appropriate to your needs.

```
*************************************************
*                                               *
*  THERE IS NO ONE RIGHT WAY TO DEVELOP          *
*  SELF-INSTRUCTIONAL MATERIALS.                 *
*  BUT THERE ARE LOTS OF WRONG WAYS.             *
*  I HOPE THIS BOOK WILL HELP YOU AVOID THEM.    *
*                                               *
*************************************************
```

2. ORGANIZING FOR COURSE DEVELOPMENT

What is a course ?

To avoid undue discussion here, let's say that a course is a planned sequence of "learning experiences", occupying several learning sessions, and involving some form of assessment of the learner's work. Thus, a course may occupy the learner for a few hours only or for several months; and the assessment may be provided by you (the course developer), by a tutor who may or may not be guided by you, or by some external body. You may be responsible for producing all of such a course or just for part of it. Either way, what stages of production will the course need to pass through ?

WHO IS TO PRODUCE THE COURSE ?

Solo or teamwork ?

Either you will be producing the course on your own or you will be working with one or more colleagues.

Individual Authorship

On your own

Working on your own may appear to have certain clear advantages, along with a number of disadvantages.

Advantages.

o You will have maximum freedom as to content, treatment, treatment, sequence, level, production schedule, etc.

o The course will hang together as a coherent whole, with no obvious gaps or undue repetitions.

o You will not need to use up time in discussions with other authors, or emotional energy in defending your chosen content and method.

o So, you may produce the course using fewer hours, in total, than if several people were working together.

o Since you will know the course as a whole you should be in a better position to adapt and up-date various parts of it in response to learners' experience with it.

Disadvantages.

o You may feel exposed and isolated, especially if
   self-instruction is a new venture in your institution
   or department.

o you may feel that biases or limitations in your
   subject-matter knowledge or teaching experience may
   lead to the course being less effective than you
   would wish.

o You may feel the lack of technical experience in
   such areas as typography, graphics, or audio-recordin

o You may feel you cannot carry out all the tasks
   connected with producing the whole course within
   the time period available.

Getting help

Perhaps you could overcome some of these disadvantages by
obtaining some **informal** help. That is, while retaining
full responsibility for the course yourself, you could
invite comments and advice -- which you would be free to
disregard ! -- from other subject-matter experts, from
educational specialists, from editors, designers, and so on

Commissioning contributions

You could even commission other authors to produce
materials for **your** course, working to a more-or-less precis
specification that you have provided them with. You may
even retain the right not to use their material or to
edit it as you choose.   For some of the readers of this
text, I expect, the boot will be on the other foot; that is
you may have been engaged on just such a basis to
contribute to someone else's course

Course Teams

Working with colleagues

When colleagues join together in a more democratic,
equal-status group to produce a course, they form what is
generally known as a course team. Course teams were
pioneered by the Open University and have become popular

elsewhere. A team may include one or more course authors and one or more of the people listed below:

Course team roles

o   *Convenor/Chair.* Person responsible for overall quality of the course (both in subject-matter content and in educational effectiveness) -- and for getting it produced within a budget. May also be a course author and may have no formal power over other team members.

o   *Course authors.* Subject specialists, maybe from more than one department or institution who will be responsible for planning the course, writing texts, devising audio-visual materials or practical exercises, as well as producing assessment and examination materials and perhaps preparing to act as tutors once the course is being used by learners. Some may be seen as part of the "central" or "core" course team, some as "externals", with the latter perhaps having little influence in how the course develops.

o   *Media producer.* Professional with special skills in the technical production of television material, audio-tape, film-strip, models, etc.

o   *Educational technologist/developer.* Professional with a special interest in the improvement of teaching and learning who may be able to give the authors disinterested help (as a "critical friend"), e.g., in clarifying their educational purposes, in choosing appropriate teaching strategies or assessment procedures, and in improving the course as a result of evaluation.

o   *Transformer.* A skilled communicator who can liaise with any subject specialists whose writing is obscure, winkling out their key ideas and re-expressing them in ways the learners will be able to understand.

o   *Editor.* Professional who can help authors in polishing their texts and ensuring consistency of useage among authors, and in preparing their final drafts for printing (including copyright clearance).

o *Graphic designer.* Professional who can advise authors on layout, typestyle and the overall graphic design of their texts, as well as suggesting ways of supplementing or even replacing text with illustrations and executing whatever illustrations are agreed upon.

o *Secretary/co-ordinator.* Administrator who can take over the day-to-day routine -- arranging meetings, relaying necessary information to course team members between meetings, chasing authors who have missed deadlines, etc. -- leaving the convenor freer to concentrate on the management and quality control of the course.

The pros and cons of teamwork

In deciding whether to set up a course team of the type mentioned above, we again have both potential advantages and potential disadvantages to consider:

Advantages.

o Sharing the work means the course can be produced more quickly.

o Individuals may work faster because they know their colleagues have expectations of them.

o Discussion and mutual criticism can be stimulating and improve the quality of the course.

o Course team members can specialize, to some extent, in those aspects of course production each is best at and/or enjoys most.

o The individual is saved from feeling isolated and alone in facing potential hostility or lack of support from people not concerned with the course.

Unfortunately, course team operation is sometimes ruled out or else spoiled by one or more of the following:

Disadvantages.

o Specialists of the kind listed earlier are not available or the project cannot afford them.

o Course team members may dislike having to cope with criticisms, or even suggestions, from colleagues.

o   Individuals may waste too much time in personal or
    ideological dispute and in trying to protest their
    own interests in the course.

o   Individuals can opt out of unpopular tasks -- e.g.
    writing assessment materials -- and shrug off
    responsibility for the course as a whole.

o   Individual authors may dislike the pressure of
    having to negotiate their own roles, contribute to
    frequent meetings, and abide by majority decisions
    (especially those that impose deadlines by which
    work must be produced).

o   It can be difficult to find a convenor with the
    right management skills to handle such a group,
    especially when his or her responsibility is
    unaccompanied by any formal authority.

CO-ORDINATING GROUP ACTIVITY

It is worth noticing that such disadvantages can begin to
appear (as can the advantages) even when the "course team"
consists of no more than two authors trying to work
together as equal partners.

*Benefits can
outweigh costs*

Despite the potential disadvantages of course team
operation, many institutions have now found ways of
minimizing them, while making the most of the advantages.
It is **possible** to have many hands making light work
rather than too many cooks spoiling the broth. Unless you
are working entirely on your own, some means needs to be
found by which members of the working group (whether

*Depends on
co-ordination*

democratic equal-status members or not) can co-ordinate
their activities:

Decision-making

*Who
decides
what ?*

Numerous decisions have to be made during the development
of a course, e.g. about whether particular content should
be included or whether certain materials are of an

acceptable standard. Who is to make such decisions ? Here are **three** possibilities:

o The convenor makes decisions on behalf of the group.

o Decisions are made by consensus among the group (or certain "core" members of it) after full discussion.

o Each member makes decisions about his/her "own" area of the course, taking account of group discussions.

Laying down the ground- rules

Some types of decision may best be taken by one method, some by another. But the sooner the "ground-rules" are discussed, the less chance is there for bickering and resentment to spring up later.

Naming the authors

Another issue: Will the author(s) of each individual section be separately named on the relevant materials ? Or will the course team take **collective** responsibility for all sections, with the authorship of individual sections being left unstated ?

Communications

Keeping one another informed

How is the course team to communicate with itself ? Even if the members of the team are acquainted with each other (and some may not be), they may never have worked together with the intimacy that successful course creation is likely to demand.

The need for communication

So what can be done to ensure that all are on much the same wavelength, sensitive to (if not always sharing) one another's assumptions, values, perspectives, terminology, intentions, and so on ? How are they to get to trust and accept one another ? How are they to profit from one another's insights and experience ? How are they to judge what may realistically be expected from one another ?

Two approaches

There are at least two ways of encouraging appropriate communication -- meetings and documentation.

Meetings. How often can/should the team get together ?
With what purpose ? Some of your meetings may be strictly
business occasions, e.g. brainstorming sessions or
discussions of schedules or the first draft of a member's
plans or course materials. Some may be professional in
a wider sense, e.g. a seminar, perhaps with outsiders
invited, on a topic related to the course, or a visit to
a factory, farm or college. Some may be purely social,
e.g. parties, lunches, visits to theatres, concerts or
football matches. Some meetings may be a mixture. In
fact, any meeting of two or more members of the course
may be expected to contribute towards getting the course
developed or the team members better acquainted.

*Business,
professional
and social
meetings*

Documentation. Groups and committees everywhere are
regularly accused of producing too much paperwork.
Nevertheless, if more than a couple of people are involved
in producing a course, they'd be well advised not to
stint on paper. Every important decision, e.g. about
schedules, or intended content, or allocation of tasks,
should be written down and circulated to all members.

*Make sure
it's in
writing*

Every member should also receive a copy of the
"specification", outlining the content, treatment, etc.,
proposed for each section and, later, a copy of each draft
of every member's materials. Even if it has been agreed
that not everyone will produce detailed comments on each
draft, **all** should see any materials that might influence
them in how they'd want to plan their own. In fact, those
members who are going to produce detailed comments on a
draft might well receive **two** copies. They could then give
their annotated copy back to the author, keeping one
copy as a reminder.

Allocating Tasks

*Who is to
do what ?*

Try to reach early agreement as to what tasks will need to
be performed and how they might be shared out fairly. Who

will do what ? Try not to overlook tasks such as:

Whose are
these tasks ?

- writing study guides and assignment questions;
- setting examinations;
- commenting on one another's materials;
- briefing other teachers;
- publicizing the course; and so on.

If early decisions are not made, someone is likely to end up doing more than a fair share -- and vital tasks may be neglected until it is too late to do them properly. In particular: Who will be responsible for looking after the course once it is **in operation** -- and making whatever adjustments and improvements may be necessary ?

And once the
course is
complete ?

Constraints

The demands
on each
individual

Each member of the group needs to know the constraints within which he or she is to work. How much freedom does each one have to determine content and treatment ? How much learner-time is each responsible for ? Does each one have sufficient time available to spend on the course at all the relevant stages of production ?

How many
author-hours ?

Does the group have enough resources, especially of author-hours, to produce a course of satisfactory quality ? Every hour of learner-time may take 50-100 (or more) hours of course team time to develop.

Media, money
and other
resources

What teaching media are available ? What physical facilities for meetings, laboratory preparation of materials, workshop testing of prototype equipment, etc ? Can specialist help be brought in ? Is there money available for revising the course (and reprinting) after it has been in use for a while ? And so on.

The Production Schedule

Deadlines
for draft
materials

Agree on a schedule for production so that individuals know when their contributions are expected. This is especially vital if some authors need to see drafts of another's work before they can proceed with their own.

Allowing for commenting

Ensure there is time for each author to have his or her plans and draft materials studied and critically commented upon by **at least** one other member of the group -- and perhaps by an external assessor -- before they are finalized.

Make contingency plans against the possibility that production might slip behind schedule. Are there parts

If things should go wrong

of the course, for instance, that might be jettisoned ? Or are there extra resources that might be drawn on, however reluctantly, in an emergency ?

It may not be good for group morale, however, to dwell too long on discussing how possible failures might be

Be realistic

retrieved. Far better for the group to assure itself that its forward planning is as thorough and realistic as possible, so as to minimize nasty surprises up ahead. For instance, course teams routinely **under**-estimate the amount of time individuals will need to produce acceptable materials. Though it is possible that some of us would be too discouraged to write anything at all if we ever admitted to ourselves at the outset just how long it was really likely to take us !

Key events in course production

Figure 2.1 overleaf shows some key events for a typical schedule, and also how individual authors and the full course team might need to interact. Several of the activities shown will be going on at once. For example, few course teams will be able to wait to see and approve **all** first drafts (D1s) before work starts on **any** second drafts (D2s). Thus, a given course team meeting may be discussing a D3 of one section of the course, a D2 of another, and a D1 or even a revised specification of a third. Authors need to know, for each piece of work they are responsible for, where their personal deadlines appear on the overall schedule.

Figure 2.1: Key Events in a Typical Production Schedule

Full Course Team (CT)   **Individual Authors**

- o Decides overall aims, objectives and structure of course.
- o Decides which authors are responsible for which sections/tasks.

- o Write specifications or outlines, detailing the content and treatment for each section, on basis of earlier CT discussion.

- o Discusses specification and agrees changes.

- o Write first draft (D1) of each section's materials, incorporating changes agreed by CT.

- o Discusses D1s, comparing them with amended specifications and with one another.
- o Suggests more changes (probably minor ones).

- o Write second drafts (D2) incorporating agreed changes.

- o Arranges for D2s to be tested by typical learners and critically appraised by outside experts in the subject.
- o Discusses D2s in light of learners' feedback and experts' comments.
- o Agrees further changes.

- o Write third drafts (D3)

- o Discusses and approves D3.
- o Suggests any "fine tuning" changes.

- o Liaise with editor and designer in getting final "handover draft" of materials printed, taped, or otherwise reproduced by the agreed date.

Even the much-simplified example of a schedule in Figure 2.2 below shows that complications can arise when different authors are responsible for different amounts of material -- especially when each may need different amounts of time to produce any given amount of material; and may be completing their drafts in some order different from that in which they will ultimately be studied by the learners.

Figure 2.2: Part of a Simple Schedule for Course Production

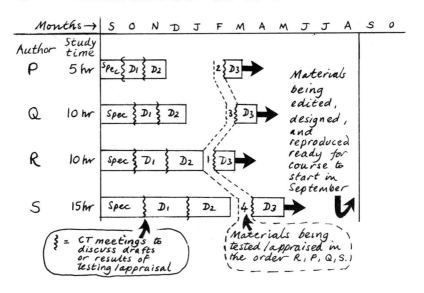

The schedule above, for instance, shows a 40-hour course being produced by four authors, P, Q, R, and S, responsible for, respectively, 5, 10, 10, and 15 hours'-worth of learning materials. If all four start together, we see that authors P and Q will, at one point, have a break of two months or more before they can start on their D3s. This is because learners must study Author R's D2 material before theirs, yet it will not be available for testing until some time after theirs. If it were not essential for learners to read the D2s in a set sequence then, of

course, P's and Q's material could be tested earlier;
they could thus get their D3s completed earlier, so

spreading the load on the editor, designer and production
facilities. As it is, P and Q might be asked to use some
of their slack time in giving assistance to S who looks
like the most hard-pressed member of the course team.

Needless to say, the sample schedule above does not
pretend to illustrate all the problems that can emerge
in attempting to draw up such a plan. It is simply meant

to show that such scheduling **can** indeed throw up problems
and issues about which decisions need to be taken early
in our course planning.

COULD YOU ADAPT AN EXISTING COURSE ?

In view of the many costs and complexities involved in
developing a course from scratch, we are bound to ask this
question: Can you take over a course that has **already**
been produced by some other institution ?

In the past, this has generally been discouraged by
the "not-invented-here" syndrome. (If we didn't produce

it ourselves, then it can't be any use to our learners !)
But financial cut-backs have led many institutions to
take a more hospitable view. Someone else's course
materials and/or system **may** be suitable for your learners.
If so, consider using them. The staff-time you'll save
by not producing your own version might better be invested
in developing self-instructional courses in worthwhile
topics that no-one has yet effectively dealt with.

Figure 2.3 suggests some questions to ask about any
existing course you think might be worth adapting to suit
your institution. Remember that, even if the course
turns out not to be suitable as a whole, **parts** of it may
be. (So indeed may existing books, videos, audiotapes,
etc., that were not produced with self-instruction in mind
at all. I'll say more about building such material into
your own courses in Chapter 5.)

Figure 2.3: Questions to Ask About Adapting a Course

o *How suitable ?* Are its objectives, methods and
   outcomes appropriate to our learners ?

o *How effective ?* Does it achieve satisfactory results ?

o *How big ?* How much time, staff and resources does it
   need ? How many topics ? What range of learners ?

o *How complete ?* Does it need extra supporting material ?

o *How complex ?* Is it difficult for teachers and
   learners to work with ?

o *How flexible ?* Is there room for teachers and learners
   to adapt it to their special needs ?

o *How different ?* Is it sufficiently different from
   other available approaches -- in outcome, method,
   cost, or whatever ?

o *How importable ?* Are there any special features (e.g.
   unusual teachers or local facilities) that we could
   not match ?

o *How compatible ?* Would it fit in or interfere with
   the rest of our existing system ?

o *How ready ?* Can it be started this term/year ?

o *How "samplable" ?* Could we give it a trial run and
   abandon it if unsatisfactory ? Or would the decision
   have to be all-or-nothing -- e.g. if it involved
   heavy investment in capital equipment ?

o *How expensive ?* What are the initial costs and the
   running costs -- both in time and money, and for both
   the institution and the learners ?

o *How comparable ?* How does it compare, on all the
   above factors and any others we think important,
   with the course we might produce for ourselves ?

COURSE MAINTENANCE

Who will maintain the course ?

Finally, whether you are adapting a course or producing one from scratch, we must come back to a question I mentioned earlier: How will the course be maintained **in use** ? In particular, who is to be responsible for its week-by-week operation, once learners ahve begun studying it ? Maybe the full, original course team will still be involved; maybe only one or two of its members -- with or without some new helpers. At all events, the **maintenance** of the course should be planned quite early.

There is certainly no shortage of tasks for the "maintenance team" to undertake during the life of the course. Here are some of them; you may be able to think of more:

Some of the tasks in course maintenance

o Supervizing the storage and delivery to learners of the course materials.

o Arranging for the production of new copies of the course materials as stocks run low.

o Tutoring, both by correspondence and face-to-face.

o Selecting, training, and monitoring the work of other people who are acting as tutors.

o Producing new assessment materials and/or examination papers (together with notes of guidance for markers) for each run of the course.

o Liaising with institutions providing facilities for associated face-to-face teaching.

o Publicizing the course and recruiting learners for it.

o Liaising with other institutions who are interested in adopting or adapting the course for their own learners.

o Dealing with problems and queries raised by learners (and perhaps other tutors) concerning difficulties they are having with the course.

o Providing learners with a statement that they have worked through the course -- e.g. a "letter of course completion"; or with an indication of their level of achievement -- e.g. an examination grade or a verbal profile.

o Evaluating the effects and effectiveness of the course, both by continuous monitoring and by occasional special studies -- e.g. of learning habits or of drop-out.

o Making minor improvements in the course, in the light of evaluation and changing circumstances, for the benefit of current learners -- e.g. by giving them details of current events or issues relevant to the course, and by correcting errors in the materials.

o Identifying areas of the course where more substantial improvements might be made for the benefit of future learners.

o Maintaining records concerning the operation of the course.

```
*********************************************
*                                           *
*  AGREE ON COURSE TEAM ROUTINES AND        *
*  RESPONSIBILITIES AS EARLY AS POSSIBLE    *
*  -- BEFORE IT IS TOO LATE.                *
*                                           *
*********************************************
```

3. PLANNING YOUR TEACHING -- LEARNERS AND CONTENT

As we know, self-instruction differs from conventional instruction in a variety of ways. Three of the most significant, from the **teacher's** point of view, are:

How S-I differs

o *The need to "teach in one's head" --* to **anticipate** how future learners one may never meet might come to terms with the subject, and provide them explicitly and consciously with all the necessary explanations and encouragements that one would be giving almost unconsciously if one were interacting with them face to face.

o *The "public" nature of the teaching.* What may have formerly been a private, transient communication between teacher and learners, behind a closed classroom door, is now to be embodied, recorded and "published" as a package of materials which colleagues (and rivals) as well as learners can peruse and evaluate.

o *The relative inflexibility of self-instruction.* That is, once the materials have been developed and committed to paper or tape, it may be prohibitively costly, in time and money, to change them or substitute others for them in response to unanticipated needs and difficulties among the learners.

Explicit plans

If we are working with colleagues, there is an additional factor -- the need to make our plans and decisions quite **explicit**.

A FRAMEWORK FOR PLANNING

These factors seem to press us towards one inevitable aim -- that of making sure our materials are as effective as humanly possible before we finalize them. That, in turn, depends not only on teaching experience and imagination but also on open and thoughtful planning. I suggest a

Systematic planning

systematic framework for course planning that revolves around four inter-connected aspects. These are shown in Figure 3.1 below:

Figure 3.1:   The Four Aspects of Systematic Planning

Consider all four aspects

In planning any self-instructional teaching -- whether a complete course or a relatively brief package -- all four aspects must be given proper attention. We can begin our planning with any one of them. For instance, a new course may arise out of the evaluation of a previous one. But we cannot think about any one of the four aspects for more than a few minutes without needing to ask how the other three might be affected. The four aspects can be presented as four questions:

Four basic planning questions

1. What are we trying to accomplish with this teaching

2. What activities must we get learners to engage in i we are to accomplish this satisfactorily ?

3. How shall we evaluate the effects and effectiveness of what we have decided to produce ?

4. In the light of evaluation, how can we improve the teaching and learning, e.g. by modifying 1, 2 or 3

****
*   *
*   KEEP ALL FOUR QUESTIONS IN MIND BEFORE, DURING   *
*   AND AFTER PRODUCING YOUR TEACHING MATERIALS.   *
****

Courses and Lessons

At this point, I need to introduce a new piece of terminology. The four questions we've just looked at are equally relevant whether you are planning a course that is going to occupy the learner for months, or sizeable sections within such a course, or merely an hour's worth of learning -- which may or may not be part of a bigger course.

From courses...

Self-instructional teachers call the sections within their courses by various names -- blocks, modules, units, sessions, and so on. (Some people's blocks etc., are bigger than some other people's courses, but that is by the way.)

to blocks, etc...

Of course, you may be concerned with planning not lengthy courses but comparatively short packages. Either way, it may help you to think in terms of what I shall call **lessons**. By this, I mean the minimum amount of material that provide for a self-contained and coherent chunk of learning. I would usually plan for such "lessons" to occupy the average learner for about **one hour**.

to "lessons"

Each lesson would then represent the minimum amount of material a learner might usefully tackle at a single study session. This notion is useful both to learners in scheduling their learning sessions and to the developers of materials in planning their teaching. (You may prefer a term like "session" or "unit" to indicate your smallest building brick of self-instruction -- but "lesson" seems preferable to me because we all, whether in education or training, have an immediate image of the kind of time-span and coherence of learning implied by the term.)

"Lesson" = a single study session

Subject v Learner-oriented Approaches

Teachers differ in how they like to approach the planning of their teaching. To a large extent, their habitual approach depends on whether they think primarily of their

How to plan

Subject v learners

subject-matter or primarily of the **learners**. Figure 3.2 below presents two lists of ways you might start planning. One is largely subject-oriented, the other learner-oriented I do not imagine that either list is complete.

Figure 3.2: Two Sets of Approaches to Planning

Contrasting approaches

SUBJECT-ORIENTED	LEARNER-ORIENTED
o Study any relevant examination syllabus and question papers from previous years.	o Establish and analyse the aims and learning objectives.
o Review your own knowledge of the proposed subject.	o Ask prospective learners what topics they would like to see tackled.
o Discuss it (e.g. by interviewing or by brainstorming) with other subject specialists.	o Discuss with prospective learners their existing knowledge and understandin of the key concepts of the subject.
o Analyse similar courses elsewhere.	o Think of learning activiti that learners logically must, or just usefully could, engage in.
o Read textbooks pitched at what you regard as the appropriate level.	o Analyse the knowledge, skills and attitudes displayed by 'master performers' (or just very competent learners) in your field.
o Read more advanced books and articles on the subject.	
o Review films, television and audio tapes, articles in newspapers and popular journals.	o Recall where previous learners have had learning difficulties, or fallen into error, in the subject
o Select books (or other source materials) around which the teaching will be organised.	o Consider how learners' attainments as a result of the course or lesson might sensibly be assessed.
o Identify and analyse the key concepts of the subject.	o Study other people's reports of learners' work on related courses in previous years.

Try both:

```
********************************************************
*                                                      *
*   FOR EFFECTIVE PLANNING, YOU WILL PROBABLY          *
*   NEED TO TRY AT LEAST SOME APPROACHES FROM          *
*   BOTH LISTS.                                         *
*                                                      *
********************************************************
```

Seven Major Questions

More detailed planning questions

There are at least seven major questions we need to ask in planning a self-instructional course or lesson:

1. Who will be the learners ?

2. What are the aims and objectives ?

3. What will be the subject-content ?

4. How will the content be sequenced ?

5. What teaching methods and media will be used ?

6. How will learners be assessed ?

7. How will the course or lesson be evaluated with a view to improvement ?

Some now, more later

These questions will all be looked at in this chapter or the next. However, as you may have noticed from the book's contents pages, questions 5, 6 and 7 are discussed at greater length later, in Chapters 11, 13 and 14.

WHO WILL BE THE LEARNERS ?

Who are you catering for ?

What do you know about the learners who will be studying your course ? What do you need to know ? Are you developing materials and a system that will cope with whatever variety of learners happen to be attracted ? Or do you have to produce comparatively inflexible materials, e.g. to fit in with the requirements of a particular examining body, and then **recruit** only those learners who can be expected to cope with the demands of your system ?

Flexibility v selection tests

To some extent, most courses can be flexible; to some extent, all learners must do some coping. If you wish to put more emphasis on the former, you will need to build in alternative content or treatment to suit individual differences. If you need to emphasize the latter, you will need to think of **selection tests** -- what abilities do learners need **before** they can **begin on your materials** ?

Useful Information

There are four types of information you might need
about your prospective learners:

*Four types of
information
about
learners*

Demographic. How many of them ? What age range ? Both
sexes ? Marital status ? Employed ? What occupations ?
Other courses being studied ? Home area ? etc.

Motivation. Why might they wish to study your subject ?
Why choose self-instruction (or distance or open
learning) ? What do they expect ? What do they hope to
get from the course ? etc.

Learning factors. How intelligent and capable are they
as learners ? Have they had prior experience with
self-instruction and especially, if appropriate, with
distance learning ? Prior level of general educational
attainment ? Attainment in whatever abilities will be
needed in coping with your teaching ? Do they have
adequate time and facilities available for study ? etc.

Subject background. What knowledge, attitudes and skills
do they already have relating to your subject ? Which of
their personal interests and background experiences have
a bearing on the subject ? (Such information may help
you decide on ways into the subject and may provide a
useful source of examples and analogies.)

*Thumbnail
sketch*

Needless to say, by the above criteria, your learners
may well be a very mixed bunch -- especially if they are
adults. All the same, it is worth trying to write a
"thumbnail sketch" of your typical learner. Better still
if you can get a colleague to do so also, and compare
notes. Figure 3.3 opposite is an example of such a
thumbnail sketch of the typical learner on a business
management course for farmers and horticulturalists.

Figure 3.3:   Thumbnail Sketch of a "Typical" Learner

The typical learner runs a small farm or market garden.
He is male, between 30 and 40 years of age, and is
married with one or two children living at home. He
left school at 16 with a few examination certificates
and has done no systematic studying since. He will not
be worried about the cost of books or travelling to
course meetings and will be ready to obtain playback
machines for audio- and video-cassettes if he does not
have them already. However, he is unwilling to
commit himself to attending even occasional class
meetings at a fixed time (because of the unpredictable
demands of his work); and, in fact, this is why he is
choosing a distance learning course.

   He is enrolling for the course in hope of improving
his efficiency and profitability and avoiding hassle
from his bank manager, accountant and tax inspector.
He will be perfectly capable of learning on his own,
provided the materials are flexible enough for him to
find his own level and he is allowed fairly ready access
(at least by telephone) to a tutor or other learners
if he gets into difficulties. The tutor will need to be
scrupulous in providing support rather than criticism.
Needless to say, the learner is very familiar with the
subject-matter of the course; he will be scathing about
anything he regards as "unrealistic" in our examples or
suggestions, and will not stick with the course unless it
remains clearly relevant to what he perceives as his needs.

Finding Out

With self-instructional courses and packages, especially
when learners are studying at a distance, we need to obtain
information about them **before** they begin. Otherwise it
cannot affect the teaching as much as it should. There

Early
enquiries
needed

Figure 3.4: Questionnaire for Prospective Learners

Questionnaire (Put a tick in the box alongside each answer you choose)

1. **What is your sex?**
   (a) Male
   (b) Female

2. **How old are you?**
   (a) Less than 20
   (b) 20-25
   (c) 25-30
   (d) 30-40
   (e) 40-50
   (f) Over 50

3. **Why do you want to take this course?**
   (a) Because you think it will be interesting
   (b) Because you want to be able to plan better meals for yourself or your family
   (c) Because you want to be able to help or supervise other people who plan meals but without wanting some professional qualification
   (d) Because you want to get some sort of professional qualification in dietetics
   (e) Because you have been told to by your employer or a teacher
   (f) Because it completes your timetable of courses for a qualification not primarily in dietetics
   (g) Some other reason (please specify)

4. **What is the most important reason for wanting people to eat a reasonably balanced diet?**
   (a) To make sure they get enough to eat
   (b) To make sure they get the right sort of food
   (c) To keep them healthy
   (d) To make sure that the food is appetising
   (e) To ensure variety in meals
   (f) To make sure their bodies get enough of each of their requirements
   (g) To avoid waste of food and unnecessary expense

5. **Do you think your own present diet is adequately balanced?**
   (a) Yes
   (b) No
   (c) Don't know

6. **Do you think it is important to be able to judge how well a diet is balanced?**
   (a) Yes
   (b) No

7. **Have you ever planned and prepared a meal for others?**
   (a) Yes, regularly
   (b) Yes, occasionally
   (c) No — only part of a meal
   (d) No — only helped others to do so
   (e) No — only watched others do so
   (f) No — never

8. **Which of the following have you studied in the last three years?** (Tick as many as apply)
   (a) Cookery
   (b) Elementary biology
   (c) Elementary physics and/or chemistry
   (d) Basic arithmetic
   (e) Elementary statistics
   (Write in any examinations you have passed in any of these subjects and the year you passed them.)

9. **How many different classes of nutrient are found in food?**
   (a) 1   (b) 2   (c) 3
   (d) 4   (e) 5   (f) 6
   (g) 7   (h) More than 7

Here is a list of terms used in connection with nutrition.
(Put the appropriate letters in the boxes below.)

A	Ascorbic Acid	G	Fibre	M	Obesity
B	Beri-beri	H	Iron	N	Pellagra
C	Brassica	I	Kwashiorkor	O	Protein
D	Carbohydrate	J	Methionine	P	Scurvy
E	Energy	K	Mineral	Q	Tryptophan
F	Fat	L	Nicotonic acid	R	Vitamin
				S	Water

Questions 10-14

10. Which of the above constitute major classes of nutrient?

11. Which of the above are names of diseases caused by a deficiency of some ingredient in food?

12. Which of the above are major sources of energy?

13. Which of the above, apart from 'vitamin' itself, are either vitamins, sources of vitamins, or are associated with vitamin deficiency?

14. Which of the above, apart from 'protein' itself, would you associate directly with protein or protein deficiency?

are three main ways of building up a picture of your
prospective learners:

o   Rely on your previous experience of those learners,
    or supposedly similar ones, or on that of colleagues.

o   Meet some of the prospective learners and discuss
    with them (individually or as a group, or both)
    what you have in mind to teach, and what they
    already know/feel about the subject and what they
    would like from the course.

o   Send a questionnaire to prospective learners, trying
    to elicit the information you need. If this can be
    followed up by discussion with learners, whether
    face-to-face or on the telephone, so much the better.

*A sample
questionnaire*

Figure 3.4 shows a sample questionnaire compiled by a
colleague of mine, Roger Harrison, for a distance learning
course on Diet and Nutrition. He now would point out
certain weaknesses, e.g. the possibility that too many
"technical" questions, like 9-14, might scare off some
potential learners, especially if they got the impression
that the implied knowledge were being expected as an entry
requirement. The purpose of the questioning could,
however, be made clear in an accompanying letter.

*Try out
a draft*

```
*****************************************************
*                                                   *
*     DON'T USE A QUESTIONNAIRE IN EARNEST           *
*     UNTIL YOU'VE TRIED OUT A PILOT VERSION.        *
*                                                   *
*****************************************************
```

WHAT AIMS AND OBJECTIVES ?

*What are
aims and
objectives ?*

It is useful to start thinking about aims and objectives
as early as possible in the process of planning a course
or an individual lesson within it. The difference
between aims and objectives is as follows:

Aims -- a general statement of what you hope the course (or lesson) will achieve, perhaps expressed in terms of what you, the teacher, will be presenting to the learner.

**What are
aims and
objectives ?**

Objectives -- a statement of what learners should be able to **do** (or do better) as a result of having worked through the course (or lesson).

Examples

Aims (from different courses/lessons):

**Examples
of aims**

o To explain the concept and importance of energy; to provide practice in carrying out surveys and experiments relating to energy studies; to engender a sense of concern about the depletion of fossil fuel reserves; and to give guidance on the planning of an energy policy.

o To introduce the learner to healthy eating habits.

o To foster an appreciation of the novels of D.H. Lawrence.

Objectives. (Note: It is customary to preface a list of objectives with some such phrase as "By the end of this course/lesson, learners should be able to, or have improved in their ability to...").

**Examples of
objectives**

o 1. List the various forms of energy.
   2. Describe how one form may be converted into another.
   3. Distinguish between energy and power.
   4. Identify the principal energy flows in a given situation.
   5. etc...

o 1. List the principal components of a balanced diet and describe the function of each in the body.

   2. Name six diseases caused by inadequate or unbalanced diet.

   3. Calculate the amounts of energy, protein, certain vitamins, and calcium and iron in a given diet, using tables of food composition.

   4. etc...

   o 1.   Relate Lawrence's viewpoint to his or her
own experiences.

       2.   Analyse the literary elements that have
provoked his/her involvement.

       3.   Make and justify a personal statement as
to Lawrence's "meanings".

       4.   Seek out and read more of Lawrence's writings
than are set for assignments.

       5.   etc...

Another
example

Look also at the aims and objectives for the book you
are reading now (pages 15 and 16).

Writing Objectives

Emphasize
doing

In writing objectives we are trying to indicate what
successful learners should be able to **do** (or say) to
demonstrate that they have learned. So it is better
to avoid introducing objectives with words like those
on the left below. (They hint at non-observable states
of mind.) Instead, begin an objective with a **verb**
like those on the right below:

AVOID words like:	**USE** words like:
know...	State...
understand...	Describe...
really know...	Explain...
really understand...	List...
be familiar with...	Evaluate...
become acquainted with...	Identify...
have a good grasp of...	Distinguish between...
appreciate...	Analyse...
be interested in...	Outline...
acquire a feeling for...	Summarize...
be aware of...	Represent graphically...
believe...	Compare...
have information about...	Apply...
realize the significance of...	Assess...
learn the basics of...	Give examples of...
obtain working knowledge of...	Suggest reasons why...

Types of Objective

Objectives can be classified in many different ways.
I find it most useful to do so on the basis of the kind
of benefit that learners are being expected to get from
a course or lesson:

*Three kinds
of objective*

o **Knowledge.** In what ways, and regarding what
subject-matter content, do you want learners to
demonstrate the knowledge they have gained from the
course/lesson ? -- e.g. "the learner should be able
to explain the significance of 'half-life' in the
prescribing of drugs".

o **Skills.** In what respects would you wish learners
to be able to demonstrate their ability to work with
and apply their knowledge of the subject-matter ? --
e.g. "The learner should be able to diagnose the
patient's ailment". Skills can be intellectual,
physical, or social (or a mixture).

o **Attitudes.** What attitudes or beliefs or dispositions
would you wish the learner to develop in respect of
the subject of the course/lesson ? -- e.g. "The
learner should show a desire to find out how the
patient feels about the illness and the treatment
being proposed".

Combinations Note that many objectives may combine two or all three of
the aspects listed above.

The Value of Objectives

*Plan early
but review ?*

Don't expect to be able to finalize your objectives before
you start writing your course materials. (Unless they
have been given to you ready-made by someone else). But
you are recommended to start thinking about them as early
as possible and expect to revise them from time to time
as your planning proceeds. This should help you in four
main ways:

*Four
advantages
of objectives*

Communication. Objectives can help make clear your educational intentions -- to yourself, to colleagues and, eventually, to the learners.

Content and sequence. Thinking out objectives can help you distinguish between possible and essential content and to identify ways of sequencing it.

Media and methods. An awareness of your objectives can help you decide on the most appropriate teaching media and the most appropriate learning activities.

Assessment and evaluation. Objectives can help you decide on suitable ways of testing what learners have gained from the course/lesson and of evaluating the effects and effectiveness of your materials.

Course v Lesson Objectives

*From course
objectives...*

Once you know your objectives for the course as a whole, you will need to know how they relate to the objectives for individual lessons. Learners will be expected to achieve some objectives as a result of a particular lesson, e.g. "learn to distinguish between ridges and valleys on a contour map". Others they will be expected to get better and better at, lesson by lesson, e.g. "learn to visualize the physical features of an unknown region from a topographical map".

*to lesson
objectives*

So, lesson objectives can be arrived at by asking:

o Which of the course objectives will be **fully attained** during this lesson ? and

o Which of the course objectives (or which aspects of which of them) will learners **improve** their ability in during this lesson ?

```
*******************************************************
*                                                     *
*    WRITING OBJECTIVES IS MEANT TO HELP YOU PLAN     *
*    YOUR TEACHING.  WHETHER YOU MIGHT LATER WANT     *
*    TO SHOW THEM TO LEARNERS IS A SEPARATE ISSUE.    *
*                                                     *
*******************************************************
```

DECIDING ON CONTENT

What are the main topics, concepts and principles to be
covered in your course/lesson ? Many thoughts about
content will arise in the process of thinking about
objectives. Alternatively, or as well, the approaches
already listed in Figure 3.2 (page 38) should be a rich
source of ideas. Two further approaches may be useful --
concept analysis and diagramming.

Two further
approaches

Concept Analysis

Concepts are the basic elements of our teaching. In
various combinations they make up the "main ideas" we
shall be trying to teach in our lessons. Even within
this chapter I have already touched on concepts such as:
motivation, objectives, assessment, media, and so on.

Main ideas

We need to be alert to the kinds of difficulties and
confusions that attach to the concepts we plan to teach.
One way of thinking about these is to apply some of the
techniques of concept analysis. I have space here only
to mention them; but the list below should be reasonably
suggestive:

Difficulties
and
confusions

Techniques of
concept
analysis

o *Isolate the concepts* -- from the facts, principles,
   examples, etc., of our subject-matter.
o *Define each concept* -- dictionary-type definitions
   to begin with, perhaps.
o *Examine model examples* -- to sharpen the definition
   by deciding which features of the examples are
   essential to the concept and which are incidental.
o *Examine counter examples* -- to further establish the
   essential character of the concept by identifying
   features that would negate it.
o *Examine border-line examples* -- to clarify our
   understanding of the crucial features of the
   concept by considering cases where it "almost"
   applies or applies only "in a way".

o *Consider invented examples* -- testing the concept
by inventing imaginary cases that might really
stretch the features we have identified for
the concept.

o *Compare social contexts* -- to consider the extent
to which people from different places and/ortimes
might disagree with our examples and non-examples.

o *Compare personal contexts* -- in recognition that
the concept will have different connotations for
different individuals (which may or may not
hinder communication).

o *Examine related concepts* -- studying one concept
leads us to see how it fits into the
surrounding network of concepts.

o *Elucidate the principles* -- concepts are related
to other concepts in the form of principles (rules,
theorems, axioms, laws, generalizations, statements)
which constitute the "message(s)" of the
subject-matter and give rise to the "teaching points".

Choose from techniques

There is, of course, no need to work through all of these
techniques with every concept in your course. Life is
too short. Usually a concept will be clarified
sufficiently for teaching purposes after you have been
through three or four of them. But all are at hand for
the main concepts that are to underpin your course --
like "distance learning" and "self-instructional materials"
in this book.

Diagramming Your Subject-matter

Picturing content

Many teachers find they can best get to grips with their
course content by drawing a picture of it. Of the many
possible forms of course diagram we might discuss, I have
picked out just five that I have found particularly useful:

Spray diagram. To draw this widely-used form of diagram, we start by taking the name of a main topic from our course or lesson and writing it at the centre of a piece of paper or chalkboard. Then we spray out lines from the centre -- one for each major aspect of the topic that occurs to us. These lines will then be branched to illustrate sub-aspects, and so on. Figure 3.5 is a spray diagram showing relationships among the ideas in a book chapter whose content is listed in Figure 4.4 (on page 71).

Branching from main topics

Figure 3.5: A Spray Diagram (based on *Learn How to Study* by D. Rowntree, Macdonalds, 1976)

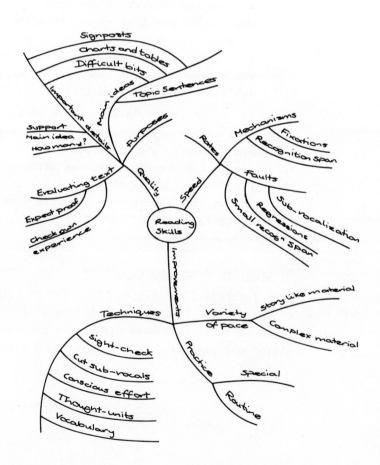

A looser diagram

Concept map. A similar, but looser form of diagram is produced when we simply start with the name of a key topic or concept (e.g. 'educational technology") and draw lines from it to a number of related concepts. Then we write in the names of concepts related to these and join them up with lines also. Figure 3.6 is such a concept map of the field of educational technology as seen by my colleague, David Hawkridge.

Figure 3.6: A Concept Map of Educational Technology
(from D. Hawkridge, *British Journal of Educational Technology*, 12, 1, Jan 1981, pp 4-18)

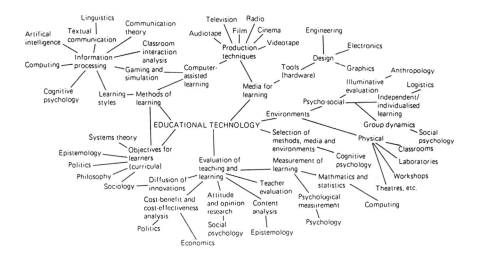

In this kind of diagram, as David Hawkridge says: "lines connect words, reflecting connections of some kind without revealing exactly what. Moreover, many other lines could be added to show additional connections".

Variations possible

Furthermore, he points out that the map of educational technology "could be drawn differently...by other educational technologists". I bring attention to this

perhaps obvious remark because many people setting out
to draw a concept map seem to get obsessed with uncovering
the "true, underlying structure" of the subject. Even if
such a structure exists, there is no need for that degree
of dedication. Drawing such diagrams is a personal and
subjective activity whose purpose is simply to help you
externalize your own understanding about how the concepts
within your field connect up. So long as you find it
helpful in your own course planning, there is no need to
worry that others might have mapped the territory
differently.

As long as
it helps you

```
***************************************************************
*                                                             *
*    AS WITH OBJECTIVES, YOU MAY OR MAY NOT WISH              *
*    TO DISCUSS YOUR DIAGRAMS WITH YOUR LEARNERS.             *
*                                                             *
***************************************************************
```

Another
example

Figure 3.7 shows the first sketch of a concept map
I drew up for a course on diet and nutrition. I started
with "Food" in the middle and then began to identify
chains of connected concepts. I put down the ideas more
or less as they came to mind, without wondering too much
about whether all would be needed in the eventual course,
or what else might be needed in addition. Again, I drew
lines wherever there seemed to be a connection, of
whatever kind -- though the broken lines indicate links
I was less sure about than others.

My perception

   I would admit, of course, that other people would map
the field differently. But so might I on another
occasion. The fact is, the diagramming served its
purpose, at the time, as a course planning device. It
enabled me to see my way around the field **as I perceived it**

Figure 3.7:   Initial Concept Map for a Course on Diet and Nutrition

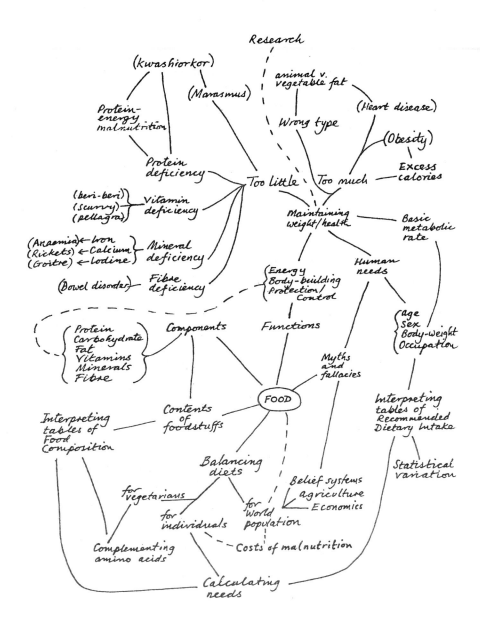

*Causes and
effects*

Statement network. Sometimes a much more structured
diagram may emerge from this kind of process. Figure 3.8
is a well-developed network illustrating the
relationships between climatic factors and the growth of
trees. In this case, arrows link causes with effects.
The column of double arrows down the centre indicates
the primary chain of causation. To the right of it are
factors affecting food storage, while the direct effects
of growing-season climate on growth are to the left of it.

*Statements/
principles*

This chart can be seen to incorporate principles --
that is **statements** involving the concepts -- as well as
the concepts themselves. For example, "Less root growth
causes less water absorption" or "Rapid evaporation and
low soil moisture lead to increased water stress in
the tree".

Figure 3.8: A Cause-Effect Network for Tree-ring Growth
(From Fritts, *Science*, 25 Nov 1966, 154, pp 973-9)

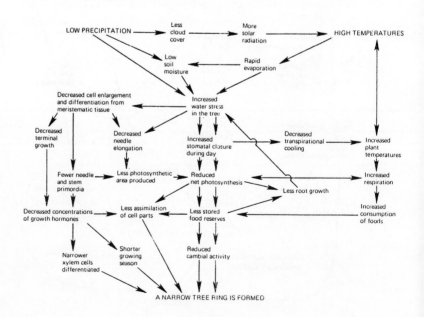

Algorithm. This is another form of diagram in which the
arrows express very explicit connections between ideas.
Such a diagram can be invaluable in sorting out a
subject-area in which the emphasis is on classifying cases

*Classifying
or deciding*

or examples, or deciding what action to take, on the basis
of a number of yes/no decisions as to whether each of a
limited number of characteristics applies in a particular
case.

Examples

For instance, if you want to classify a soil specimen
as loam, clay, sand, or whatever, you'll need to notice
what combination of attributes it possesses from among
such attributes as grittiness, silkiness, and resistance
to deformation. (See Figure 9.4 on page 186 for an
algorithm that deals with this task.) Similarly,
diagnozing patients' ailments may depend on which
combination each patient presents from a range of
standard signs and symptoms. Figure 3.9 overleaf shows
part of an algorithm concerned with the diagnosis of
blood-vessel disorders in patients whose limbs have
turned an unusual colour.

Yes/No ?

Working out an algorithm is a useful way of exploring
subject-matter that can be boiled down to yes-no
decision-making. Such charts are useful not only as
course planning devices; they may also be used as part
of the teaching.

*Algorithm
instead of
teaching ?*

Indeed, you may sometimes decide to provide an
algorithm **instead** of teaching. Why teach in advance a
procedure that is used so rarely that learners are likely
to have forgotten it before it is next needed -- especially
if it can easily be "looked up" when it is needed ?

Figure 3.9: Part of a Medical Diagnosis Algorithm (Redrawn from Lewis and Woolfenden, *Algorithms and Logical Trees*, Algorithms Press, 1969)

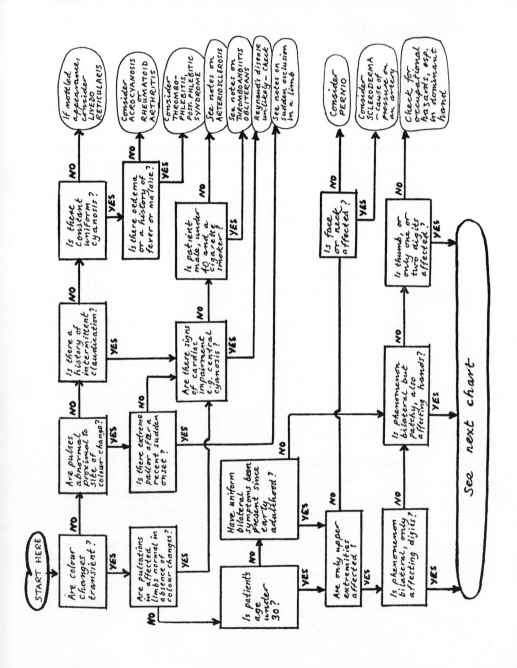

Two-way
classification **Matrix.** This is the final form of diagram I want to mention here. A matrix may suggest itself when you are dealing with a body of knowledge that can be classified and discussed with more than one set of categories in mind. For example, in planning a course for school governors, I found the following matrix was useful:

Figure 3.10: Part of a Matrix for a Course for School Governors

LEVEL of concern

	School	Local	National
Curriculum			
Staffing			
Pupils			
Organization			
Resources & Finance			
Community			

TYPE of concern

This matrix helped the course team be systematic in asking what are the **school** aspects, the **local** aspects, and the **national** aspects of each of the six topics: "curriculum", "staffing", "pupils", and so on. (In fact, we had a third categorization to juggle with also -- how do governors of "voluntary" schools differ from those of "county" schools in all of those concerns ? -- but I have *Could* *be 3-D* refrained from turning the matrix into a 3-dimensional block.) For an example of a filled-out matrix, depicting *Example* a complete course, see Figure 8.1 on page 166.

*Further
diagrams*

A final caution. As you will appreciate, a great variety
of diagrams can be drawn to represent a subject area.
There are many other kinds of diagram I could have shown;
indeed, there are others we must look at later in the
chapter. Furthermore, you may well have your own ways of
diagramming that are more suited to your particular
purposes.

Be flexible

Like any tool in educational planning -- like schedules
and objectives, for instance -- diagrams can be a useful
servant or a dangerous master. Their purpose is to help
you generate ideas. If some form of diagramming seems
helpful on a particular project, then use it. If different
forms seem suitable for different parts or phases (e.g.
matrix followed by concept maps) then use more than one.
But don't let the diagrams dictate to you.

*Diagram
mustn't
dictate*

For example, the matrix in Figure 3.10 gives eighteen
possible categories of course content to think about. It
would be dangerous, however, to assume that every cell of
the matrix must necessarily have something in it. Some
cells may be empty and some may be considerably fuller than
others. Nor should we allow the neat boxes of the matrix
to blind us to the possibility that some important topics
may lie outside its boundaries or even be obscured by this
quite powerful way of carving up the conceptual territory.

*Process v
product*

Finally, remember it is the **process** of drawing such
diagrams that is meant to be helpful, rather than the final
product. It may be, on occasion, that your diagrams will
be so revealing of the structure of your subject (as with
an algorithm, for instance) that you will want to share
them with your learners. On the other hand, you may think
it more to the point to help your learners develop their
own pictures of the subject-matter.

Enough is Enough

*Avoid
overload*

However you decide on the possible content of your course,
don't overload it. Too many self-instructional courses
contain far more content than learners can possibly cope

with in the time available. And nothing causes them more dismay, especially if they are working at a distance. Unlike on-site learners, they cannot easily pick up hints from you or fellow learners as to which bits of the content can safely be ignored when time presses. Under stress, their learning may become superficial, or they may drop out altogether.

...and its dangers

So, don't feel obliged to include everything you happen to know about the subject area, however much that might amaze your friends and affright your enemies. Tell your learners what they need to know to attain acceptable learning objectives, and no more than that. Given such a solid foundation, they will then be able to seek out any further content they feel they need, under their own steam and in their own time.

How little need they know ?

IT MAY BE BETTER FOR LEARNERS TO FULLY UNDERSTAND **HALF** THE CONTENT YOU WOULD IDEALLY LIKE TO INCLUDE THAN TO HALF UNDERSTAND ALL OF IT.

Learners' Own Content

Can learners choose ?

Finally, before we leave the subject, it is worth noting that some self-instructional courses require learners to decide **their own** content -- at least for some portion of their time on the course. Thus, for example, after several packaged lessons in a poetry course, learners might be asked to gear their next week's work to preparing an essay on a poet of their own choice.

Projects

Taken further -- perhaps occupying several weeks of work -- such a learning task may be called a **project**. Here, instead of working through course materials, learners will be guided in doing some kind of

*Tutor
guidance*

investigation of their own. They may, for example, carry
out a local pollution survey or document the history of
a local building. Such a topic would need to be agreed
with a tutor, who would also advise on useful approaches
and source materials and would eventually comment on the
results.

*Worth
doing ?*

Such a course would save money on preparing and
producing teaching materials; but extra might need to be
spent on tutorial support to learners. How far the
approach might be justified would depend on the nature of
your objectives and on the degree to which your learners
are able and willing to take responsibility for what and
how they learn.

These final paragraphs serve to highlight two questions
that reflect back on the whole of this chapter:

```
*************************************************
*                                               *
*  WHAT DO YOU KNOW ABOUT YOUR LEARNERS ? and    *
*                                               *
*  HOW DO YOU KNOW WHAT THEY NEED TO LEARN ?     *
*                                               *
*************************************************
```

4. PLANNING YOUR TEACHING -- SEQUENCE AND METHODS

*Four more
planning
questions*

Having identified your learners and thought about aims and
objectives and content, you still have four questions to
consider at the planning stage:

o How will the content be sequenced ?

o What teaching methods and media will be used ?

o How will learners be assessed ?

o How will the teaching be evaluated and improved ?

We shall look at all four questions in this chapter; and
all but the first will be explored further in later chapters.

SEQUENCING THE LEARNING

*Most
helpful
order ?*

Once you've got some notion of possible content, you need
to think about sequencing it. How might the ideas best
be ordered within your course or lesson ?   How do we
identify a sensible teaching sequence ? To the best of
our ability, we must ensure that the ideas our learners
meet early in the teaching are those that will help -- or
at least not interfere with -- their later learning.

*Looking for
a storyline*

Your problem here is akin to that of the novelist or
playwright at a similar stage of their writing. Like them,
you need some kind of vision of your course or lesson **as
a whole** -- yet not so rigid a one that your preconception
prevents it from developing in useful but unforeseen ways
once you get involved in writing the actual learning
materials. What you are looking for is the equivalent of
"narrative drive" or **storyline** -- a broad flow of ideas,
sufficiently coherent for you at least to be able to begin
writing with some confidence about where you are heading.

It may help, when trying to envisage your storyline, to
be aware of some of the kinds of sequence that I have
noticed in self-instructional materials:

Varieties of Sequence

Here are some of the possible types of sequence that may
be needed within your course. More than one type will
usually be evident within any one course, and sometimes
within one lesson.

*Nine types
of sequence*

Topic-by-topic. What we might also call the "parallel
themes" approach -- involving the study of a number of
related themes or topics which (after an initial
introduction to the overall purpose of the course) could
have been studied in any order. The topics are independen
-- parallel rather than forming a necessary series.
Within the lesson(s) on each topic, however, other types
of sequencing would probably be needed.

*Independent
topics*

Chronological sequence. In such a sequence, happenings,
events, or discoveries over a period of time are presented
in the order in which they occurred. This order will
obviously suggest itself when your subject-matter is
historical -- and this is not confined to "history"
courses. Chronological sequence may be necessary in
dealing with the development of institutions, or of
economic or social theories, or of scientific discoveries
-- wherever understanding of one event or of one stage
depends on the understanding of what had occurred
previously. I have recently used chronological sequence
in writing lessons about a staff appraisal system. Here,
the sequence followed that of the separate activities
that managers and staff engage in at intervals over
the "reporting year".

*The
"historical"
approach*

Place-to-place. This is the spatial equivalent of
chronological order. Start talking about one place or
situation, and work your way from place to adjacent
place. In writing about ailments of the human body,
for example, you might start with the head and work
your way down to the toes.

*Adjacent
places*

Concentric circles. This is a variant on place-to-place in which one "place" is included in the next, and that in another, and so on. For instance, colleagues and I developed a management course in which the sequence of the blocks was as follows:

*Like
onion
skins*

1. You as a manager.
2. You and your team.
3. Your team within the organization.
4. Your organization within the wider world.

Beginning with the basic techniques required of a manager, the course goes on to discuss how these need to be blended with social considerations in coordinating the activities of the members of the manager's team; then on to how the work of the team is affected by the structure and culture of the organization that it forms part of; and finally to how the work of the organization is affected by social, legal and economic changes in the outside world.

Causal sequence. This kind of sequence is also closely related to the chronological. Learning based on a causal sequence will follow a chain of cause-and-effect for an event or phenomenon -- so that when learners reach the end of the chain they can explain the final effect, the event or phenomenon itself. It applies where you are teaching cause-and-effect relationships -- especially if your objective is that the learners should be able to work out and explain such a relationship.

*Cause-
effect
chains*

This kind of sequencing might be relevant in meteorology or in geomorphology, where the learner is establishing the cause-and-effect relationships that result in different weather patterns or in different landscape formations. You might use a diagram like that shown in Figure 3.8 to explore the possible causal sequences that might be followed.

(On page 54)

Structural logic. Here we are talking about a sequence dictated by the logical structure of the subject. Sometimes it is clear that a certain topic cannot be learned without

*Subject's
own logic*

prior understanding of some other topic. For instance, in
basic arithmetic, the idea of multiplication will not make
sense unless you have already learned addition. And in
order to carry out division you need first to be able
to subtract.

Most subjects have a certain amount of "structural
logic" in them -- either in the connection between one
major topic and the next or at least **within** such topics.
Thus, in learning a new language, it may be clear that
learners must learn to distinguish between sounds in that
language before they can hope to imitate them in their

*Beware
spurious
logic*

own speech. Conversely, what we often take to be "the"
inner logic of a subject is sometimes nothing more sacred
than the order in which we once happened to have learned
it ourselves !

Problem-centred sequence. You may sometimes be able to
structure a course, or lessons within it, around the

*Seeking
solutions*

exploration of an issue or problem. If you present your
learners with a problem and then engage them in developing
solutions or interpretations, you may be providing them
with a realistic context in which to learn the essential
knowledge and skills of the subject.

Examples

For instance, an in-service course for family doctors
might focus on the problem of "What do patients really
expect from doctors ?" An interdisciplinary humanities
course might develop a variety of approaches to the
problem "Is man free ?" A technology course on the
properties of materials might have a section based on
the problem "What is the most suitable material from
which to mass-produce car bodies ?"

Spiral sequence. In this kind of sequence, learners will
meet a concept again and again during their progress

*Repetition
plus*

through the course -- each time at a more complex or
demanding level. This may appeal to you if your subject
is of a kind where learners cannot get deeply into any one

topic or concept unless they already have some familiarity
with most of the others. Thus you may decide to give
your learner a brief tour of the main conceptual landmarks
before coming to examine them closely and, later still,
going on to analyse them in yet greater depth. At each

Increasing
sophistic-
ation

new level, the learner will treat the concepts in more
sophisticated ways, relating them to a growing network
of more recently acquired understandings.

An example from elementary physics: The concept of
"force" might first be introduced as "push" or "pull";
then discussed in terms of acceleration, using graphs;
and, later on, it might be represented symbolically.

Backward chaining. Whenever objectives involve the learning
of sequences (or "chains") of activity or decision-making --
whether simple chains (like tying a knot) or complex (like

Last
step
first

applying a problem-solving routine), it may be useful to
teach the **final** step in the chain first. You might then
teach the second to last step, and so on.

For example, you might teach your learners to interpret

An example

the results of a chemical test before you teach them how
to carry out such a test. And you might then teach them
to do such tests (which they can already interpret) before
teaching them how to select the appropriate test. Figure
4.1 below shows how such a sequence would work with a
chain of five steps:

Figure 4.1: Sequencing a Five-step Chain

Run	Steps in chain	Key
1	E→	☐ = Student learns step
2	D→Ⓔ→	
3	C→Ⓓ→E→	◯ = Student is reminded of step
4	B→Ⓒ→D→E→	
5	A→Ⓑ→C→D→E→	No box or ring = Student performs step unaided
6	Ⓐ→B→C→D→E→	
7	A→B→C→D→E→	

Such backward chaining offers an unusual advantage -- it
can provide your learners with the satisfaction of master#
Good for
motivation ?
the final stages of the job at the outset of instruction.
This can also help motivate their further learning in that
they now see the relevance of each step they then need to
learn in order to reach the stages they have already
mastered.

Logic v Psychologic

Whatever types of sequence you go for, do so on the
grounds of how you believe they will appeal to your
What is
best for
learner ?
learners and help them learn. Don't just follow the
traditional "logic of the subject" as enshrined in the
textbooks. This will be the logic of people who are
already expert in the subject. It may or may not appeal
to newcomers.

What you should be looking for is not so much the best
logical order as the most satisfying **psychological order.**
Psychological
order
For instance, despite the usual advice to go from simple
to complex, concrete to abstract, learners may sometimes
enjoy **starting** with something fairly complex, e.g. as a
challenge or as an indication of what the basic work will
be leading up to. (Backward chaining would be one example
Similarly, while one might traditionally start at the
beginning of some chronological subject-matter and work
towards the present, the psychological order might be to
work backwards from the present.

I hope you feel I have been reasonably "psychological"
in my ordering of the chapters in this book. If not, I am
Learners'
choices
sure you will read them in the order you find most
appropriate ! (That's what our learners often do, no
matter how carefully we've tried to think out the "ideal"
sequence.) I leave you to decide what kinds of sequencing
I have used within chapters -- and whether it is logical,
psychological, both, or neither.

From Topics to Teaching Points

*What are
your main
topics ?*

Within the subject-area you have defined -- whether by
concept analysis, diagramming, or any less formal methods --
you should be able to identify the main topics. Figure
4.2 shows the main topics I picked out from my initial
concept map for diet and nutrition (Figure 3.7 on page
53). It is a hierarchy (yet another form of diagram !).
That is, it shows which topics must be explored before
certain others can be understood ("structural logic").
Clearly, knowledge about "components of food" appeared
to me as the cornerstone of understanding here.

Figure 4.2:   A Hierarchy for **Diet and Nutrition Course**

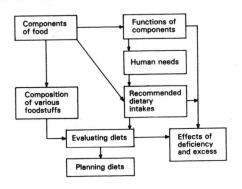

In Figure 4.3 below, I took the analysis one stage further
looking for linear sequences through the topics. In fact,
I identified at least two. After an introduction to "the

*Possible
sequences*

components of food", learners might work down the
left-hand side of the diagram first, as far as "analysing
sample diets", and then down the right-hand side as far
as "interpreting tables of recommended dietary intakes"
(always following the broken line) -- or they might work
through the right-hand set of topics first (following the
solid line). Either way, they must have followed both
chains of topics **before** going on to "evaluating diets".
Yet a third possibility is for the sequence to take, as

it were, a "middle path" -- pursuing dietary needs and
dietary sources both at the same time, combining ideas
from both sets of topics.

Figure 4.3: A Flow Diagram for Diet and Nutrition Cour

Teaching point outlines. In fact, a list of ordered topi
may not provide a clear enough framework upon which to
begin writing. Preferably, once you have decided on the
topics you'll be tackling within each lesson, you should
decide what **teaching points** you want to make about each.
These should be arranged in sequence as a **teaching
point outline.**

*List of
topics not
enough*

Your "teaching points" are the main statements you wa
to make about the subject-matter, e.g. definitions,
factual observations, relationships, judgements, and so
For instance, you might begin your teaching point outlin
for a lesson on Diet and Nutrition by drawing on the

*List your
teaching
points*

topic "components of food" as follows:

   o Food has six main components.

   o These components are...

   o They can be divided into the following categories...

Teaching points from topics

At this juncture we would need to decide whether to draw our next teaching point from the topic "functions of food" or from the topic "foodstuffs in which each is found". Alternatively, we might draw on both, making our next point an integrative statement, e.g.

   o In order to balance a diet, you need to know
          how much of each component is required, and
          how to obtain it.

An example

For a completed example of a teaching point outline, see Figure 4.4 which formed the basis for one chapter in a self-instructional book about studying. Compare it with the spray diagram in Figure 3.5 (page 50). If you have not already diagrammed your subject-matter, this kind of teaching point outline can be produced (as can a concept map, for that matter) by starting out with a number of topics, e.g. "speed of reading", "quality of reading", "improving reading" -- and deciding what statements you want to make about each.

From teaching points to paragraphs

Once you have got your list of statements arranged in what seems like a sensible order, you can use it as a framework for your writing. Each teaching point may form the basis for a paragraph or two (rarely more). Remember, however -- as with all aids to course planning -- not to let your teaching point outline dictate to you. Be prepared to delete, add, re-write and re-sequence your teaching points as you get ahead with the writing of your lessons. The process of writing may bring to mind points that had escaped you earlier. Incidentally, AFTER you have written a lesson, it can be a useful check on the

*Checking
your
points*

lesson's structure to read through it -- or get someone
else to -- making a list of the teaching points you have
actually covered, paragraph by paragraph.

The Learner's Own Sequence

One final thought before we leave the subject: The
sequence in which you finally decide to present your ideas
may not be the sequence in which some learners choose to
tackle them. Even within an individual lesson, some may
begin by reading the final few pages -- and then skim

*Learners
vary*

through the rest of the text, stopping wherever they see
something that catches their interest. They may or may
not then go on to work through the text, paragraph by
paragraph from the first page. And within a course, some
learners may choose to start with the lessons they expect
to be most rewarding (or most threatening) rather than
follow the published sequence.

With some courses and subjects, it may be quite
practicable for learners to decide their own sequences.
With others, the way you've written the course materials
will make this difficult, if not dangerous. You need to

*Encourage or
discourage ?*

decide whether to encourage learners in choosing their
own sequences -- e.g. by clear contents lists, section
headings, index, etc. (see Chapter 8) -- or whether to
warn them against it.

IF YOUR COURSE CONTAINS A **PROJECT** (SEE PAGE 59)
LEARNERS WILL BE REQUIRED TO DECIDE NOT ONLY THE
SEQUENCE BUT ALSO THE CONTENT OF THEIR STUDIES.

Figure 4.4: A Teaching Point Outline (based on *Learn How to Study* by D. Rowntree, Macdonalds, 1976)

1 Despite 'experience' few college students read as well as they might. (Too slow, can't concentrate, forget.)
2 For *better* reading (improved comprehension):
   (a) Apply SQ3R to get sense of purpose.
   (b) Look for topic sentence in each paragraph:
       (i) Usually first or last sentence, and
       (ii) Contains the *main idea* of the paragraph.
   (c) Look for important *details*:
       (i) e.g., proof, example, or support for main idea.
       (ii) Usually at least one to each main idea.
   (d) In hunt for main ideas and important details:
       (i) Watch out for signposts: visual (Layout and typestyles), verbal (Clue words and phrases).
       (ii) Study all charts and tables.
       (iii) Don't skip difficulties.
   (e) *Evaluate* the text:
       (i) Be sceptical (expect author to prove).
       (ii) Look for applications in your own experience.
3 Towards *faster* reading: (most people could read half as fast again and still understand just as well).
   (a) During reading:
       (i) Eyes jerk left to right in series of *fixations*.
       (ii) At each fixation, brain decodes group of words, making up its *recognition span*.
   (b) *Poor* readers:
       (i) Have small recognition spans, therefore make many fixations
       (ii) Regress frequently (backward glances).
       (iii) Read aloud (or make sub-vocal noises).
4 Can improve reading (speed *and* understanding).
   (a) Five basic steps:
       (i) Check whether you need specs.
       (ii) Stop saying words aloud.
       (iii) Consciously try to read faster.
       (iv) Read in thought-units (2 or 3 words at a time).
       (v) Build-up vocabulary (reading, speaking, writing) by reading widely, learning Greek and Latin roots, noting new words, using dictionary, making glossaries.
   (b) Practice (absolutely essential) by:
       (i) Nightly sessions (15 to 30 min.): read articles of known length, time yourself (w.p.m.) (Progress chart?), test your comprehension.
       (ii) Reading *all* study material faster.
   (c) Vary your reading pace:
       (i) Faster for 'story-like' material and main ideas.
       (ii) Slower for complex argument and for important detail.

CHOOSING YOUR TEACHING MEDIA

Early planning needed

Although Chapter 11 deals with media in some detail, I include a few paragraphs here. This is to persuade you that choice of media is worth thinking about **early** in your course planning. The most urgent question for consideration is likely to be:

Which media do you and your learners actually have access to ?

Available Media

Print (plus AV ?)

In most self-instructional courses -- whether on-site or at a distance -- the main medium is **print** (the written wor together with pictures). This may be supported by **audio-visual** material -- especially audio-cassette tapes, and slides or filmstrips. Occasionally, moving pictures in the form of television or film will be available. In some cases, television or radio teaching will be broadcast

Other media

Practical work can be arranged, if necessary by providi learners with their own "kits" of material and equipment, or by enabling them to use laboratory or workshop faciliti at some convenient location. **Personal interaction** -- between learners, or between learners and a tutor -- may be possible, at least occasionally, either face-to-face or on the telephone.

A list of media

Figure 4.5 is a list of four broad categories of media. I leave you to decide which of them might be available for your course.

The Functions of Media

Compensating for your absence

If you were meeting your learners in class, you would be performing a number of teaching functions. Since you are **not** meeting them face-to-face (or not often), you will need to make your chosen media perform these functions **instead of you**, viz:

Figure 4.5: Types of Media

PRINT

o Textbooks and "readers" -- already published, or else specially written.

o Specially written commentaries or supplements to already published material.

o Specially written "correspondence texts" or "tutorials-in-print" (see Chapter 5).

o Worksheets (or media notes) for use with audiotape or videotape material, practical work, etc.

o Study guides, tests, notes on assignment requirements, bibliographies, etc.

o Maps, charts, photographs, posters, etc.

o Newspapers, journals, and periodicals.

o Handwritten materials passing between learners and tutor.

o Computer-learner "conversations".

AUDIO-VISUAL

o Audiotape (or disc).
o Radio broadcasts.
o Slides or filmstrip.
o Film or film loops.
o Videotape.
o Television broadcasts.
o Computer displays.

PRACTICAL WORK

o Materials, equipment, specimens for learner's individual use -- e.g. home experiment kits.

o Field-work or other use of learner's local environment -- e.g. social or ecological surveys, collection of local plant specimens, etc.

o Work in local laboratories, farms, workshops, etc.

o Assignments based on learner's place of work.

HUMAN INTERACTION

At-a-distance

o Telephone conversation between learner and tutor (supplementing written communications).

o Learner-learner telephone conversations (or exchange of letters).

o Several learners in telephone contact at the same time, with or without a tutor, by means of a "conference call".

Face-to-face

o Learners' self-help groups.

o Contacts with local people with relevant knowledge or skills.

o Occasional seminars, tutorials, lectures by tutors or other group organizers.

o One-day, one week, weekend, or other short duration group sessions (residential or otherwise).

Tasks for
your media

o Catching the learners' interest.
o Reminding them of earlier learning.
o Stimulating new learning.
o Explaining, and provoking thought.
o Getting learners to respond actively.
o Giving them speedy feedback to their responses.
o Encouraging them to practise and review.
o Helping learners assess their own progress.

Types of Learning Stimuli

Between them, the various available media can provide
several different types of stimuli to learning. These
appeal to different senses or ways of understanding in
our learners. The different stimuli are:

Five types
of stimulus

The written word	-- print, typescript and handwritin
Pictures	-- diagrams, photographs, maps, graphs, etc. (still or moving).
Recorded sound	-- music, speech, etc., that can be listened to away from the preser of the person who produced it.
Human interaction	-- responsive communication with other people, either face-to-fac or on the telephone.
Real objects and events	-- and, where they are being observed rather than interacted with, real people.

Essential
stimuli

For certain learning objectives, some types of stimuli are
essential. For example, learners could not be expected
to learn **how to read** blueprints without pictorial help.
Nor could they learn to identify soil specimens (e.g. as
sandy, loam, or clay) without getting their hands on some
real specimens.

For other objectives, one stimulus may simply be
preferable to another, though either might be serviceable.

Preferable stimuli

For instance, learners' attitudes can be affected by the
written word -- but human interaction is likely to affect
them more deeply.

Several types of stimuli can be combined in a
particular medium. For example, both the written word

Combining stimuli in one medium

and pictures can be contained in a book; a video-tape can
combine pictures (still or moving), recorded sound, and
(as captions) the written word; practical work can combine
real objects or events and human interaction; and so on.

The Essential Questions

Here is a set of key questions to ask yourself when
choosing media :

Questions to ask

o   Which media are available to me **and** to the learners ?

o   Do any of our learning objectives imply particular
    types of stimuli and particular media ?

o   If so, how and to what extent (e.g. what proportion
    of the learner's time) would I wish to use each of
    the preferred media ?

o   What would it cost me **and** the learner (in money, time
    and flexibility) to use these preferred media ?

o   Would less expensive media be **acceptably** effective ?

o   Do the chosen media offer the learner sufficient
    variety of stimulus and activity ?

o   How can I **combine** media for maximum effect (e.g.
    audio-tape plus real specimens) ?

ASSESSMENT AND EVALUATION

More later

These two topics are also given chapters of their own
later in the book. Again, however, I am spending a
few paragraphs on each here -- simply to emphasize that
they should be given early consideration in the planning
of a course.

Assessing Your Learners

As part of your planning, you should decide on:

*Courses v
lessons*

(a)   an assessment strategy for the course as a
      whole; and

(b)   an appropriate way of assessing learners on each
      lesson, within this overall strategy.

*Questions
to ask*

Key questions. Here are some of the key questions you
might consider:

o What knowledge, skills and attitudes will be assesse

o At what points in the course will they be assessed ?
   -- e.g. sometimes learners can usefully be assessed
   lesson by lesson, while with some objectives we need
   to know whether learners can **integrate** what they hav
   learned over a **number** of previous lessons.

o How **will** learners be assessed ? (This is an importa
   question to ask early on because some forms of
   assessment, e.g. a project report, will influence ho
   the course is to be taught).

o Who **will** think up the assessment **activities** and
   prepare any necessary materials ? -- e.g. assignmen
   questions, examination papers, guidance notes for
   markers, etc.

o By whom will the assessment be carried out ? -- e.g
   by the individual learner, by other learners, by the
   person who produced the course, a tutor, an external
   examiner, etc.

o   Will the assessments "count" towards any form of
    certification ? -- e.g. a certificate of "course
    completion", a course grade, a diploma, or a degree

o   If different standards of learner performance are to
    earn different grades, how will these standards be
    decided upon ?

o   What kind of feedback will learners be given as a
    result of assessment ? -- e.g. marks, grades, comments
    on their strengths and weaknesses, model answers, etc.
    And can this be given in time to help them improve
    before they finish the present course ?

o   Can data from assessment be used to improve the
    course for present or future learners ?

```
*******************************************************
*                                                     *
*  NB.  EVEN IF YOUR LEARNERS WOULD REJECT ANY KIND OF *
*  FORMAL ASSESSMENT (e.g. ON A HOBBY COURSE), YOU     *
*  WILL STILL NEED TO PROVIDE THEM WITH THE MEANS      *
*  OF SELF-ASSESSMENT.                                 *
*                                                     *
*******************************************************
```

Assessment is discussed further in Chapter 13.

Evaluating Your Teaching

Evaluation is dealt with more fully in Chapter 14.
However, like assessment and the choice of media, it

*Start
planning
early*

is not an issue that can be safely left on one side until
after you've produced your course or lesson. Right from
the beginning, you need to be thinking about how you will
check on its effects and effectiveness -- with a view to
making modifications and improvements, where necessary.

*Overall
strategy
needed*

As with assessment, you need an overall strategy for
evaluating the course -- within which, plans can be made
for evaluating each individual lesson or type of learning

activity. What kinds of data will be sought and how might it be collected ? There are two main areas about which you may wish to collect evidence:

Two aspects to evaluate

1. *Subject-matter credibility*. Is the course content accurate, relevant, up-to-date, balanced, etc. ?

2. *Educational effects/effectiveness*. Can the course enable reasonably productive learning within the time learners have available for it; and what unexpected problems/opportunities arise during its operation ?

There are four main ways of collecting evidence. Crudely speaking, the first two mentioned below will be chiefly concerned with 1 above, and the second two with 2. But all four are likely to yield at least some insights about both subject-matter and educational factors:

Four ways to collect evidence

Critical commenting. What arrangements will be made for one or more members of the course team to study and critically comment (constructively, of course) on the materials produced by each of the other members ? Have realistic amounts of time been budgetted for this activity ?

Commenting by external readers/assessors. These may be external to your institution or just to the course team. By whom are such people to be chosen ? How will they be rewarded ? What guidance will they be given as to the nature and depth of commenting required ?

Developmental testing. What plans are there for trying out materials on typical learners in time to modify and improve before producing a final version ?

Continuous monitoring. Once the course is in operation, how can the knowledge gained in running it be used to make further improvements and refinements ? Who will take responsibility for "maintaining" the course ?

A LESSON SPECIFICATION

So, I'll assume that, for the course within which you are writing, decisions have been made, **and** properly documented, about:

Documented decisions

o Prospective learners

o Aims and objectives

o Content

o Sequence

o Media

o Assessment

o Evaluation

The idea of a "lesson"

I'll further assume that you are responsible for developing one or more sections of the course. These I would recommend you to think of as sets of "lessons", each lesson being meant to occupy the learner for, say, 1-2 hours. Experience indicates that both learners and teachers find this amount of study time to be the most manageable unit when planning how to get to grips with the course content.

Specification or blueprint

Before launching into the first draft of your first lesson, you should ideally produce **a specification**. This will be essential as a means of conveying your intentions to fellow-authors if you are working in a course team. But even if you are working alone, you may find such a "blueprint" worth drafting to remind yourself of your own earlier intentions.

The blueprint or specification for each lesson, or set of lessons, within a course might usefully indicate the following:

Points to include

o Proposed title of lesson.

o Name of author(s)

o Dates by which materials are to be made available -- e.g. for commenting by colleagues, for developmental testing, and for final production.

o Names of any course team colleagues who have been specifically enlisted as commenters.

o   Names of external readers/assessors.

o   Relationship of material to rest of course -- e.g. any prerequisite knowledge/skills/attitudes expected of learners. Entry test needed ?

o   Aims and objectives.

o   Outline of content -- main theories, concepts, processes, procedures, etc., to be included.

o   Sequence -- list of main teaching points in order, or a flow diagram.

o   Teaching media to be used -- e.g. textbook plus notes, audio-cassette, practical work, etc.

o   Chief types of learner activity -- e.g. reading, problem-solving, project work, etc.

o   Types of assessment required -- e.g. learner-marked objective tests, tutor-assessed essays, exams, etc.

o   Evaluation plans -- e.g. how will material be tested and improved ?

o   Total estimated study time, including assessment activity.

You should now be ready to begin writing your first lesson, the subject of Chapter 5.

```
*******************************************************
*  BUT TRY NOT TO SPEND TOO MUCH TIME PREPARING       *
*  YOUR LESSON UNLESS YOU KNOW THAT THE REST OF        *
*  THE COURSE HAS BEEN AGREED IN OUTLINE OR YOU        *
*  ARE QUITE CONFIDENT THAT YOUR LESSON CANNOT         *
*  LATER BE DECLARED "SURPLUS TO REQUIREMENTS".        *
*******************************************************
```

5. WRITING A SELF-INSTRUCTIONAL LESSON

Print is the basis ?

Having thought about the purposes and content of your self-instructional lesson, you should now be ready to begin writing it. In this book I am assuming that the chief medium you will be using is **print** -- written words and (still) pictures. Print is the most-used medium of self-instruction and, in any case, any advice I have to give about it can easily be adapted for use with other media also. (In Chapter 11, I do give some advice about developing an audio-visual lesson and using other media.)

TEACHING THROUGH SELF-INSTRUCTION

Teaching the unseen learner

Teaching a learner through self-instruction is different from any other kind of teaching you may have done. It is not like lecturing -- where the learner is there in front of you and can ask you to clarify a point or give more examples. Nor is it like a classroom lesson or a tutoring session -- where you can see that the learner needs extra help or more practice. You won't be around to advise the learner on how to tackle the work -- and, if the learner is studying alone, nor even will other learners. So:

```
************************************************************
*                                                          *
*   EVERYTHING YOU MIGHT HAVE WANTED TO SAY TO             *
*   LEARNERS STUDYING IN YOUR PRESENCE WILL NEED           *
*   TO BE THOUGHT OF AND PUT DOWN IN WRITING INSTEAD.      *
*                                                          *
************************************************************
```

What kind of writing ?

Unfortunately, even the kind of writing required is quite different from anything most teachers will have done previously. It is not like writing lecture notes, journal articles, training manuals or textbooks.

Lecture notes are clearly not written with solo learners in mind; and journal articles are usually written for fellow-specialists rather than learners. Training manuals

Your writing must teach

and textbooks may seem closer to the mark. But they are usually written for teachers, or for learners working closely with a teacher. Usually they will provide learner only with a **reminder** of the **bare bones** of the course conte -- and with a source of exercises to which the teacher wil provide the answers. That is, they are rarely written as a **substitute** for the teaching. Those that are we might prefer to consider as self-instructional texts !

The Tutorial-in-Print

Tutoring in print

It is vital that you keep in mind the learners you are writing for. But do not imagine them as part of a lecture audience -- nor as textbook readers whose teacher is hovering somewhere in the vicinity. Imagine instead that you are **tutoring** one individual learner for between one and two hours. Everything you might want to say to this individual will need to be written down -- forming what I have called a **tutorial-in-print**.

What your writing must do

This is what you will need to do in your tutorial-in-print if you are to teach your individual learners:

o Help the learners find their way into and around your subject -- by-passing or repeating sections where appropriate.

o Tell them what they need to be able to do before tackling the material.

o Make clear what they should be able to do on completion of the material (e.g. in terms of objectives).

o Advise them on how to tackle the work (e.g. how much time to allow for different sections, how to plan for an assignment, etc).

o Explain the subject matter in such a way that learners can relate it to what they know already.

o Encourage them sufficiently to make whatever effort is needed in coming to grips with the subject.

o   Engage them in exercises and activities that cause
    them to work with the subject-matter -- rather than
    merely reading about it.

*(More about
activities in
Chapter 6)*

o   Give the learners feedback on these exercises and
    activities -- enabling them to judge for themselves
    whether they are learning successfully.

o   Help them to sum up their learning at the end of
    the lesson.

How Much to Write ?

Perhaps I ought rather to say "How **little ?**" Newcomers
to self-instruction are often surprised that learners take
so long to work through their materials. It is rare to
find an author who **under**-estimates the amount of material
learners can get through in a given time.

*Less than
you think ?*

When reading for entertainment -- say the latest Judy
Collins or John le Carré -- people may be able to read
two or three hundred words per minute. But research
indicates that people **studying** a self-instructional text
will read much more slowly. As **learners**, they will be
pausing to take notes, or to answer questions, or simply to
reflect on how their own experience or beliefs relate to
the ideas being discussed in the text. They may even need
to read certain sections several times.

*Reading v
learning*

As a **very** rough-and-ready estimate, you might reckon
on your average reader working through self-instructional
materials at the rate of about:

*A rough
estimate*

```
*****************************************
*                                       *
*  50 - 100 WORDS PER MINUTE, OVERALL   *
*                                       *
*****************************************
```

For a one-hour tutorial-in-print, this suggests a **total**
of (50 x 60) to (100 x 60) = 3000 to 6000 words.

*Variable
speeds*

With straightforward, narrative material (like this), some of your readers may exceed 100 words per minute. But with a complex, closely-reasoned argument -- especially when the ideas are new to your learners and take some coming to terms with -- their speed may drop to 50 words per minute, or less.

*Activities
take time*

As for the questions, exercises and activities you build into your text -- and these are essential in self-instruction -- they can reduce the reader's overall speed yet further. Some activities may be particularly time-consuming. For instance, just the **four** following words -- "Now interview six customers" -- would be quite enough to keep your learners busy for an hour or more.

*No formula
figures*

So, one cannot simply give a formula figure for the number of words that learners might be expected to cope with in a given time period. It depends on what you are wanting them to do with those words. For example, if you're wanting them to do practical work, you'll need to give them less reading to do. Likewise if you want them to study from an audiotape or draft an assignment to send to a tutor. Remember also that if you want your learners to read from some **other** book or printed materials, you will need to subtract the required number of words from what you might otherwise have reckoned to write yourself.

*Difficult
to predict*

*...so try out
your drafts*

Even when the materials have been completed, it is sometimes quite difficult to predict how long the average learner will take over them. Your ability to predict will improve with practice, of course. Meanwhile, the best way to ensure you don't make unreasonable demands is to try out an early draft of your lesson on some typical learners. If they take too long, prune it fearlessly ! Early drafts often need to be reduced by 50% or more as a result of such tryouts.

*Dangers of
overload*

It is so easy for the self-instructional author to get carried away and generate far more work than learners can cope with in the time available. This can cause them considerable distress -- and they may even drop out of the course. After all, unlike classroom learners, they cannot easily confirm with their teacher (or even with one another) that some of the material (and which ?) can safely be skimmed or ignored altogether. Yet I have many times seen evidence that courses are overloaded -- and never the reverse.

How Long to Write ?

This is another much-asked question for which there are no cut-and-dried answers. How much time you'll need to develop a given set of self-instructional materials will depend on so many factors -- like, for instance, on:

*What your
speed depends
on*

o How much new thinking/learning you need to do about the subject-matter.

o How much you need to find out about the needs of your learners.

o Whether your materials are meant to be truly self-instructional or just a prelude or follow-up to other teaching.

o The extent to which you can have your learners work from already-published material.

o How easy it is to think up appropriate and effective teaching strategies.

o What kinds of activity you are setting your learners.

o What media you are using.

o How many drafts you need to go through -- and how many learners you need to try them out on -- in order to get a version that produces satisfactory learning and is acceptable to colleagues.

*Some
examples*

For example, if you base your lesson on having your learners read a chapter in an existing textbook, it will clearly take you less time than if you had to write the chapter yourself. And very much less than if you had to produce computer software or a piece of interactive video.

*More
examples*

Similarly, if the subject-content is clearly defined and well known to you, you should be able to produce your material faster than if the subject is new to you and/or has to be "created" in debate with colleagues -- as often happens in interdisciplinary courses with titles like *Health and Environment, Images of Women,* and *Science in Society*. On the other hand, you may know so much about the subject that you take an inordinate amount of time deciding what to **leave out** -- or else write it all down and then lose time later by having to rewrite (and rethink) it more succinctly.

*Another
broad
estimate*

All the same, one needs **some** idea of how long it's all going to take (even if it usually takes longer). Various estimates are to be heard among self-instructional writers -- from one day per hour of learning time to several weeks per hour. I would suggest you'll need to allow, on average, **at least 50 hours** of development time per hour of learning time. Some lessons may need less -- but some may need twice as much (and maybe more, especially if they involve computers).

*Can we
afford to
be quick ?*

As with most things in life, you get what you pay for. Quality learning materials need thoughtful planning, writing, testing and rewriting until they **work**. This takes time. Inferior materials (the "quick and dirty") can be produced more cheaply -- by skimping on or omitting some of those stages. This is what happened with programmed learning in the 1960s, when bad (but cheap) material drove out the good (but expensive) -- leading to the discrediting and collapse of programmed learning. I hope we can ensure that history does not repeat itself with distance/open learning in the 1980s.

WHY NOT USE EXISTING MATERIALS ?

*Already
published
materials*

Instead of writing your own lessons, why not make up the
learning package from existing texts and/or tapes, together
with some specially written notes on how to study them ?
(I am not talking here of taking over a complete **course**,
which is an option I discuss in Chapter 2.)

*Could save
time and
add quality*

This can seem like an attractive way of saving time.
And, in theory, it might provide your learners with more
authoritative teaching materials than you could produce
from your own resources alone. Material of quality does
exist, and some of it you may be able to turn to the
needs of your learners.

*Questions
to ask*

However, in view of the essential features of
self-instruction I listed earlier, we must demand answeers
to a number of searching questions. These are set out
in Figure 5.1 overleaf.

*Don't trust
titles*

We certainly cannot rely on authors' and publishers'
claims that their materials will substitute for a teacher.
Nor can we base our trust on titles like *Lion-taming Made
Easy, Learn Hypnotism in Your Sleep,* or *Teach Yourself
Brain Surgery.* Too often they are simply jazzed-up
textbooks.

*Sources of
information*

A more promising way to track down useable materials
(at least in Britain) would be to consult the materials
catalogues of the Open University or the National Extension
College -- or the Materials and Resources Information
Service (MARIS), set up by the Open Tech Unit of the
Manpower Services Commission. But the questions
overleaf will still need to be asked.

```
****************************************************
*                                                  *
*   NB.  IT MAY BE WORTH YOUR WHILE ENLISTING THE HELP  *
*   OF PROSPECTIVE LEARNERS IN VETTING SUCH MATERIALS.  *
*                                                  *
****************************************************
```

Figure 5.1:   Questions to Ask About Books or Other
              Potential Learning Materials

Coverage   Is the subject-matter appropriate for our
                learners ? Is it broad enough ? Deep
                enough ? Any serious omissions ? What
                proportion is irrelevant to our needs ?

Teaching   Does it teach -- or merely act as a
approach   reference, or as a reminder of what has
                been learned elsewhere ? Is it geared
                to a learner working without other help ?
                Does it require learners simply to read
                and remember ? Or must they interact with
                the material through exercises and
                activities ? Are they given adequate
                feedback ? Summaries ? Glossary ?
                Tests ? Index ?

Style   Is the style of the material suitable
                to our learners, e.g. vocabulary,
                sentence length and structure, use of
                graphs and other pictorial material ?
                Is it interesting ?

Reputation   Does the material have a "track record"?
                Have we used it before ? Do we know how
                well it has been received by other
                teachers/learners ?

Physical   Is it attractive in appearance ? Durable
format   enough to survive likely use ? Easily
                carried about, if necessary ? Useable
                anywhere it might be needed ?

Treatment   Is it acceptable to the specialist or
              expert ? Accurate ? Up-to-date ? No
              distortions or over-simplifications ?
              Well-argued ?

Audience   For whom is it written ? Is its target
              audience (so far as we can identify it)
              sufficiently like our prospective
              learners ?

Starting   What prior knowledge and skills (e.g.
point   numerical, technical or social) are
              required of its audience ?

Costs   How much does it cost to hire or buy ?
              Are additional costs attached to using
              it, e.g. a video play-back system ? Is
              this within our budget and/or that of
              learners ? Is the study-time it would
              entail for learners reasonable ?

Availability Can we rely on its being available
              (e.g. staying in print) throughout the
              intended life of the course ?

Alternatives How does the material compare on all
              counts with other existing material and
              with what we might produce ourselves ?

Supplementing Existing Materials

*Using what
you can*

It is unlikely that any existing material will be
completely suitable for your learners. Even so, material
may still be useable **within** your package, e.g. as a
"set book". Or you may decide to write your package

around the material in such a way as to overcome or compensate for any weaknesses it may have.

A study guide. For instance, you might produce a "study guide" to help your learners get the best out of a not altogether satisfactory text (or tape). Such a study guide might include items like the following:

Possible study guide contents

o Your overviews and/or summaries of the subject-matter.

o Concept maps or other diagrams showing how the main topics and ideas are related.

o Learning objectives.

o An annotated bibliography.

o Guidance as to which chapters/sections to study and which to ignore.

o Specially-written (or audio-taped) alternative explanations -- to be studied instead of sections in the materials that you think are inaccurate, biassed out-of-date, confusing, etc.

o Local or topical examples or case studies -- which you have prepared because they will be more appealin than those (if any) in the existing material.

o Your paragraph-by-paragraph commentary on the argument expressed in the text.

o Questions and exercises based on the materials, section by section.

o Model or specimen answers to questions, and written discussion of criteria whereby learners can evaluat their own responses to questions or exercises that seem likely to be answered in diverse ways.

o Suggestions for practical work or experimental activity, e.g. guidelines or worksheets.

o A glossary of technical terms.

o A self-assessed test related to the objectives.

o Instructions for an assignment to be sent to a
   tutor for comment and/or marking.

Your study guide supplement to the existing materials may
be minimal or extensive. At the very least, you must
ensure your learners are provided with:

The bare
essentials

- guidance on how to approach the materials;

- a means of assessing their understanding of the
  materials; and

- additional help on any topics they have failed
  to understand.

At some point, you may find yourself not so much
supplementing existing materials as writing your own

Writing
your own ?

lessons and merely incorporating those materials. At
what point ? Perhaps at the point where learners must
spend more than 50% of their time on "your" material.
But no matter. In the following chapter, I assume that
the lesson you are producing will be sufficiently "yours"
to be called a tutorial-in-print. Even if you are
merely supplementing existing materials, however, much
of what I have to say will still be relevant.

SAMPLE PAGES FROM SELF-INSTRUCTIONAL TEXTS

Anyone who wants to write -- whether epic poetry,
sexsational best-sellers, or self-instructional texts --
would do well to study what others have written in the
chosen genre. So, in the remainder of this chapter, we'll

Extracts
for
analysis

look at twelve extracts from tutorials-in-print. They all
come from Open University courses, some at undergraduate
level, some from post-experience training and vocational
updating. I shall be referring back to these examples in
later chapters.

N.B. The sample pages are some 40% smaller in area than the
originals, and some of the originals had colour.

The Culture of an Organization

3   Four kinds of organizational culture

In this section, I am going to ask you to work on the first ten pages of the material entitled 'On cultures and structures' in Charles Handy's *Understanding Organizations* (pp 176–185). He describes four different kinds of organizational culture and the kinds of structure associated with each. (He then goes on to look at the factors influencing an organization's culture and structure, and to consider the implications for organizational change; this will form the substance of Session 10.2.)

Introduction
Read the introduction now (pp 176–7) asking yourself the following questions. (Jot down your answers in the margin alongside.)

Activity F ▷
- To what extent does Professor Handy's idea of 'culture' seem similar/different to those we have been working with so far?
- Does he approve/disapprove of different organizations having different cultures?
- What is the key concern that Professor Handy says links his 'cultures/structures' approach to describing organizations with the systems approach and contingency theories?

- Charles Handy seems to be much in agreement with the way we have been talking of 'culture' so far. He mentions 'sets of values and norms and beliefs'. Where he seems to be moving us into new territory, however, is in his emphasis on the close link between culture and structure.
- He approves of cultural and structural variety amongst organizations.
- The concern that links his 'cultures and structures' approach to the systems approach and contingency theories is with *appropriateness*. (Even when it would be pointless to look for the one best way of doing something, we should still be looking for an appropriate way, even if it is one of several such.)

Section 2 The cultures
Section 2.1 (pp 177–8)
Now read Charles Handy's paragraph introducing cultures (pp 1.77–8), asking yourself the following questions. Note your answers in the margin.

Activity G ▷
- How many different cultures does he mention? Are these all he thinks possible?
- Does he suggest that just one of these cultures will be found throughout any one organization?

- Charles Handy mentions four cultures, labelling them *power, role, task,* and *person.* He seems to imply that only these are possible.
- He asserts that 'even within organizations cultures will differ'.

Now we shall look at the four 'possible cultures' one by one. In the discussion, Professor Handy talks of the various types of power – personal, resource, expert, position – which you should recall from his treatment of them in Session 8.2.

Section 2.2   The power culture (pp 178–9)
Read this section.

Activity H ▷   What kind of manager would be happy in a power culture?

To get on well in a power culture, Professor Handy says that people must be 'power oriented, politically minded, risk taking, and rate security as a minor element'. They

◀ **Figure 5.2A**

This extract comes from a "post experience" course for managers (P670). It illustrates a "low cost" approach, based on a previously published textbook. Not all of the textbook is appropriate to the objectives of the course. Nor was it written with self-instruction in mind. So, in a separate booklet from which this sample page is taken, learners are asked to read a couple of pages of the book at a time. Each time, they are given one or more questions and are asked to write their answers in the wide margin of the booklet.

After each of these "activities", there is a line across the page -- a "reader stopper", reminding learners not to read on until they have answered the questions. There then follows the course author's answers, so that learners can verify their understanding of the text.

This fairly basic approach can be applied to **any** existing material -- from the blurb on a packet of breakfast food to a full length feature film. Essentially, you are asking the learner "What are they saying ?" and/or "What do you make of it ?". Thus, you can get your learner to engage with you in the detailed analysis of published materials.

Units 2B and 9   Uses and Abuses of Argument

Recently a friend wrote to me that he had been reading Solzhenitsyn's account of conditions in Soviet Russia. 'It's incredible,' he commented. Well, so it is. But just a minute. Did my friend mean that he couldn't (i.e. didn't) believe what Solzhenitsyn had written? That is what 'incredible' (like 'unbelievable') means, strictly speaking. It means that it is not possible to believe. But perhaps my friend was using 'incredible' in a devalued sense; perhaps he merely meant 'hard to believe' or 'very surprising'. The word is often used in this way, and mostly – but not always – the meaning is clear enough and no harm is done. However, on this occasion I really was uncertain: did my friend believe it or didn't he? Did he mean *literally* incredible? That is what I found myself asking in my letter to him. But then it struck me that 'literally' too is used in a devalued way! Thus if my friend had said that he found it 'literally incredible', I might have had to ask: But do you mean 'literally' *literally*? And so on.

Sometimes the desire for hyperbole leads one to choose an expression which is not simply an exaggerated version of the truth, but which actually means something different. I suppose that the writer of A meant to use 'slave' by way of hyperbole. It is stronger, more dramatic, than such words as 'badly off', 'underpaid', or 'exploited by the employer'. The trouble is that 'slave' is *not* just an extreme version of these; it means something rather different. (Of course there are also resemblances, which make it plausible to use that word.)

The word 'claustrophobia' in C is a more subtle case. It is, again, an impressive word: and again there is a certain satisfaction, a feeling of 'speaking out', in declaring that 'all city-dwellers' suffer from claustrophobia. Still, isn't it true at least of some city-dwellers? (Let's not argue here about 'all' and 'some'.) Take those people crowding into a tube-train at rush-hour. They are, literally, like sardines. (Well, perhaps not *literally* . . .) Do you mean to tell me they are not suffering from claustrophobia?

What should we say? Is it correct to use the word 'claustrophobia' of these people? If not, why not? (If necessary, consult your dictionary.)

No doubt conditions in a rush-hour train can be very unpleasant. And the same may be said of certain other aspects of city life today. We may feel quite strongly that people living in these conditions are suffering harm, that they are losing something very important. And no doubt 'claustrophobia' may seem to carry the right sort of punch to drive this home. But it would be driving in the wrong direction. For the point of a word like 'claustrophobia' (as with other 'phobias' and 'manias', for example agoraphobia, kleptomania) is that it refers to an *abnormal* response. And there is nothing abnormal in feeling frustrated, irritated and sometimes enraged, if you travel in rush-hour trains, get stuck in traffic jams and dwell in crowded conditions. If we are going to use the word 'claustrophobia' for this sort of thing, what will we use for cases of claustrophobia?

They are, literally, like sardines

22

◀ **Figure 5.2B**

This extract comes from an undergraduate humanities course (A101).
But for the box in the middle of the page (and perhaps the cartoon),
this might appear, at first glance, like an extract from an
"ordinary" book. It presents a sequence of paragraphs in which the
author tells of his experience, analyses it, and draws conclusions
from it -- all in a quite informal yet closely-reasoning style.

Where it differs from an ordinary book is in what it expects of the
reader. The reader is not treated as a passive sponge -- one who
will merely "read, learn and inwardly digest". Rather, the reader
is seen as an **active** partner in a **dialogue** or conversation. This is
revealed by the question in the middle of the page. It is not
rhetorical -- not just a stylistic device. The reader really is
expected to think out a personal response to the author's question --
and write it in the box provided. Having paused for the reader to
make a contribution, the author then goes on to comment on the
question.

A couple of technical points: Notice that the "activity" -- the
question about the use of the word "claustrophobia" -- is not
labelled as such. However, the box will immediately indicate to
readers that this is an activity to be answered. Below the box,
you will notice that there is a double line across the page to
act as a "reader stopper" -- though we may feel that the box itself
is adequate for this purpose.

The governors' roles and responsibilities

You can find out about your role with regard to curriculum by looking at your Articles of Government. Here are extracts from three sets of Articles:

Model Articles

8. (a) The Local Education Authority shall determine the general educational character of the school and its place in the local educational system. Subject thereto the Governors shall have the general direction of the conduct and curriculum of the school.

8. (c) (ii) All proposals and reports from the Head affecting the curriculum and conduct of the school shall be submitted formally to the Governors....

Liverpool's Articles

The headteacher in consultation with the Authority and the Governors shall be responsible for the direction of the conduct and curriculum of the school.

Birmingham's Articles

...the Governing Body in consultation with the Head Teacher shall be responsible to the Authority for exercising general oversight of the conduct and curriculum of the School.

🔺Which of the three extracts above seems to give governors most responsibility for curriculum and which of the Articles is most like yours?

It seems to us that the Model Articles give governors greatest responsibility for curriculum: they are to be responsible for its *general direction*. Liverpool's Articles, however, see the head exercising the direction, and only needing to *consult the governors* (and the local education authority). Birmingham's Articles are almost the reverse – this time the governors *consult the head*, but general 'oversight' sounds like rather less responsibility than general 'direction'.

As for the Articles which are most like yours – the chances are that the Model Articles come closest. Most governors will find their Articles expect them to exercise general direction (or general oversight) of the conduct and curriculum of the school.

General direction/oversight

Many local education authorities (LEAs) issue 'Notes of Guidance for Governors' which indicate what general direction/oversight actually means.

🔺Look at the extracts from two sets of 'Notes' that follow (one from East Sussex and one from Walsall). Underline all the words and phrases that indicate what governors should be doing about the curriculum.

East Sussex

The Governors must therefore be kept well informed by the Head about the curriculum and in particular about any new developments.

It is important that Governors should take an active interest in this key aspect of the school's work. They should not hesitate to ask questions and should ensure that these questions are fully and properly answered.

Walsall

The Governors usually exercise their influence in three ways:
(i) by seeking information
(ii) by requiring to be consulted, and
(iii) by giving advice.
The Governors have a right to be informed about all matters concerning the life of the school. The Head and other teaching staff are trained and expert professionals but this need not cause the Governors to hesitate to ask questions: indeed, if they ask questions enough and listen carefully to the answers they will be in a fair way to becoming experts themselves.

In the East Sussex 'Notes' we underlined 'well informed', 'active interest', 'ask questions' and 'ensure that these questions are properly answered'. In the Walsall notes, we underlined points (i), (ii) and (iii), and again noticed also 'ask questions'.

Exercising your role

Perhaps we can sum it up by saying you can exercise your general direction or oversight of the curriculum by:
● Expecting to be consulted
● Seeking information (asking questions)
● Offering comments or advice
● Taking any necessary action.

Consultation   It is perhaps when *changes* are in the offing that you are most likely to get involved. To be usefully involved it is essential for you to *know about* the proposed change.

🔺Suppose there *is* to be an important curriculum change in your school, maybe a new method of teaching reading is to be introduced, or maybe the teaching of separate science subjects is to be dropped in the first three years in favour of combined science.
(a) At what stage do you think the governors *should* first hear about such a change?
(b) At what stage do you think the governors of *your* school actually *would* hear for the first time?
Tick the appropriate boxes in the (a) and (b) columns below.

The head first consults governors	(a) Should?	(b) Would?
1 Before consulting staff	☐	☐
2 After consulting staff but before making decisions	☐	☐
3 After decisions but before letter informing parents	☐	☐
4 At same time as parents by sending them copy of letter to parents	☐	☐
5 At next governors' meeting by a reference in his report	☐	☐
6 The head never mentions the change to the governors	☐	☐

◄ **Figure 5.2C**

This extract comes from a course for school governors, helping them
come to grips with their new roles and responsibilities (P970).
The most obvious feature of the page is its two-column layout (and
the narrow margins).

Perhaps the next things to strike the eye are the three symbols
(a white letter "A" on a dark square) that indicate activities.
The first two activities get the readers to analyse extracts from
other governors' documentation (and, in the first case, compare
these with their own). The third activity gets them to relate the
general principles expressed in the documentation to how things are
actually handled in their own schools.

Notice the variety of the questions asked. The first activity is,
in effect, a multiple-choice question -- requiring readers to notice
the key words in three brief texts and make a couple of overall
comparisons. Readers are not told whether merely to think their
answers or to mark them somewhere on the page.

In the second activity, readers are given a couple of brief texts
and are asked to pick out all the words and phrases that touch on
a certain matter. They are to record their answers by underlining.

The third activity is a two-fold task: readers are asked what they
think should happen and what they think would happen. The form of
the question is multiple-choice, and readers are asked to indicate
their two answers by ticking boxes.

Notice that the authors' answers are given immediately after each
activity. Notice also that there are no "reader stoppers" on this
page. On the original, however, the activity material was printed
in red, and this might have reminded learners not to read on until
they'd answered the question -- but for the fact that the authors'
answers were also printed in red !

Overall, nearly two-thirds expected a prescription. On being asked what they expected the doctor to do for them, they might reply:

> 'More than he did last time. Last time he just gave me paracetamol under another name.'

or
> 'I've been coming for my blood pressure, and he'll ask me how I've been in the last month. I'll tell him I've been feeling weak in the legs and he'll take my blood pressure. I expect he'll give me the usual pills but he might change the dose.'

or
> 'What I've come for now is more tablets. Well, the doctor might examine me a bit, have a chat and I'll leave feeling better, feeling the doctor is doing me good.'

Once the patient comes into your surgery, your prescribing is likely to be influenced, not just by the physical signs and symptoms, but also by the *social interaction* between you and the patient. In particular, you are liable to be influenced by the patient's expectations and by your estimates of how he is likely to respond to various forms of treatment.

Here is a consultation (quoted by Byrne and Long, 1976, page 12) with an elderly man who has recently had varicose veins removed from his leg. The doctor seems to be reacting to the patient's concern about his pills.

But is there anything you feel he is missing? Underline any of the patient's statements that you feel should have been pursued further by the doctor before he wrote what was, in fact, a repeat prescription.

Doctor: 'Well now, here you are again. How are things?'
Patient: 'Oh, doctor, I have not been taking all those pills you gave me. They didn't seem to agree with me.'
Doctor: 'Ah ha. Have you been getting your exercise every day?'
Patient: 'Oh, yes, doctor. Every morning I walk to work and I walk home at night. That's nearly four miles a day.'
Doctor: 'Mmm. Now then, how about this leg?'
Patient: 'Oh, that's much better now. The scar is still there though. I expect it will go in time.'
Doctor: 'How about the wife? Is she getting about all right?'
Patient: 'Yes. She gets out of a morning and goes down to the shops. She takes the bus down to the station, you know, and walks from there.'
Doctor: 'You're sleeping all right, aren't you?'
Patient: 'Well, I still take those tablets, doctor.'
Doctor: 'Good. Well now. Take this to Mr Green and get it made up. There are some different pills. Different colour, you know. Let me know how things are getting on. Don't forget your umbrella. 'Bye-bye.'

We have underlined 'I have not been taking all those pills you gave me. They didn't seem to agree with me' and (referring to his ability to sleep) 'Well, I still take those tablets, doctor'. The doctor does not investigate what happened to the patient that made him stop following the prescribed medication. Furthermore, he seems to have completely ignored or misinterpreted the patient's admission that he is not sleeping all right – and with it the implied expectation, perhaps, that the doctor should be doing something about it. The patient may also be seeking praise and reassurance, both on his own account (e.g. the scar) and on that of his wife, but he does not get it. We can only speculate as to why this doctor was either ignoring or not noticing the patient's 'social' messages (tiredness, boredom, irritation?) – whatever the reason, it resulted in less than optimum treatment.

◀ **Figure 5.2D**

This extract comes from an in-service course for family doctors, aimed at improving their prescribing habits (P550). Its most striking feature is its use of quotations from "real world" patients and the activity based on a mini case study.

Notice that the presentation is not academic and detached. It is job-related, specific in its examples, and it clearly expects the reader to relate its ideas to his or her own **practice**. Notice also that the text is not merely presenting knowledge but is also working on the reader's **attitudes**.

The "activity" is signalled by bold print (on a coloured background in the original) and a line acts as a "reader stopper". Readers are asked to analyse the situation presented and to indicate their responses by underlining appropriate statements. The authors then go on to say which statements they regard as significant, and why.

2.3 Extraction

The amount of a substance that dissolves in a particular solvent is a function of the solubility of that substance. Solubility is a physical property: its value depends on the nature of the substance being dissolved, on the nature of the solvent and on the temperature. So different substances will have different solubilities in the same solvent (at the same temperature). We can make use of this property in the technique of extraction.

If we take a liquid mixture of substances which we want to separate and add to it a solvent which is fairly insoluble in the mixture then, after shaking the container, we will find that some components of the mixture will have been preferentially extracted into the solvent phase.

For example, pentane-1,5-dioic acid is prepared from pentane-1,5-dinitrile according to the following reaction:

$$NC(CH_2)_3CN \xrightarrow[H_2O]{H_2SO_4} HOOC(CH_2)_3COOH$$

(Don't worry about the chemicals involved in the reaction — all we are interested in is the extraction procedure.)

At the start of the reaction there are two liquid layers present; an aqueous layer containing the sulphuric acid and an organic layer consisting of the dinitrile, as shown in Figure 4. The product, pentane-1,5-dioic acid, is soluble in water in the presence of H_2SO_4 so the reaction is continued until the organic layer disappears. At the end of the reaction there are several substances present in the aqueous layer.

Can you think of a way of extracting the organic acid from this solution?

In Unit 1 you were told that 'like dissolves like'. This organic acid has both polar and non-polar parts to the molecule, neither of which dominates the other, so the acid should dissolve in both polar and non-polar solvents. Therefore if we add a non-polar solvent to the mixture the organic acid should be extracted, to some extent, into this solvent leaving the sulphuric acid, water and other polar substances in the aqueous layer. Non-polar solvents commonly used are diethyl ether, toluene and trichloromethane (chloroform).

The procedure adopted for this particular reaction reads as follows:

> *Reflux* (i.e. continuously boil, returning the condensate to the reaction flask) the mixture for 10 hours and allow to cool. Extract with diethyl ether (four 150 cm³ portions); dry the ethereal extracts with anhydrous sodium sulphate. Distil off the ether.

So the organic solvent chosen in this example is diethyl ether. The aqueous solution is transferred to a separatory funnel like that shown in Figure 4. A 150 cm³ volume of diethyl ether is then added and, after shaking, the two liquids are allowed to settle. As diethyl ether is insoluble in water, a distinct boundary will be observed between the water and the ether. By running off the lower, aqueous, layer into a separate container until the boundary approaches the tap, we achieve a partial separation.

Why, in this example, do we extract four times with 150 cm³ portions of the ether rather than extract once with 600 cm³ of ether?

Extracting with four lots of 150 cm³ of solvent is much more effective than extracting with one lot of 600 cm³. We know this from everyday experience; to quote one example, if we were extracting paint from paint brushes, much cleaner brushes would result from washing with five lots of 20 cm³ of white spirit than with one lot of 100 cm³ of white spirit.

After extracting four times with 150 cm³ of diethyl ether, the ether extracts are combined. Water is not completely insoluble in diethyl ether and so the water is removed from the ether by shaking with a solid drying agent (anhydrous sodium sulphate). Finally the solvent is removed from the required organic substance by distillation over a hot water bath. The resulting residue is fairly pure pentane-1,5-dioic acid.

10 hours under reflux

start of reaction

two liquid layers

one liquid layer

end of reaction

transfer liquid to separatory funnel

add 150 cm³ of ether and shake

two liquid layers

running off lower layer

aqueous layer

ethereal layer

transfer aqueous layer to separatory funnel.

add 150 cm³ of ether and shake

aqueous layer

ethereal layer

extract twice more with ether

distil off ether

ethereal layer

collect residue

product

FIGURE 4   The preparation of pentane-1,5-dioic acid.

◄ **Figure 5.2E**

This extract is from an undergraduate course on chemistry (S246).
The layout is very striking, with the wide right-hand margin
entirely occupied by a sequence of diagrams. These diagrams
illustrate an "extraction procedure" described in the text alongside.

Within the text, there are two "activities" -- about one-third and
three-quarters of the way down the page. They are indented and have
more space above and below them than there is between normal
paragraphs. The first asks learners to suggest a method of
extraction, while the second asks them to explain a step in the
procedure. The author's comments follow directly, after a space.

The activities do not exactly leap to the eye on this page. Partly
this is because they are not followed by "stoppers". Partly it is
because their layout is not distinctive enough; they have exactly
the same appearance as the item that begins with the word "Reflux"
and much the same appearance as the reaction equation near the top
of the page. Might it have been better to print the activities in
bold type or a second colour ?

Incidentally, the extraction procedure illustrated in the diagrams
is the kind of sequence that some course developers might expect to
demonstrate with **moving** pictures -- using video. A series of still
pictures (together with text or audiotape commentary) can sometimes
provide an acceptably effective low cost alternative.

eighteenth-century music whereby two bars of ¾ become one of ³⁄₂.[1] afford a welcome relief from the prevailing rhythmic pattern and also yield an apparent extension of the phrase. Examples of hemiola cadences may be found in this air at bars 36–7 and 65–6; less obviously perhaps at 46–7.

At first sight the B section (bar 47), while continuing the dotted accompanimental rhythms, appears to have a new vocal line. However, after two bars the familiar melodic contour with its dotted rhythms recurs:

Ex. 10

Seeks she the groves,   or bathes   in   crys - tal   foun - tains?

(cf. bars 35–8)

showing that Handel regarded this as a continuation of the same, rather than a calculated contrast as one might expect to find in a B section of a *da capo* movement.

EXERCISE

Play the air now. Observe the points I've made (basic 'affect', dotted rhythms, hemiolas) and ask yourself whether the tonal scheme is conventional. The movement is in C minor, so we would expect the following keys to be reached and probably clinched by substantial cadences: E♭ major (relative), G minor (dominant minor), B♭ major (one degree sharp), F minor or A♭ major (flat side). Does this happen? If so, where?

ANSWER

I identify the following principal cadences: E♭ major (relative) 17–18; F minor (subdominant) 23–4; C minor (tonic) 37–8 and, following the ritornello, again at 46–7. The B section begins on the sharp side, B♭ major, and cadences in that key 50–51; in E♭, 54–5; and moves to the dominant minor (G minor), where it cadences (no third in the chord, incidentally) at 66–7.

DISCUSSION

The A section has a tonal scheme of tonic–relative–subdominant–tonic; the sharp side, G minor or B♭ major, is entirely absent. I assume this is because Handel is reserving both these keys for the B section.

3.5 No. 6, Recitative: 'Stay, shepherd, stay!'
No. 7, Air: 'Shepherd, what art thou pursuing?' (Damon)

The delightfully brief and pertinent recitative leads to an Italianate ritornello-based *da capo* air which could serve as the archetype for the hundreds of such movements found in works by Handel and his contemporaries. 'Shepherd, what art thou pursuing?' seems to me first class in every respect: form, tonal movement, melody, accompaniment and deftness of orchestration, all of which are persuasively realized by the St Martin's Academy/Marriner performance we have chosen, especially in the tasteful but thoroughly characteristic embellishments, vocal and orchestral, found in the repeat of the A section. **Listen to the movement now.**

Fairly obviously, the piano accompaniment to the vocal score lacks the finesse of Handel's scoring which is, incidentally, for first and second violins in unison,

---

[1]That is, ³⁄₂ ♩♩|♩♩♩♩ |becomes in effect ³⁄₂ ♩♩♩|♩♩♩ |. You will remember from Unit 3, Section 4.2, that this is a characteristic and prevailing feature of the courante in the French suite.

◄ **Figure 5.2F**

This extract is from an undergraduate course on music (A314).
The page bristles with terminology that may be unfamiliar to most
of us -- "hemiola cadences", "dotted rhythms", "ritornello", etc --
though this "jargon" is clearly presumed to be familiar to learners
who have got this far through the course. (Notice the footnote
referring readers back to an earlier lesson.) Despite the technical
vocabulary, the tone of the prose in which it appears is energetic
and personal.

The discussion centres around listening to recorded music. In this
section of the course, learners are listening to a commercially-
produced gramophone record. (In other lessons they listen to
audio-cassettes specially prepared by members of the course team.)
A pair of symbols appear in the margin at two points on the page --
signalling to readers, the moment they turn to this page, that they
will be needing their gramophone record and (the symbol on the right)
their printed score. An additional prompt is given by printing the
instruction to play the record in bold type.

The first use of the gramophone record and score relates to an
activity (or "exercise" as it is labelled here). Readers are asked
whether the tonal scheme is conventional in the piece they are
listening to -- and to locate the expected cadences in their score.
The author's answer follows immediately, the heading "Answer" perhaps
acting as a "reader stopper". A paragraph headed "Discussion"
follows the answer, and the whole activity block is preceded and
followed by a line across the page.

The second "listening" has no exercise associated with it. Readers
are given information and judgements about the piece but are not
asked questions about it. We can no doubt think of reasons why the
course author might choose sometimes to direct the learner's
listening and sometimes not, but we cannot confirm them from this
extract alone.

B4;J.3   11

and is noticeably less spread out. There appears to be a marked peak just below 60 in the sampling distribution whereas it is difficult to identify a peak in the population distribution.

You may also have commented on the fact that the heights of the vertical lines in the sampling distribution are smaller than those in the population distribution. This is due to the fact that the vertical lines measure proportion and in each case the sum of the heights of *all* the vertical lines is equal to one. Because there are many more lines in the sampling distribution, the heights of the individual lines are correspondingly smaller. (This is rather like what happened in Section 3 of Unit B1 when we looked at various probability distributions. Recall that the greater the number of possible outcomes, the smaller the corresponding probabilities.) ■

In fact we are really interested in what happens to the sampling distribution as the sample size increases. So we shall now look at the sampling distribution of the mean for samples of size 5.

Notice that there are about 10^{17} possible samples of size 5.

Activity 1.5   Find the sample mean of each of the following samples of size 5

(a)   10, 20, 45, 62, 91
(b)   82, 24, 33, 33, 60
(c)   52, 61, 73, 61, 43
(d)   79, 64, 46, 59, 91.

Solution

(a)   sample mean $= \dfrac{10 + 20 + 45 + 62 + 91}{5} = \dfrac{228}{5} = 45.6$

(b)   sample mean $= \dfrac{232}{5} = 46.4$

(c)   sample mean $= \dfrac{290}{5} = 58$

(d)   sample mean $= \dfrac{339}{5} = 67.8.$ ■

This activity demonstrates that there are many more possible values of the sample mean for samples of size 5 than there are for samples of size 2. This means that the vertical lines in the sampling distribution will be *extremely* close together, in fact so close that it is impossible for us to differentiate between them. For this reason we just concentrate on the *shape* of the distribution as indicated by the *tops* of the lines and we obtain the following picture of the sampling distribution, Figure 1.8.

Figure 1.8   *Sampling distribution of the mean for samples of size 5*

Compare with Figure 1.7. Here we have changed the scale on the vertical axis in order to make the picture as clear as possible.

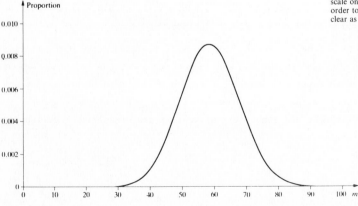

◄ **Figure 5.2G**

This extract comes from an undergraduate course on Statistics
(MDST 242). It begins part of the way through the "feedback" to an
"activity" in which learners have been asked to comment on a graph.
(The black square signals the end of the feedback.) A brief
paragraph links this with the next labelled activity -- a set of
calculations. Notice that there is no "reader stopper". However,
as in Extract F, the next heading, "Solution", may be enough to
remind learners not to read on.

With numerical answers of this kind, however, it is quite easy for
readers to catch sight of them inadvertently before having attempted
the calculations themselves. You may or may not consider this worth
worrying about. If you do, you may ask learners to guard against
it by covering the page below each activity with a sheet of paper.
Alternatively, you can print the answers elsewhere in the book.

After the worked solutions have been presented in the extract
opposite, the black square again signals the end of the feedback.
Then follows the author's comments on the results, leading on to
the next step in the argument which is illustrated with a new diagram.

Notice how the wide margin is used both to show a calculator-symbol
(signalling to readers that they are about to be asked to do some
computation) and to offer comments on the main text and the diagram.
Compare this with Extract F in which review material is given as a
footnote. The use of footnotes and marginal comments needs thinking
about in writing self-instructional texts. Are they optional
reading ? Or are they meant to be looked at as soon as they are
referred to in the main text ? If the latter, why not incorporate
them into the main text ? How can they best help the reader ?

Section 8A:2

METALLURGICAL EXAMINATION OF THE BRAKE ROD

A metallurgical examination of the brake rod was performed at the Safety in Mines Research Establishment (SMRE), Sheffield. This examination included: visual inspection, non-destructive inspection, chemical analysis, metallographic examination and mechanical testing. We shall proceed in a similar fashion with our examination.

8A:2.1 Visual examination

Before we consider the observations made at SMRE, cast yourself in the role of a metallurgical Sherlock Holmes and carry out a visual inspection of the material evidence.

Take Replica 6 (not labelled) from your Home Experiment Kit. It is moulded from the fracture surface of the larger piece of brake rod. Spend at least three or four minutes examining it under a table lamp both with your naked eye and using the magnifier. Pay particular attention to the texture of the fracture surface and to any features on the perimeter of the cross-section. Try to find answers to the following questions (I suggest you cover up the answers in the margin).

How many areas of distinguishable surface texture can you see?

> You should be able to see at least two with the naked eye. The circular fracture surface consists of two segments; the larger one (seen in the lower part of Stereoslide 7) is rather smooth, dull and flat, whereas the smaller segment is rougher and more reflecting. Both segments lie approximately perpendicular to the axis of the rod.

Compare the fracture of the brake rod to the fractures of Replicas 1–4 (the Charpy impact specimens). What conclusion can you draw?

> Replicas 1, 3 and 4 have shear lips and are not similar to Replica 6. The brake rod fracture is similar to that of Replica 2 in that the fracture is flat and lies perpendicular to the side surfaces. In texture, the Replica 2 fracture is similar to the smaller segment of the brake rod fracture. Since you know that Replica 2 is a brittle fracture (Section 6A:1.1), this suggests that the smaller segment of the brake rod surface is a brittle fracture too. This is consistent with it being reflecting.

What is the significance of the path taken by the perimeter of the rod's fracture surface?

> The perimeter follows the root of a screw thread; since this follows a helical path there is a step on the perimeter of the fracture surface (at the top of Stereoslide 7). Clearly the larger fracture segment has followed the screw thread.

14

◀ **Figure 5.2H**

This extract is from an undergraduate course on materials (T351).
The layout of the page is striking. After three introductory
paragraphs, the learner is presented with a sequence of three
"activities" -- indented and underlined -- each of which has its
own feedback in the margin (also underlined). Notice that readers
are asked to cover up the answers.

Notice also that this extract includes practical work.
The activities call for the learner to examine replicas of
fractured materials from a "Home Experiment Kit". Among other
things, this kit contains a magnifier which learners are expected
to use in this "visual inspection". The Kit also includes a simple
device for viewing pairs of slides that give a stereoscopic (3D)
image. (These slides are referred to in the feedback to the first
and third activities.)

The questions that learners are asked to consider involve identifying
features on one specimen, comparing it with other specimens, and
making deductions from the evidence. The feedback talks the learners
through what they ought to be seeing. Sometimes, to save the
learners needing to flip their focus back and forth between the
specimen (or slides, filmstrip, etc.) and the explanatory text, it
can be worthwhile putting such commentary on audiotape -- thus leaving
the learners' eyes free to concentrate on the objects.

2   THE MANSFIELD THEATRICALS

(Chapters 13–18, see Introduction pp. 26–31).

At the bottom of page 147 Jane Austen makes the observation that 'a love of the theatre is so general, an itch for acting so strong among young people that he [Mr Yates] could hardly out-talk the interest of his hearers'. But Edmund and Fanny hold out against this general enthusiasm. What are their reasons?

We are told Edmund's reasons first. He is worried by the scale of the upheaval that is threatened, and feels it to be particularly improper while his father is absent (and possibly in some danger) and Maria is in a state of semi-official engagement. Sir Thomas, Edmund is convinced, would 'totally disapprove' (p. 152). Fanny 'had . . . borne Edmund company in every feeling throughout the whole' (p. 153). So does she disapprove simply because Edmund does? I don't think Jane Austen puts this explanation entirely out of the question. She exalts the values of Fanny's love for Edmund (see Chapter 4) but this does not put her above being slightly amused by her devotion. However, Fanny has been considering the situation independently, and has come to the conclusion that if scruples about Sir Thomas won't stop the actors, their own egocentricities may. Edmund's words are very fine, but quiet Fanny is the more down-to-earth, perhaps.

Edmund's resistance begins to crack very quickly. Where do you first see signs of him weakening, and what do you think Jane Austen intended us to understand by it?

When Mary Crawford announces her desire to be useful, Edmund is 'obliged to acknowledge that the charm of acting might well carry fascination to the mind of genius' (p. 154). I'm not sure whether his tone here is meant to suggest stilted pomposity, or ironic overstatement; but it certainly conveys his embarrassment. I don't think this indicates that we are called on to condemn Edmund downright as a hypocrite; what Jane Austen is doing is establishing with masterly care the mixture of his motives. Look at the exchange with Fanny on page 175 where he finally capitulates. Are we meant to praise or blame him? Or is a more complex assessment required of us?

Surely, what we are asked for is richer than simple praise or blame: Jane Austen wants us to see all the irony of the situation. Poor Edmund, not only forced out of his opposition, but made to take one of the leading, and most improper, parts! And his motives hopelessly divided between preserving the sanctity of his father's household, and pleasing Mary Crawford!

◀ **Extract 5.2I**

This extract is from an undergraduate course on the nineteenth
century novel (A302). In a way, it is similar to extract A in that
it is guiding learners through their reading of a separate,
already-published book. In this case, however, the book (Jane
Austen's *Mansfield Park*) is not the source of the teaching (as was
Charles Handy's *Understanding Organizations*) but rather the **subject**
of the teaching.

Learners are here being involved in a detailed analysis of a chapter
they have already read through on their own. The author of the
lesson proceeds by asking readers to say what they see in the
chapter (e.g. "Where do you first see signs of him weakening ?")
but also to interpret Jane Austen's intentions (e.g. "Are we meant
to praise or blame him ?").

The author's feedback to these activity-questions is careful in
giving the facts (complete with page-references); but she also states
her own opinions. These latter are often questing and tentative
(e.g. "I don't think...", "perhaps...", "I'm not sure...") as befits
a teacher who is helping learners respond to irony and ambiguity --
rather than memorize some received view of what Jane Austen is
all about.

Visually, the page is dominated by the prominent and elaborate
"stoppers". Together with the decorated initial letter, they
perhaps lend a period flavour to the design of the page; but they
are heavier than they need be to remind learners not to read on --
and, in fact, they were reduced in size in later editions of
the course.

J

Activity 4.6   **Allow 5 minutes**

Active listening

This activity, like the last one, uses photographs and is quick and easy to do. These photographs are intended to make you more consciously aware of the non-verbal messages associated with listening.

As you look at the following two photographs, imagine that you are the patient. State, in each case, whether you think that the nurse is listening to you in a way that really makes you feel she is concerned to hear what you have to say. Write down what it is about the nurse that tells you whether or not she is listening.

PHOTO 1

PHOTO 2

Authors' comment

PHOTO 1: this nurse appears to be paying attention to what the patient is saying, for she is looking directly at her. However, the nurse is standing up and has placed herself further away from the patient than is usual for someone who is genuinely interested in developing a conversation. The nurse also has her arms folded so that she is unconsciously creating a physical barrier between herself and the patient. The message which the patient receives from the nurse is to keep her conversation brief and superficial.

PHOTO 2: this patient is being listened to. The nurse has positioned herself close to the woman and at her eye level. She shows no sign of hurrying

away. She is looking directly at her patient and her face shows that she is concentrating on what is being said. The way the nurse is leaning slightly towards the woman suggests genuine interest, and her touch shows warm concern. The patient should be aware that the nurse wishes to hear what she has to say and indeed, she appears to be quite relaxed and comfortable in the conversation.

Communication is a two-way process. Once you have perceived what your patient is telling you, you need to respond in a way that shows you understand.

You can convey empathy in your words and your actions. For example, you can use words which simply reflect an understanding of what is being said:

"I can see that is very painful for you to talk about."
"You are really very worried about going home."

You can avoid words that imply an opinion or judgment and thereby focus attention away from the patient and onto yourself.

"That's good", "That's wrong", "I think you should . . ."

Touch can convey a great deal of warmth and understanding, but needs to be used sensitively. Inappropriate invasion of personal space can be discomfiting and irritating and will not be received as an empathetic gesture. However, holding the hand of a woman in labour or a patient undergoing a painful procedure, cuddling an unhappy child or literally providing a shoulder for a distressed patient or relative to cry on are examples of ways in which touch can be used to give comfort. Touch can also be invaluable in conveying empathy when there are major communication barriers, as with a blind person, a patient being artificially ventilated, or a patient who cannot understand English.

Allowing the patient to cry, or to express anger or any other emotion is important. "There, there don't cry", or "try to calm down" imply that you don't think that the emotions being expressed are appropriate, or at least that the person shouldn't be sharing them with you.

Of course, empathy isn't something which you deliberately set out to create – it evolves within a relationship; but a deeper understanding of the elements of communication involved and a heightened self-awareness can make you a much more effective partner to your patient. If this material is new to you, further study in the field is strongly recommended (see *Further Reading* at the end of the module).

Activity 4.7   **Allow 10 minutes**

Getting involved with your patients

This activity aims to help you think about the practicalities of forming close relationships with your own patients and their families.

List any practical difficulties or personal anxieties which you think may occur if you get more closely involved with your patients and their families.

◀ **Figure 5.2J**

This extract comes from a professional updating course for nurses
(P553). As in Extract D, the discussion is clearly job-related and
concerns human relationships and is seeking to influence the reader's
attitudes and behaviour (as well as understanding). The author gets
readers to analyse the behaviour of two particular nurses (in the
photographs) before going on to make a more general statement about
what is involved in attaining empathy with patients.

There are two activities on this page. Each is labelled "Activity"
and numbered. In the original, this label is printed in a coloured
block. The presentation of the activities has three features that
do not appear in any of our other extracts, viz:

- readers are told about how long to spend on each activity;
- each activity is given a descriptive heading; and
- readers are told what they are expected to get out of
  each activity.

In the first activity, readers are asked to identify with the patients
in two "micro case studies" and pick out significant aspects of the
nurses' behaviour. (Such an activity might suggest a moving picture
treatment, on videotape; but obviously much is possible using still
pictures only.) The second activity asks readers to anticipate likely
difficulties in applying the approaches being discussed to **their own**
situation. As feedback to the first activity (headed "Author's
Comments"), the author shows how **she** would respond to the activity.
The feedback to the second activity (not shown on this page)
lists five points that readers may have written down, together with
an acknowledgement that they may have written others.

The two-column format is neither "portrait" nor "landscape" -- for
the text area is as broad as it is high. Notice the variety of
typestyle. Apart from the main text, different typefaces are used
for headings to the two activities (bold), for the statement of
purpose for each activity and for "speech" within the main text
(italics), and for the feedback to activities (light italic). Notice
also that all these typefaces, unlike those in our other extracts,
are "san serif" (no little tails on the letters).

K

2 PERSON TO PERSON

Asserting yourself

Relationships are a matter of give and take. You tell

people what you want. You try to understand what they want.

How can you do it without falling into the traps we talk about in the earlier topics? Look at the cartoons on these two pages and decide which is most typical of you when you try to stick up for yourself.

Passive, hostile or assertive?

The first cartoon shows a passive exchange. Mabel approaches Bill timidly. She is apologetic. She is vague about what she wants. Bill hardly bothers to listen. He doesn't even register that there is a problem.

The second cartoon shows a hostile exchange. Mabel is really steamed up. She attacks Bill but she doesn't really say what she wants him to do. The conversation escalates. They exchange insults. Bill slams out of the house.

In the third cartoon strip, Mabel gets what she wants. Bill agrees to 'talk about the problem'. Why? What has happened that is different? Mabel has asserted herself. She has worked out beforehand what she wants to say. She is concrete about exactly what she wants Bill to do. She persists. She is not put off.

Asserting yourself or asserting your rights is part of good, clear communication. People sometimes think that being assertive means being pushy, selfish or manipulative. It doesn't.

You are more likely to be manipulative if you adopt a passive role like Mabel in the first cartoon. This Mabel will probably get back at Bill by sulking, crying or secret acts of revenge. She might 'forget' to wash his socks.

You are more likely to be selfish and pushy if you adopt the hostile approach. The hostile approach assumes that no compromise is possible. The only gains will be those won by force. Blaming, anger and making others feel guilty are the weapons in both cases.

Asserting yourself means first working out what you want, then saying it clearly and negotiating with others. If you are assertive, you retain your dignity and leave others the chance to retain theirs.

56

What do you do?

Most people have times when they find it difficult to assert themselves. Someone puts you down. Someone takes advantage of you. You get bad service in a shop. You can't stand up to someone in authority. You feel timid, anxious, or shy. You find a 'good reason' for not making a fuss. And you don't get what you want.

Think of some occasions where this sort of thing has happened to you recently. Write them down, on a separate piece of paper, like the example from Mabel below. For each one make sure you write down what happened, who you were with, where you were, when it happened, how often this has happened before.

Think of at least four events of your own to write down.

What happened?	Who with?	Where?	When?	How often has this happened before?
When I made a	Bill	At a	Last	Every time we meet
comment about		party	week	his friends
politics to Jane,				
Bill said 'Oh				
Mabel, you don't				
know what you're				
talking about'				

ASSERTING YOURSELF

For the four events you have written down, tick any of the following feelings you experienced at the time:

	1	2	3	4
sad				
hostile				
bewildered				
frightened				
shy				
resigned				
inadequate				
self-conscious				
stupid				
inferior				

Tick any of the following bodily reactions you felt:

	1	2	3	4
'butterflies in the stomach'				
blushing				
going weak at the knees				
dry mouth				
increased pulse				
heart thumping				
shallow breathing				
hot flushes				
sweating				

And any of the following rationalisations you made to yourself:

	1	2	3	4
it's not worth making a fuss about				
perhaps I'm being selfish				
it's only once				
no-one else is complaining				
it won't make any difference				
I don't want to make a scene				

You now have the information you need to start changing your behaviour to become more assertive. Look through your list of situations. Decide which was the most threatening to you.

Decide which was the least threatening. And which came in between. The more ticks you made on the three checklists above the more threatening or upsetting the situation probably was. Use this as a rough guide to help you judge.

Now pick one of your medium-threat situations. This is the situation you are going to work on for the rest of this topic. If you choose a very threatening situation to work on it is likely to be too upsetting for you to do much about at first. If you pick one with very little threat it will be such a pushover that you won't learn anything.

Comments overleaf ▶

◀ **Figure 5.2K**

The previous extract is a "double page spread" from a continuing education course called *Health Choices* (P921). In this case, the course team found a commercial publisher (Harper & Row) to produce the self-instructional text, and it achieved a massive readership in addition to registered students of the Open University.

The format is similar to that of many popular magazines and "part publications" -- three-column layout, prominent titles and subtitle "trailers", "human interest" illustrations that cut across several columns, questions and quizzes and checklists to tick, and resolutely reader-directed language (look how frequently the word "you" appears). Unlike many popular publications, however, the emphasis is clearly not on entertainment or even on giving information: it is on helping readers to understand themselves better and to act more effectively.

There are two activities in this extract. The first asks readers to identify four events in their own lives of the kind being discussed. As an example, they are shown how Mabel (who appears in the cartoon) might have answered. The second activity asks readers to analyse their responses to the four events, using checklists.

No feedback is provided for the first activity (though Mabel's answer can be seen as a kind of "feed-forward", against which readers can assess the appropriateness of their own answers). Feedback on the second activity is a comment helping readers to interpret their responses ("The more ticks you made on the checklists above, the more threatening or upsetting the situation probably was"). As the lead into the next activity, readers are then asked to pick out one of their "medium threat" situations.

Incidentally, these pages illustrate the impediments to smooth reading that can result from abandoning single-column layout. Did you ever find yourself reading material out of the sequence intended by the authors (e.g. in the right-hand cartoons or in the text below them) ? If so, how might the design have been modified to guard against this ?

Figure 5.2L ▶

The following and final extract consists of two consecutive pages
from an undergraduate course on biology (SDT 286). It concerns
the analysis of two experiments about the role of learning in
influencing simple behaviour. The course author presents the
facts, but the activities require learners to do the analysing.

The first activity asks learners to formulate a suitable hypothesis
for the first experiment. The second activity asks them to interpret
the results of that experiment as displayed in a bar chart. The
third activity invites readers to formulate a new hypothesis about
a related experiment. Finally, in the fourth activity (SAQ 7),
readers are asked to compare the two experiments and come to a
conclusion about the underlying principle.

The layout of the first three activities is similar to that in
Extract H -- with the activity-question indented and underlined,
and the feedback (also underlined) in the margin. The fourth
activity is treated differently. This course is one of several
that insert what are labelled as "self assessment questions"
(or SAQs) -- perhaps as well as, perhaps instead of other activities
-- and print the answers or feedback all together at the end of the
lesson. In this course, the activities labelled "SAQ" are those
that test attainment of major objectives. In SAQ 7, learners are
reminded (by reference to a number in an earlier list) that the
objective here is "to evaluate experimental evidence concerning the
ontogeny of simple behaviour".

Notice in this extract (as in Extract J) that the pictures are
essential to the teaching. They alone present the key information
on which the activities are based.

L

relative of our own sea gull. When newly hatched, the young Laughing Gulls are fed by their parents, who regurgitate food in response to the young birds pecking at their beaks; the parents then pick up some of the food and present it to the young. Hailman presented juvenile Laughing Gull chicks with several different models of gull heads, to investigate their stimulus preferences.

In the first part of the experiment, Hailman presented newly-hatched naïve Laughing Gull chicks with the cardboard models shown in Figure 8.

Figure 8   The gull-head models used by Hailman (see text for details).

Model A closely resembles the parent Laughing Gull.

Model B has the standard red beak but with an irregular head shape.

Model C is a standard red beak shape with only a fragment of the head.

Model D is the standard red beak shape alone.

Model E is the standard Laughing Gull head without a beak.

Hailman measured the number of pecking responses given to each model in thirty seconds; each chick was, however, only presented with one model and was tested only once.

On the assumption that the instinctive behaviour enables a 'biologically appropriate response' to be made, which model do you expect the young birds to prefer?

Clearly a 'biologically appropriate response' would be one made to the model that most closely resembles the parent's head. The results of this experiment are given in Figure 9.

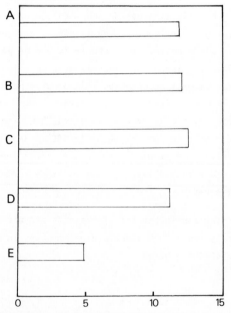

Figure 9   The responses of the newly hatched Laughing Gull chick to the five model heads (see text for details.)

◀ Comments overleaf

The results of these experiments indicate that the chicks did not discriminate between models A to D, but showed a marked preference for these four models in comparison with model E.

On the basis of these results, which features of the models appear to be important in eliciting the naïve chicks' begging responses?

The differences between the group of models A to D and model E indicate that some feature of models A to D is the important determinant for this begging response, since models A to D all have the head and beak, but E does not have the beak, it seems that the important common feature is the beak itself.

From Hailman's first experiment we can isolate the parent bird's beak as being the important stimulus in eliciting the naïve juvenile birds' begging responses. As a second part of this experiment, Hailman presented the same model to experienced, older Laughing Gull chicks which had been wild-reared.

On the assumption that the begging behaviour is 'instinctively determined,' which of the models do you predict will elicit the most begging responses from the wild-reared chicks?

Since, in the first part of the experiment, the naïve chicks all gave similar responses to models A to D, if the food begging behaviour is truly instinctively determined, you might expect experienced birds also to show a preference for models A to D—because they all contain the standard red bill shape. The results of this experiment are shown in Figure 10, together with the results of the previous experiment.

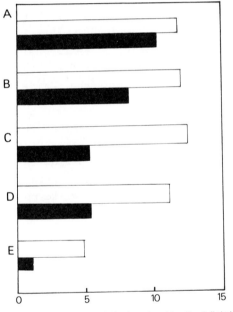

Figure 10   *The responses of newly hatched and experienced Laughing Gull chicks to the five model heads (see text for details).*

SAQ 7 (*Objective 8*)

Are there any differences between the responsiveness of the newly hatched chicks and that of the older experienced chicks? If so what implication does this have for the idea that the chicks' behaviour is instinctively determined?

This experiment, then, has demonstrated how learning can influence the course of development of stereotyped, species-typical behaviour, such as the food-begging response, that is thought to be instinctively determined. This, of course, is just one example of the modification of stereotyped behaviour, but there are many other such examples and one will be discussed in Unit 14. In general, it is

role of learning

In Conclusion:

Issues and samples

In this chapter, I have asked you to consider some of the issues involved in writing for self-instruction and, in particular, to look with me at some sample pages from self-instructional texts.

Variety but...

The sample pages we looked at were all from Open University texts but, neverthless, we were able to see considerable variety in subject-matter, in types of objective and/or learner being aimed at, in layout and typography, in teaching approach, in integration with other media, and (a subject we explore further in Chapter 6) in the forms of "activity" -- from simple questions of the "What do you see ?" or "Is this an example ?" type up to those requiring the learners to evaluate, interpret or explain.

seek out more examples

It may be that none of the sample pages comes very close to your own subject area. This, however, should not have prevented you from picking up useful insights. Again, you might have liked to see longer extracts from some of the courses; but it is instructive to notice just how much of interest one can glean from a single page. All the same, it is obvious that these pages represent only a tiny sample of the world's (or even the Open University's) self-instructional materials. So:

```
**********************************************
*                                            *
*  START MAKING YOUR OWN COLLECTION OF        *
*  SELF-INSTRUCTIONAL TEXTS (OR EXTRACTS)     *
*  THAT SEEM TO YOU TO HAVE IDEAS OR          *
*  APPROACHES YOU MIGHT SOME DAY USE IN       *
*  WRITING YOUR OWN LESSONS.                  *
*                                            *
**********************************************
```

6. PROMOTING ACTIVE LEARNING

Active learning ? This is the most distinctive feature
of the kind of self-instruction we are thinking about in
this book. As I argue in Chapter 5, we should not treat
the writing of a tutorial-in-print as an opportunity
to lecture at our readers -- pouring out a stream of
information for them to register and commit to memory.

Drawing out responses

Instead, we should be working to draw responses out of
our readers.

```
************************************************
*                                              *
*  OUR AIM SHOULD BE TO PRODUCE THE WRITTEN     *
*  EQUIVALENT OF A ONE-TO-ONE TUTORIAL.         *
*                                              *
************************************************
```

The tutorial approach

Imagine how you might operate as a tutor, working with
just one learner. You would not expect to ramble on at
length about your subject (as you might in a lecture).
You would make sure your learner was working with you.
You would perhaps present some provocative ideas or
launch a line or argument -- but every few minutes you
would stop and encourage your learner to contribute

Ways of encouraging contributions

something. For instance:

o You might simply check that the learner understood
   what you had been getting at.

o You might ask the learner to suggest examples
   from his or her own experience.

o You might get the learner to apply the principle
   being discussed to a new situation or example.

o You might invite the learner to evaluate an idea
   or to compare it with another, or to show how it
   might be applied in practice, And so on.

Giving feedback

As a tutor, you would be drawing active responses from
your learner. You would then **comment** on each response.
You would give your learner **feedback** as to the strengths/
weaknesses of his or her response -- or at least say what

you found interesting about it. Perhaps also you might
mention other possible responses that could have been
made to the same question or invitation. You might then

*Building to
next point*

build upon your learner's response in moving on to the
next substantive stage in the discussion.

TEACHING THROUGH ACTIVITIES

*Interaction
in tutorial-
in-print*

In short, such a tutorial is an **interaction** between tutor
and learner. This is what we are trying to simulate in
the tutorial-in-print. Experience indicates that learners
are kept more alert and involved -- and learn better --
when they are required actively to **use** ideas rather than
merely reading (or hearing) about them. Bear in mind the
old Chinese proverb:

> *I hear, and I forget;*
> *I see, and I remember;*
> *I do, and I understand.*

*The
importance
of activities*

This is why **activities** -- questions, tasks, exercises --
are a vital feature of self-instructional material. (See
Figure 5.2/A-L on pages 92-117.) They are meant to keep
learners purposefully engaged with the material. Without
them, our learners would be denied an advantage that "face-
to-face learners" take for granted -- the opportunity to
come up with ideas of their own and see how they compare
with other people's. Without such activities, our
learners might assume that the only objective was to
memorize our multitudinous words of wisdom.

Frequency of Activities

*Getting the
learner
to do*

So, just like a face-to-face tutor, we structure our
discussion around getting the learner to **do** something.
We build in frequent activities. These activities need
to be built in throughout the text, so that the learner
can learn from them. It is not enough to stick them on
at the end, where their only role is to check whether or
not he or she has learned.

SAQs
and ITQs
Some writers of self-instruction distinguish between what they call:

- SAQs (Self-assessment questions) -- which may appear, perhaps several together, testing major objectives, at the end of perhaps an hour or so's reading; and

- ITQs (In-text questions) -- which may be used at frequent intervals in the text **between** SAQs, generating the running dialogue between author and reader.

This terminology may not seem very helpful -- since **both** types of activity are really "in-text" and "self-assessed" (and they may take forms other than questions).
Two uses
Nevertheless, the distinction between these two **uses** of activities is worth bearing in mind.

How often ?
Of course, there are no rules about how frequently to insert an activity. You may have noticed, however, that some of the examples shown in Figure 5.2/A-L had several activities to a page. Some topics may lend themselves to more activities per hour of reading than do others. All the same, I would be surprised if you managed to offer your learners more than two or three pages of reading without there being something of significance they should be asked questions about before reading on. And if more than four or five pages went by without your requiring the learners to do anything but read, then I'd suggest you'd forgotten about them. And I'd expect them to have dozed off !

Varieties of Activity

There are many ways we might categorize activities in a self-instructional text. Three aspects worth considering are:

Three aspects
of activities
o How much time are learners expected to spend on each activity ?

o What do they have to do to arrive at a response ?

o How are they to record their response (if at all)?

Duration
of task

Some activities require the reader to do little more than "stop and think". These may require a pause of but a few seconds. Other activities may demand a few minutes' calculation or a brief written answer. Yet others may send the reader away from the text for quarter of an hour or more to carry out some kind of practical work.

Arriving
at response

What do readers have to do to arrive at their response to the question or instruction ? Readers may be required, for example, to:

o Reflect on what they have read or on their experience of the world.

o Read a new piece of text -- or view a video, listen to a tape, etc -- in the light of such reflection.

o Engage in an interview or discussion with other learners or with workmates, family members, etc.

o Carry out practical work with equipment and materials -- either at home or "in the field" -- and record their results.

o Keep a diary or log of work done or observations made over some period of time prior to some subsequent lesson.

o Develop a workable proposal -- e.g. for a device or procedure to help handicapped people.

o Imagine what they would think/feel/do as one or more of the participants sketched out in the text, -- e.g. as a farmer faced with a change in the government's agricultural policy.

Recording
the response

Some of the ways in which they might be asked to record their responses -- rather than just thinking them -- are as follows:

o Ticking boxes to indicate agreement or disagreement with a number of statements.

o Answering a multiple-choice question, perhaps again by ticking boxes.

o Matching items in one list with items in another,
   by drawing lines from one list to the other.

o Underlining relevant phrases in a piece of text.

o Completing a form or questionnaire.

o Providing the missing word/phrase/number(s) to
   fill the blank(s) left in a sentence.

o Writing a word/phrase/number in the margin or in
   a box provided within the body of the text.

o Writing a longer answer, on the page of the text or
   in a separate notebook (perhaps for sending to
   a tutor).

o Making additions to a printed diagram, chart,
   graph, etc.

o Drawing a graph, chart, flow-diagram, etc.

o Making a tape-recording -- perhaps for the benefit
   of other learners or a tutor.

*Which ways
for you ?*

(Pages 92-117)

Such possibilities as those listed above are but a few of
the many ways in which we might engage the learner's
active participation. (I leave you to check which of them
are represented among the sample pages shown in Figure 5.2
and elsewhere in this book.) You will need to decide on
ways that are appropriate to your subject, your objectives,
and your learners.

Levels of Difficulty

*How
demanding ?*

You may also like to consider how difficult or demanding
your activities should be. Different types of activity
will engage the learner's mind at different levels --
making varying demands on his or her ability to apply the
ideas that you are discussing.

Below, I have listed five types of activity I have
noticed in self-instructional material. To me, each of

the later ones seems likely to be more demanding than
those that precede it in the list. What do you think ?:

So, the learner might be expected to:

1. Report his or her observations or experience
    in everyday terms (usually as a preliminary to
    learning new ways of seeing them):
    > *e.g. "Who carries out these procedures in your Department
    > and how often are you involved ?"*

2. Pick out, restate, or remember important facts,
    concepts or principles to which he or she has
    been introduced:
    > *e.g. "What is meant to be the chief purpose of the
    > new system ?"*

3. Distinguish between **given** examples and non-examples
    of the new concepts and principles that are being
    presented:
    > *e.g. "Which of the following procedures would be
    > acceptable under the new system...?"*

4. Provide his or her **own** examples and non-examples
    (perhaps by reporting his or her observations and
    experience in terms of the new concepts and
    principles):
    > *e.g. "Which of your Department's present procedures will
    > be acceptable under the new system and which will not ?*

5. Apply the new concepts and principles (plus native
    wit and personal experience) to analyse, interpret
    or design a new situation (one that has not been
    discussed) -- perhaps in the process arriving at
    a **new** concept or principle (new to the learner,
    that is):
    > *e.g. "What advice would you offer to staff in the
    > Department described below if their procedures are
    > to fit in with the new system ?"*
    > *e.g. "What snags do you foresee in implementing the new
    > system in your Department, and how would you suggest
    > trying to overcome them ?"*

All these types of activity could play a useful part within a single lesson. Type 1 activities might be used where you are about to begin on a new concept or principle. Your readers will not yet have considered the new ways of looking at things. Indeed, Type 1 activities can be used as a basis for the "egrul" or "discovery" learning I discuss in Chapter 7.

Activities of Types 2 and 3 may serve the function of "comprehension questions". They can draw your readers' attention to important points in the text and enable them to check that they understand what you are saying.

Type 4 activities go beyond this -- by asking learners to relate their existing knowledge to what you have taught them. You are inviting them to classify their experience in your terms.

Type 5 activities can make the ultimate demand on the learners' learning -- by inviting them to analyse, plan and create in the new terms. They may even be faced with situations or problems that are not so cut-and-dried as those they have considered previously. This may require them to **extend** their learning. Like Type 1 activities, those of Type 5 can push the learners towards new knowledge, enabling them to **anticipate** or "discover" ideas, connections and relationships for themselves. If the activity is one (perhaps at the end of a lesson or sequence of lessons) where you don't tell the learner which of the several ideas you've discussed are most relevant to the problem -- leaving the learners to decide this for themselves -- then the activity can be extremely demanding.

I do not claim that my five types cover every possible activity you might think of. Nor do I believe they form a perfect progression of difficulty; you may be able to think up some Type 1 or 2 activities that would be more demanding than some of Type 4 and 5. All the same, even if my list does not seem to relate too closely to the

Making the different demands

Type 1

Types 2 and 3

Type 4

Type 5

Additional demands

*What
activities
for you ?*

topics you'll be teaching, I hope it will stimulate you
in thinking about how **you** might use different kinds of
activity to make the appropriate levels of demand on your
own learners at different stages in your lessons.

(Pages 92-117)

```
*****************************************************************
* WHICH OF THE ABOVE (OR OTHER) TYPES OF ACTIVITY  *
* CAN YOU FIND AMONG THE SAMPLE PAGES IN FIGURE 5.2 *
* -- AND IN ANY OTHER SELF-INSTRUCTIONAL MATERIAL  *
* YOU ARE ABLE TO EXAMINE ?                        *
*****************************************************************
```

HOW TO DEVELOP ACTIVITIES

Before we talk about developing activities, let me remind
you of the teaching context in which they appear:

*The
teaching
context*

1. You introduce or explain a particular aspect
    of your topic.

2. You ask your learners to make a response on
    the basis of:

    - what you can assume they have already learned
      or experienced elsewhere; and/or

    - what you have told them; and/or

    - what they can anticipate or else find out
      somewhere other than in your text.

3. You tell them what response you'd have expected
    and why. If there is no one correct answer,
    mention several possible answers that would have
    been acceptable -- e.g. what other learners may
    have said; and mention criteria against which they
    can judge the validity of their own responses.

4. You carry on to the next step in your argument
    or the next aspect of the topic you wish to
    introduce (as in 1. above).

*Visual
reminder*

See Figure 6.1 for a visual reminder of this context.

Figure 6.1: The Basic Unit of a Tutorial-in-Print

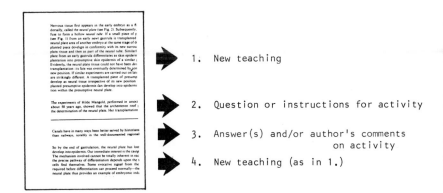

1. New teaching

2. Question or instructions for activity

3. Answer(s) and/or author's comments on activity

4. New teaching (as in 1.)

When to Think about Activities

Before and/or during ?

Some writers are able to think up likely activities even **before** they begin on their text. They can then weave these activities together with suitable exposition. Other writers prefer to launch into the text -- perhaps working through their teaching point outline -- thinking up appropriate activities whenever they reach a critical point in the build-up of their argument.

Afterwards ?

Yet other authors try to produce a "straight" version of the text first, and insert activities later -- literally as an after-thought. I used to say that this was about as difficult as inserting currants into a cake that has already been baked. However, my subsequent experience as a "transformer" of less experienced authors' first drafts has changed my opinion. I now believe it is possible to insert worthwhile activities and "study questions" into

Possible if not ideal

existing material -- even into material that was not designed for self-instruction. Though I generally feel that the materials would have been differently (and better) structured if their authors had been thinking in terms of activities at the time they wrote.

Questions
for other
people's
texts

Other people's texts.   You may need to develop activities in this way yourself, if you ever base a lesson on previously-published texts -- especially if certain passages are not as clear as you would wish.   At intervals in their reading of the texts, you could ask your learners to consider questions such as these:

Examples

o   "The writer mentioned this theory under another name on page 34.   What was it ?"

o   "In the paragraphs above, the writer seems to be talking about three exceptions to the general rule.   List them below."

o   "Draw a spray diagram of the issues discussed in this section -- and then see how it compares with mine overleaf."

More
examples

You will see that one such study question has been added to the "Introduction" shown in Figure 8.2 (on page 169). And Figures 5.2A and I (on pages 92 and 108) show study questions or activities being used to guide learners' reading of a separate text.   Clearly, such questions could equally well be applied to audio or video source materials.

Your own texts.   However, let's get back to developing your own self-instructional materials.   The kinds of activity that are easiest to think up before or after writing the material are SAQs -- questions testing the learners' grasp of the main objectives of the lesson.   If you do think up questions in advance, or if you leave it until you have a first draft, do be alert for any that might occur to you **while** you are writing it.   If you really are thinking about the learner you are "talking with", such tutorial-type ITQs are bound to come to mind as a means of focussing the conversation -- especially if you apply some of the following advice:

SAQs
to test ?

ITQs
to teach ?

Ways of Generating Activities

*Hints
and tips*
Here is a selection of hints and tips to guide you
in thinking up activities:

Objectives
o   Keep your objectives in mind while you write. As
    a rule, your activities should either lead the
    learner towards an objective through a number of
    contributory exercises (e.g. ITQs) or else give
    guided practice with that objective (e.g. SAOs).

Misconceptions
o   Consider what **mis**conceptions about the topic your
    learners are likely to be starting out with -- and
    develop an activity that will flush them out for
    discussion.

*Recall your
own learning*
o   Try to recall the experiences you went through
    yourself in coming to understand the concepts or
    principles under discussion. Try to re-create
    comparable experiences for the learners; involve
    them in activities that will help them find their
    own way through similar routes to understanding.

*How groups
have learned*
o   Think of group exercises you have used in
    face-to-face teaching and consider whether any of
    them might be translated into useful activities for
    learners working on their own (with or without help
    from their friends).

Case study
o   Take a general or abstract point you have made in
    the text -- e.g. about how people with different
    values can come into conflict -- and develop a
    case study in which the learner can be asked to
    play a certain role.

*Learners to
interpret
pictures*
o   If you are bringing graphs or tables or
    illustrations into your exposition, consider asking
    the **learners** to read and interpret them -- rather
    than merely giving your comments on the exhibits.
    Learners can then go on to read your comments as
    "feedback" after they have attempted the activity.

Make learners establish own principles

o Try not to hand your learners important principles/ generalizations/interpretations "on a plate". Where you can do so without using up a disproportionate amount of their time, enable learners to arrive at them themselves -- through an activity. Whenever you find yourself writing phrases like:

"It therefore follows that..." or

"From this we can clearly deduce..." or

"Here is a summary of the argument so far..."

you perhaps should be asking a question instead, e.g

"What would you expect to happen as a result ?";

"What can you deduce from this ?";

"What are the four main points in the argument so far ?".

Again, your deductions or summaries can then be provided as feedback against which the learners can compare their own efforts.

Activity for every important idea

o Whenever you are introducing a stream of important ideas and you want your learner to be able to use them all, make sure they are **all** made the subject of an activity. If they are all closely connected, you may be able to have your learner deal with all of them at once within one activity. Otherwise, you can group them, or even give each idea a separate activity -- even if this means several activities within a page or two (programmed learning style).

What are learners meant to do ?

o Most important of all: keep thinking about the learner you are tutoring, and keep asking yourself - page by page -- what would you like your reader to be **doing** with the material you are presenting ?

And now three important DON'Ts:

Avoid non-activities

o Don't set vague, pseudo-activities, e.g. "Think about jot down a few ideas of your own about X". The learner would probably -- and quite rightly -- ignor such half-baked suggestions.

o Don't set an activity unless you are confident your
Will it be   learners should be able to make a reasonably
satisfying ? satisfying attempt at it -- satisfying to them, that
is. Will they have the necessary knowledge, skills
or attitudes -- whether gained from previous learning
or from other human experience ? For instance: Don't
base exercises on the assumption that all your
readers are male (unless you are sure they are).
And don't demand lengthy written answers from
readers whose verbal skills are weak.

o Don't set an activity at all unless you are sure it
Don't waste   will seem **relevant to** your readers and worth their
learners' time spending time on. Learners soon learn to skip
"trivial" or "busy work" activities. Unfortunately,
they may extend the habit to activities that really
are crucial.

Technical Issues

Finally, a few technical points about setting activities:

o Right from the start -- e.g. in a "study guide" to
Explain   the course -- make sure your learners know **why** you
general   have built the material around activities. What
purpose   are they meant to do for the learners, and how are
they to use them ?

o You may also need to tell the learner why certain
..and for   specific activities -- especially the longer ones --
each activity ? are worth doing, e.g. "Completing this activity
will give you practice in the important skill of ...".

o Be clear about how long you expect the average
say how long ? learner to spend on each activity. If it is more
than a minute or two -- or if it is not obvious
from the form of the question - tell your learners
explicitly, e.g. "This exercise should take you
between five and ten minutes" or "spend no more
than half an hour...".

How big an
answer ?

o Similarly, if it is not clear from the form of
   the activity, tell your learners how extensive an
   "answer" you require and where you want them to
   write it. Perhaps you can provide a box or space
   of appropriate size in the text. If you can't
   afford the space, however -- or if you wish certain
   responses to be available for a tutor to look at --
   you may need to ask your learners to write in a
   separate notebook. In which case, you might say:
   "Write no more than a sentence" or "In not more
   than 200 words...", and so on.

Variety in
activities

o To avoid monotony, watch the balance between, e.g.:

   - brief activities and lengthy ones;

   - those requiring written answers and those merely
     requiring thought; and

   - closed questions (where there is only one correct
     answer) and open-ended questions (e.g. "In your
     experience, what are the most common causes
     of...?"), where a variety of equally acceptable
     answers may be forthcoming.

Using
"reader-
stoppers"

o Use some kind of **"reader-stopper"** to help your
   readers from accidentally "cheating" by glancing
   ahead to see your feedback before they have attempted
   the activity. There are many ways of signalling to
   readers that here is a place they must stop and do
   something before reading on, e.g.:

   - a rule across the page;

   - a row of asterisks;

   - an answer box;

   - indented text;

   - a change of typeface;

   - a standard symbol in the margin, e.g. (A) .

Masking card

Devices like the above may be used on their own or in combination. (Look back at the reader-stoppers used in the pages shown in Figure 5.2.) You may also provide readers with a **masking card**, of the same width as your page -- to shield those areas of the text they do not yet wish to read.

Placing your feedback

o As a general rule, place your feedback -- e.g. the answers and your discussion of them -- **immediately** after the reader-stopper. If your readers really wish to, they will use their masking card (or just will-power) to avoid taking a peek. If they do want to "cheat", then attempts to hide the answers -- e.g. by printing them upside-down or on another page -- will merely irritate them. Perhaps to the point where they skip the activities altogether. However, if you can use smaller type or indenting, or even italics or colour, this may be worth considering as a means of "warning off" the reader who is not yet ready to see the feedback.

Avoiding eye-catchers

The only obvious exception to this advice about printing the feedback directly after the stopper is when the answer is a graph or diagram so eye-catching that readers can scarcely avoid registering its salient features as soon as they see the page.

Feedback to open-ended questions

o When the questions you ask are open-ended (e.g. "What do you believe are the reasons why...?"), you will not be able to predict exactly what response your reader will make. However, your feedback should be able to discuss two or three **possible** answers. These you may be able to imagine from previous work with learners on this topic.

From trial learners

Alternatively, you may sometimes need to obtain them later -- from the learners on whom you try out your materials in draft form. (For an example, see Figure 6.2 overleaf.)

Figure 6.2: Activity Feedback Provided by Earlier Readers

(from *How to Tutor in an Open Learning Scheme* by R. Lewis, CET Publications, London, 1983)

How to tutor in an open-learning scheme

To meet student expectations by giving 'lectures' can lead to all kinds of problems:

(i) duplication of the course materials

(ii) waste of valuable opportunities for group interaction

(iii) a simple inability to 'cover the syllabus' in the infrequent tutorial time

(iv) the production of dependent rather than autonomous learners.

Q3
How will you (do you) deal with the problems of student expectations discussed above?

132

Face-to-face sessions

Here are some tutor responses.

'by careful structuring of the situation - setting tasks to individuals, getting pairs to work on a problem, syndicates and pyramiding.'

'by concentrating in early sessions on building up a strong sense of "self-help" in the group. This breaks down the shyness and wish to stay separate that often lead to students putting the lecturer in the role of total dominance. When students relax they don't mind admitting to weaknesses, etc.'

'by getting them to meet occasionally between tutorials. Or to ring one another up. This gets round one major problem - the long gaps between tutorials.'

Getting students to work flexibly, and together, can be difficult, especially in early tutorials and when the student population may also be tired after a day's work and reluctant to make the effort to mix and to exchange views. They may feel that it is easier to stay strangers and to be talked at by the tutor. The tutorial may also be very short, say an hour, and you may not feel there's enough time to warm the student up.

A teacher of accounting comments:

'These problems are very real, especially if we want to avoid forcing students into a regular pattern of attendance. I'd look seriously at (artificial) methods of altering expectations, eg,

- name badges (with identifying course details)
- "induction" meetings in which the sole aim was to break the ice and inculcate new expectations
- perhaps a short warm-up period before the session starts, based on a series of "Please find out from your friends" questions: in an English course: find out which poem they like best and why; in an Accounts course: whether

133

Criteria for
self-checking

At the very least, you should be able to suggest criteria -- e.g. a checklist of points that should have been mentioned in an answer -- by which your learners can evaluate their own responses. If this seems impossible, re-think the activity.

Don't stint
on feedback

o Be ample with your feedback. For learners working on their own, it may be their only way of assessing their own progress. But if your answers are lengthier or more considered than you'd have expected from them in the time implied for the activity, do let your learners know. The relevance and helpfulness of your feedback can make all the difference to how satisfying the learners find your activities and how likely they are to keep on doing them.

(Examples
on pages
92-117)

Look again at the activities included in the pages shown in Figure 5.2. Look also at any other self-instructional texts you can find. To what extent do they reflect or contradict the advice given in the previous few pages ? What other DOs and DON'Ts would you wish to add to the lists ? What decisions do you arrive at about using activities in your own self-instructional teaching ?

N.B. If this were designed as a self-instructional text, I would have inserted a "reader-stopper" at this point. As feedback, I would have followed up with some comments on the lists, provided by people like yourself who had worked through an earlier "tryout version" of the text.

```
************************************************
*                                              *
*  LATER ON, WHEN YOU TRY OUT YOUR LESSON       *
*  ON SOME LEARNERS, TAKE PARTICULAR NOTE       *
*  OF HOW THEY TACKLE YOUR VARIOUS KINDS        *
*  OF ACTIVITY -- AND OF WHAT THEY SAY          *
*  ABOUT THEM.                                  *
*                                              *
************************************************
```

7. STRUCTURING YOUR LESSON

How are you to structure your lesson so as to help the
learner learn ? Chapter 6 discusses one essential
structuring device -- the activities. But more is needed

*Structuring
the teaching*
-- the **teaching** in which those activities are embedded.
How is this to be structured ?

As a writer of self-instructional materials -- teaching
at a distance -- you will lack the feedback you would get
as a classroom teacher. You won't be seeing the puzzled
frowns or hearing the exasperated curses of learners who
are having difficulty understanding you. You will need

*Anticipating
difficulties*
to think about all their possible difficulties while you
sit at your writing. You'll need to structure your lesson
in such a way as to help learners avoid, or at least
overcome, them.

To aid you in this task, here is what I am going to

*Four
sections in
this chapter*
talk about in this chapter:

o   the importance of your teaching point outline;
o   the teaching of concepts and principles;
o   two basic teaching strategies; and
o   the need for variety of stimulus in your lesson.

REMEMBER YOUR OUTLINE

*(Discussed
in Chapter 4)*
Keep your "teaching point outline" by your side as you write
If you diverge from it, do so only by conscious decision.
Once you have started writing, you will see ways of
developing your lesson that could not have occurred to
you before you began to clothe general ideas in specific
details. Lessons tend to grow organically, like any

*Write around
your outline*
creative writing. You will not know exactly what you mean
to say until you see what you have already said. But be
critical about every diversion and change of emphasis.
Don't just wander.

You may find it helpful to stick to the basic rule of **one main idea per paragraph.** This you may state as a teaching point in one sentence -- usually the first in the paragraph. The main idea can then be illustrated, supported, or elaborated upon in the subsequent sentences.

Start from main idea...

Sometimes, however, you may prefer to lead up to your main idea, rather than starting out with it. In that case, you may hold back your teaching point until the final sentence of the paragraph.

or lead up to it ?

Incidentally, when you finish a lesson, it's worth checking how logically you've sequenced your ideas. Do they hang together, without missing steps ? You can check this by noting down the sequence of main ideas as they appear in the first (or final) sentences of your paragraphs

Check your logic later

TEACHING CONCEPTS AND PRINCIPLES

In distance teaching, as in other kinds, we are concerned with concepts and principles. Even when we teach technique and procedures -- like servicing a piece of equipment or filling in a form -- they usually depend on the learner understanding certain concepts and principles. These are our "main ideas".

What are main ideas ?

In the next few paragraphs, I'll mention eight "tasks" that seem to be necessary in teaching concepts and principles. In essence, these amount to the need to provide:

Three essentials in teaching

o   appropriate and effective examples;
o   learner activity or practice; and
o   feedback on activities.

Eight teaching tasks

Task 1:   Analyse Your Main Ideas

This you may have begun at the planning stage. (See Chapter 3.) In the case of each principle you want to teach, what kind of statement is it ? Does it define, evaluate, offer an empirical observation, or what ? How will different kinds of statement need to be presented ?

What kinds of ideas ?

Concept analysis

And what concepts does each principle involve ? What are their essential features ? Now is the time to put your concept analysis to the test (see page 48). You may even want your learner to work through the concept analysis with you during the lesson.

A simple example

Let's say the principle we want to teach is the "simple" one -- Area = Length x Width. More precisely, we should say: the area of a rectangular figure = length x width. Or, even more precisely: **one** way of finding the area of a rectangular figure is to multiply its length by its width. (Unless it is a square, of course, in which case we could multiply any two adjacent sides.)

Not so simple ?

Maybe the principle is not quite so simple after all. However, even sticking to the basic computational statement, we see that it involves the concepts of (a) multiplication, (b) length, (c) width, and (d) rectangularity. Each of these, in turn, depend on the learner having acquired certain **prior** concepts. If we feel that the learner may be weak on any of these prior understandings, we shall need to review them, or teach them, within the lesson (see Task 3).

Task 2:   Tell the Learners what they may Learn to Do

Objectives...

Let the learners know what they should be able to do -- or do better -- as a result of understanding the concepts or principles. In short, give them some idea of the purpose or objectives of the learning. Tell them they'll learn to analyse a Beethoven sonata or a company balance sheet; or to prepare a computer programme or a case in family law. With our area principle, tell them they'll learn to calculate the size of rectangles, and where this ability may prove useful. The point of this is to help your

aid learners' self-direction

learners direct their own learning and monitor their own progress.

Task 3:   Ensure Learners have all Pre-requisite Learning

What prior learning ?

Learners can grasp new ideas only by relating them to ideas they are familiar with already. Your analysis (Task 1) may have revealed concepts a learner must already possess in order to grasp the new concept or principle. These will need teaching first if learners do not already have them. To acquire even a basic grasp of a simple concept like, say, "immigrant", the learners would already need to have concepts like "birthplace", "place of domicile" and "travel". In order to distinguish immigrants from emigrants, tourists, travelling business-people, etc., they would need further concepts like "intention", "direction", and "duration of stay".

Example

In the case of our "area = length x width" principle, learners clearly need the notion of rectangularity. Without rectangularity, the calculation would be inappropriate. Learners must also be able to distinguish long sides from wide ones -- or at least recognize that these are two adjacent sides. And they must know what multiplying involves.

Understanding v applying

Furthermore, if they are to understand the principle -- as opposed to merely being able to apply it (i.e. perform a calculation) -- they must possess some intuitive concept of areas. This latter they may have acquired, for example, by grading rectangles in order of "size" -- or by comparing the number of, say, coins that can fit on surfaces they recognize as being bigger or smaller than one another.

Diagnostic testing

You may need to include some kind of **diagnostic tests** in your lessons -- to establish which of the pre-requisite concepts your learners already possess. Any they do not have already, they will need to learn. Maybe you can provide the necessary teaching within your lessons -- perhaps as an optional sequence which many or most learners will by-pass. If not, you will need to direct them to

Providing necessary help

some other source of instruction, like an earlier lesson or a better-informed colleague.

Anyway, this much is certain: lack of attention to
pre-requisite learning -- either not thinking about it
at all (assuming that learners will know whatever is
necessary) or hoping that they can somehow struggle
through without it -- can be the kiss of death to
effective distance teaching.

Task 4: Provide Examples and Non-examples of the New Idea

Here you should be able to draw on your earlier concept
analysis (Task 1). There are several more detailed points
to be made about Task 4:

*Four detailed
points*

Provide SEVERAL clear examples. Obvious as this may
seem, it is often neglected. If learners are to register
all the features of a new idea, they will usually need
more than one example. But that is often all they get,
e.g. one photograph of a river's meanders, one specimen
of a metal fracture, the recorded sound of one major
chord, and so on. If they are to appreciate the variety
of situations in which the new idea applies, they need a
variety of examples.

*Obvious
examples*

*Variety
needed*

Provide several clear NON-examples. Equally, to test
the limits of the criteria for using the idea, learners
will need several non-examples, e.g. photographs of
non-meandering rivers, specimens of metal that have been
cut, recordings of minor chords, and so on. In the case
of our "area = length x width" principle, learners will
need to recognize that it cannot be applied to shapes
that do not have four sides.

*Obvious
non-examples*

Provide BORDER-LINE examples and non-examples. Once
our learners can distinguish between clear-cut examples
and non-examples of the new idea, they can be exposed to
finer discriminations. Present them with border-line
examples -- examples they might be tempted to regard as
non-examples. For instance, they might not recognize an
eel or a sea-horse as "fish".

*Finer
distinctions*

*Under-
generalizing*

Examination of such border-line examples will help learners to avoid **under**-generalizing the idea -- being too restrictive in its use. With our "area = length x width" principle, a border-line example would be provided by showing how the principle applied to a square.

*Over-
generalizing*

Conversely, learners may need to avoid **over**-generalizing the idea. Thus, they will need to see some border-line **non**-examples. These are cases to which learners might think the idea applies when in fact it does not. Thus, with the concept of "fish", they might need to be shown that it does not apply to whales or tadpoles or sea-snakes, even though all live in water. These creatures have some of the attributes of the idea in question; but they do not have all that are necessary to qualify as "fish".

*Another
example*

Likewise, in learning about "area", our learners may need to be persuaded that the "length x width" principle will not work even on shapes with four straight sides if the shapes do not contain four right angles.

Start simple

Go from simple to complex and concrete to abstract. (But notice the warning about psychological v. logical order on page 66.) In a way, I have already touched on the simple-to-complex approach in suggesting clear examples before border-line examples. But it is worth singling out for special mention.

*Cut out
inessentials*

Make sure that your first examples of a concept or principle are not cluttered up with inessential elements. For example, in teaching the concept "immigrant", you'd do better to start with a person who has just arrived in your country intending to spend the rest of his or her life there -- rather than with people who were born in your country but whose parents had immediately taken them abroad where they had remained for the last sixty years, returning now to spend their final years in the homeland (if they can adjust to it) ! In the case of "area = length x width", an example of simple-to-complex would be to deal with rectangles having sides of, say, 3 x 2

before dealing with sides of, say, 3.42 x 0.07. Clearly,
we would not wish arithmetic to obscure the principle.

*Concrete
to abstract*

What about **concrete-to-abstract** ? Generally speaking,
you should consider offering concrete examples (and
non-examples) before abstract ones. A real fish is more
concrete than a picture of a fish. A picture of a fish
is more concrete than a verbal description. A verbal
description is more concrete than the name of the concept.

*Words v
things*

If learners start off on examples that are too abstract,
they may learn only a pallid, verbal ghost of the concept.
Conceivably, for example, they might be able to recognize
"trout", "herring" and "shark" as the names of fish -- yet
not be able to recognize any of these creatures as fish if
they were shown unlabelled specimens. Unless they had
seen specimens, or at least pictures, while supposedly
learning the concept, they would be unable to link the
name with the object.

Example

How would concrete-to-abstract apply in teaching
"area = length x width" ? Well, perhaps we'd have our
learners begin by cutting out cardboard tectangles and
covering them with cut-out squares. Then we might have
them draw squares on rectangles. Next they might do the
calculation after merely measuring the sides. Finally,
they would apply the principle to rectangles they never
see at all, being merely told the lengths of the sides.

Task 5: Relate the New Idea to Learners' Experience

*Will they
understand ?*

Whether you are giving examples to convey a new idea, or
trying to explain it by use of analogy, do ask yourself
whether your learners will know what you are talking about.
Do your examples or analogies touch on the learners'
experience ? For instance, if you wanted an example of
"cash flow", you might do better to remind the learner
about his or her household accounts -- rather than delve
immediately into the possibly remote, and certainly more
complex, worlds of commerce and high finance.

*Care with
analogies*

Analogy can be a potent means of clarifying a new idea. That is, we can point out all the ways in which the new idea is similar to one that learners are already familiar with. For example, we might tell them that "isobars are like the lines on a contour map". For this to be illuminating, of course, we have to be sure that they **already** understand contour maps.

Examples

Unfortunately, it is all too easy to find oneself trying to explain something the learners don't understand by relating it to something else they don't understand ! In the last couple of weeks I have watched two television programmes in a series about computers. The first tried to explain how computers work by analogy with a Jacquard loom. The next programme -- as if in recognition that the previous analogy may not have been totally transparent to all viewers -- tried again, this time comparing the computer with a steam organ. In both cases, however, the object of the analogy -- the loom and the steam organ -- seemed too much in need of explanation itself to contribut anything to my understanding of computers.

*Point out
limitations*

That last example reminds me of another common pitfall especially when the analogy you are using is rich or exotic. Your learner may incorrectly assume that the thing you are trying to explain (e.g. the working of the computer) shares certain characteristics with the object of the analogy (e.g. the steam organ) **in addition to** those you were identifying. Such errors, which might easily be corrected in face-to-face teaching, can be troublesome when the learner is learning at a distance. Be careful to indicate the limitations of your analogies.

Task 6: Get your Learners to Apply the Idea

*Learners
to identify*

At the beginning of the lesson, you may identify all the examples and non-examples of the new idea for your learners But, as the lesson develops, you may want them to make such identifications -- increasingly subtle ones -- for

Figure 7.1: .A Sequence of Double-page Spreads (from Open University course P912, Book 4)

themselves. If the concept or principle has several
aspects which you are teaching one at a time, get the
learners to demonstrate that they can apply those you
have taught so far before you go on to teach more.

Example

For instance, taking "fish" again, suppose you are
beginning with the fact of their living in water. You
may start with examples like salmon and sharks, and
non-examples like dogs and birds. Before going on to
attributes like "cold blood" or "scales" or "no legs", or
whatever is essential, you might well present the learner
with a set of creatures, only one of which (say a carp)
lives in water, and ask them to pick out the fish. Your
next exercise might involve them in selecting the fish,
using new attributes, from a group of creatures all of
which live in water.

*Learners
to apply*

Furthermore, once your learners' basic grasp of a
concept or principle is established, you will want them
to use it, along with others learned earlier. You may
get them to apply it, for example, in analysing a case
study, carrying out some practical procedure, or exploring
a theory. Thus, the concept of "fish" might be used in
developing the idea of an evolutionary progression of
life-forms from water to the land.

*Learners'
deductions*

Here I must briefly mention one other way of using
examples which I'll be describing more fully in the next
section (pages 148-151). That is, you may sometimes want
your learners to work out the principles for themselves --
rather than merely apply them once you have pointed them
out. For instance, you could provide the learners with a

*Work from
examples*

set of examples and ask them to pick out the features
they have in common. If they were learning about area in
this way, they might be given a series of exercises
requiring them to cover rectangles with cut-out squares.
These exercises would culminate in their making the
"discovery" that the total number of squares on any
rectangle was the product of the two sides. Such

"discovery learning" can be very effective, although it may be unduly time-consuming in some cases.

However you get your learners to apply the ideas of your lesson, appropriate **activity** is essential. This is discussed at length in Chapter 6.

ctivity

Task 7: Give the Learners Feedback on their Activity

This also sounds almost too obvious to mention. But it is often not done, even in texts that explicitly ask the reader to tackle questions and exercises. Sometimes the answers are not printed at all. Sometimes only bare answers are printed, with no indication as to the criteria by which they are justified. So learners who get the same answer as that shown in the book may be ignorant as to whether they reached it by the "best" route. And those with different answers are not told whether they were working on the right lines or where their mistakes occurred.

*ften
eglected*

Feedback is also discussed in Chapter 6. There we are considering pre-planned feedback, the same for all readers, printed in the lesson. However, it is worth remembering that learners working with self-instruction will occasionally need **individual** feedback. They may not be able to monitor their progress satisfactorily by relying solely on your pre-printed specimen answers and comments. You may need to provide a means whereby, from time to time, they can get their work inspected and commented upon -- by someone more expert in the subject than they are. I discuss this kind of feedback at length in Chapter 11 and 13. It can play a vital part in helping your learners learn.

*re-recorded
personal
eedback*

Task 8: Give your Learners Practice with the Idea

Practice will occur almost automatically in a sequential or hierarchical subject like mathematics or science. Later parts of a lesson -- or later lessons in a course -- will build on earlier parts. In tackling new ideas, the

*n
ierarchical
ubjects*

learners will constantly be using those they acquired
earlier.

*In other
subjects*

With less hierarchical subjects, you may need to make
a special effort to help your learners keep earlier idea
alive in their minds. One way of doing so is to include
them in your occasional summaries of the course (or less
so far. Another is to refer back to them by way of
contrast or analogy with concepts and principles you are
discussing in a later section. A third way to encourage
practice is to include questions relating to those
earlier ideas in your periodic tests and assignments.

```
****************************************************
*                                                  *
*  ONE OVERALL POINT ABOUT EXAMPLES, ANALOGIES     *
*  AND ACTIVITIES -- DON'T ALWAYS BE SATISFIED     *
*  WITH THE FIRST ONE THAT COMES TO MIND.          *
*                                                  *
****************************************************
```

TWO BASIC TEACHING STRATEGIES

How are you to get your main ideas across to your learner
Here I assume that your purpose is not simply to have the
read those ideas, or even to read and remember them.

*Teaching for
understanding*

Rather it is to have your learners read and **understand**
them -- in such a way that they can relate them to what
they know already and apply them in new situations. That
is, you are not telling -- you are teaching.

It seems to me that there are two basic strategies for
teaching the concepts and principles that are our main id

o We can give the learners a "rule" (e.g. a definitic
   then illustrate with an example of the rule being
   applied; and finally offer the learners an example
   to which they must apply the rule themselves; OR

*Two contrasting
strategies*

o We can show the learners a number of examples and
   non-examples of the idea we are trying to develop;
   then encourage them to notice the similarities and

differences among these examples; and finally help them to formulate the "rule" that distinguishes between the examples and the non-examples.

The first strategy is sometimes called the RUL-EG strategy -- rule followed by example. Conversely, the second is the EG-RUL strategy -- examples before the rule.

Let me give you a simple example (following the ruleg strategy). Suppose we wanted to teach the meaning of "triangle". We could start by saying "A triangle is a three-sided figure. Here are some figures. Which of them are triangles ? Now you draw some triangles". With (ruleg) practice, we'd drive the definition home.

Alternatively, we might begin by showing our learners a set of shapes, all of which have four sides, except for one that has three. We then ask the learners to tell us which shape stands out from the others. We could then give them the name "triangle" and ask them to pick out the only triangle from a new set of shapes, all but one of which have four or five sides. Then we might show our learners a number of different triangles mixed together with other shapes and again ask them to pick out the triangles. Next we ask them to draw a triangle. To do this they must actively see what attribute distinguishes a triangle from other shapes. Finally, we can ask them to put into words what makes a triangle different. So we'll have taken our learners through four stages of discovery:

1. recognition;
2. naming;
3. reconstruction; and
4. definition.

In this egrul strategy, experience comes before verbal definition.

Two more examples

Below, you will see a couple of examples of how the tw
alternative strategies might be applied in a tutorial-in-
print. (As it happens, these examples also deal with
triangles, of a sort.) Of the two extracts on the left,
dealing with spherical triangles, the first one tells the
secret and then asks learners to apply it (ruleg); while
the second encourages them to observe it for themselves.
Similarly, the first of the two alternative strategies to
Pascal's Triangle is ruleg, while the second is egrul.

In a spherical triangle, the sum
of the angles is *greater than* 180°.

So, if two angles in one particular
spherical triangle are 80° and 60°,
the third angle must be greater
than ...*(how many degrees ?)*

You are correct. This was the
only diagram showing a spherical
triangle. Every
side of the
triangle is an
arc of a 'great
circle'.

One side of this
particular
spherical triangle
is part of the 'equator'
of the sphere. The other two sides
are part of two 'lines of longitude'.

From this particular spherical
triangle, we can learn something that
is true for *all* spherical triangles:

Remembering that lines of longitude
meet a sphere's equator at
right-angles, what is the *sum of* the
angles (A + B + C) in this particular
spherical triangle ? Is it:

   (a) Exactly 180°
or (b) More than 180°
or (c) Less than 180° ?

PASCAL'S TRIANGLE
This arrangement of numbers is known as Pas
triangle:

$$
\begin{array}{ccccccccccccc}
 & & & & & & 1 & & & & & & \\
 & & & & & 1 & & 1 & & & & & \\
 & & & & 1 & & 2 & & 1 & & & & \\
 & & & 1 & & 3 & & 3 & & 1 & & & \\
 & & 1 & & 4 & & 6 & & 4 & & 1 & & \\
 & 1 & & 5 & & 10 & & 10 & & 5 & & 1 & \\
1 & & 6 & & 15 & & 20 & & 15 & & 6 & & 1 \\
\end{array}
$$

It has many interesting properties. One of the r
interesting is the rule by which rows can be added to
base of the triangle indefinitely. Notice that any num
in the triangle is the SUM of the two numbers dire
to the left and right in the row above.
Suppose we added another row to the triangle.
numbers would be: 1 7 21 ? ? 21 7 1. What are the
numbers in the middle of the row?

        28 and 28
        30 and 30
        35 and 35
        42 and 42

PASCAL'S TRIANGLE
This arrangement of numbers is known as Pas
triangle:

$$
\begin{array}{ccccccccccccc}
 & & & & & & 1 & & & & & & \\
 & & & & & 1 & & 1 & & & & & \\
 & & & & 1 & & 2 & & 1 & & & & \\
 & & & 1 & & 3 & & 3 & & 1 & & & \\
 & & 1 & & 4 & & 6 & & 4 & & 1 & & \\
 & 1 & & 5 & & 10 & & 10 & & 5 & & 1 & \\
1 & & 6 & & 15 & & 20 & & 15 & & 6 & & 1 \\
\end{array}
$$

It has many interesting properties. One of the m
interesting is the rule by which rows can be added to
base of the triangle indefinitely. See if you can work
this rule for yourself. Look at any number in
triangle; then look at the two numbers to the left
right of it in the row above. How are these three numl
related?

Write down your answer, then turn to the next pag
check.

The general idea behind the egrul (discovery) strategy
is that we try to enable the learners to formulate the
rule (or principle, or definition) for themselves.

Learners to tell us...

Somehow, we must present whatever information or experience
the learners need in order to be able to tell **us** that, e.g.:

- A is an example of B; or
- P must be bigger than O; or
- N must result from M; or
- X is the reason for Y; or
- F must happen before G; or
- R is the reverse of S; or
- D is part of B ... and so on.

then we elaborate

Once we've led our learners to notice the key point, we
can elaborate upon it just as if we'd stated it openly
for them in the first place. We'll be hoping, however,
that they will have understood it better -- because they
will have contributed more thought in arriving at it.

Not always possible

Sometimes this will be too time-consuming, of course,
both for you and for your learners. Besides, we can't
always arrange for the learners to have all the necessary
information and experience from which to derive the rule
themselves. Sometimes we have no choice but to give them
the definition or principle first and then help them
practice with examples.

Choose appropriate strategy

The important thing, though, is to keep these two
possible strategies in mind while writing your tutorial-
in-print. Be aware of which you are using from section to
section, and why. Choose whichever seems most appropriate
and practicable. You may be particularly interested to
to find out which of the two strategies is preferred by
(and works best with) your learners.

```
**************************************************
*                                                *
*   BOTH STRATEGIES ARE WORTH USING -- NEITHER    *
*   IS SUPERIOR TO THE OTHER FOR ALL PURPOSES.    *
*                                                *
**************************************************
```

VARIETY OF STIMULUS

*Don't be
boring*

Learning at a distance can be boring. Learners who are
working on their own, deprived of the stimulus of
interacting with other people, may well think print a
cold and dreary substitute. To a very considerable
extent, your use of **activities** (see Chapter 6) should
help them escape the tedium of "one damn paragraph after
another". But there is more you can do. Bear in mind
the potential loneliness of the long-distance learner.
Do what you can to build variety into your lessons.

Vary the Physical Format

*Double-page
spreads*

Try to avoid offering page after page of solid print.
Think of your text as a number of "double-page spreads".
Aim to make each one visually distinct from others. Vary
your format. This will refresh your learners with a
new image each time they turn the page. The visual
uniqueness of each spread will itself help many readers
to learn and remember. See Figure 7.1 (page 145) which
shows a sequence of double-page spreads from a
tutorial-in-print; note the variety.

*(More about
this in
Chapter 9)*

Illustrations. One way of varying the format, and making
your page more interesting, is to use illustrations. You
could use maps, diagrams, graphs, old etchings and
engravings, drawings, cartoons, and perhaps photographs.
Practically every lesson can make occasional use of one
or more of these. Some lessons can usefully be presented
almost entirely as sequences of illustrations with caption
Figure 7.2 shows a double-page spread from a "documentary
comic book" approach to Einstein's theory of relativity.

*How many
columns ?*

Layout. Be prepared to vary the layout of your printed
page. If your lesson is to be printed in two columns, fo
instance, go to a single column occasionally -- perhaps
to get a wide margin for pictures, or for readers to add
their own data. Alternatively, switch from single to
double column, if and when it makes sense.

Figure 7.2: A Double-page Spread from *Einstein for Beginners* by Schwartz & McGuiness (published by Writers and Readers Cooperative, London, 1979)

Don't feel bound to the traditional prose paragraph.
At times, you may wish to use alternatives like:

*Alternatives
to paragraphs*

o Lists -- perhaps with each item numbered (if you
intend referring back to them) or simply marked wit
a "blob" as I have done here.

o Material enclosed by a box (see below) in order
to give it special emphasis.

o

Blocks of print whose
shape reflects the subject being
discussed. For example, the block of
print in which you discuss
nuclear power
accidents
might be
mush-
room
shaped

o Blocks of print arranged
around an illustration,
with arrows leading to
those parts of the
illustration they are
commenting on.

o A sentence or two (no more) printed in white on a
dark background, for special emphasis.

o Material printed sideways   OR   uʍop-ǝpᴉsdn   OR   *in a different typef*

However:

```
********************************************************
*                                                      *
*  WARNING:  DON'T OVER-DO IT !  THESE DEVICES ARE     *
*  FOR OCCASIONAL EMPHASIS ONLY.  IF EVERY PAGE WERE   *
*  A RIOT OF GRAPHIC INGENUITY -- AS HAPPENS IN SOME   *
*  TRENDY MAGAZINES -- YOUR MATERIAL COULD BECOME      *
*  TOO "BUSY" TO COMPREHEND.  BE SELECTIVE.            *
*                                                      *
********************************************************
```

Vary Your Voice

The tutorial voice

In general, you will do well to write as if you are a sympathetic tutor explaining your subject to an individual learner. Your exposition will call for frequent responses from the learner because it will be built around activities. The extent to which your learner will find you stimulating as well as informative may depend on the extent to which you can **vary** your tutorial voice. How might you do this ? Here are three suggestions:

Avoid dreariness

Lightness of touch. So much academic and official prose is heavy, stuffy and indigestible. The exposition rolls endlessly on, talking to no-one in particular -- solemn, pedantic and remote. It seems to have been produced by a computer for consumption by a committee (or possibly vice versa). From first paragraph to last, the tone is uniform -- uniformly dreary and impersonal.

Write what you'd say

Such prose is best kept out of your tutorial-in-print. The American writer, E.B. White, spoke of writing as being "the self escaping into the open". So let your personal voice emerge in your prose. Cultivate a lightness of touch. Remember that both you and the learner have interests other than the subject you are writing about. Imagine you are talking to such a learner, and write what you might say. (More about this in Chapter 10.)

Different purposes

You should thus find yourself varying your voice from one section of your lesson to the next. Sometimes you will be exhorting your learners, at other times provoking or sympathizing with them. Sometimes you will be painstakingly explaining the inticacies of an idea; at other times you will be reminiscing about your own experiences in learning about it or using it.

Humour too ?

You may even feel sufficiently at ease to introduce humorous "asides" or even jokes if they really do illuminate the subject rather than distract from it. Unfortunately, one person's joke is often another person's wisecrack.

Good-humour and respect

Note, however, that a lesson can still be human, light of touch and **good-humoured** without any efforts after humour as such. Be friendly, be conversational, but talk to your learners with respect both for them and for the subject of your discussion. Take care to avoid the flippant chit-chat which authors sometimes inject in a misguided attempt to be matey -- and which they would never dream of using face to face with a learner.

Read aloud

One of the best safeguards against monotony in your writing is to READ IT ALOUD. If it sounds dull, it probably is. Re-write it. With a bit of practice, you may find that you can "hear" your prose in your head, without actually needing to speak it.

Dramatize your teaching. Where appropriate, try to get a bit of human drama into your writing. Rather than simply reading about abstract ideas, most of us like to hear about how those ideas impinge on **people.** Where it is relevant, develop your subject-matter in terms of people's problems, discoveries and activities. Tell what happened to them or what they made happen.

Write about people ?

Actual people...

Sometimes you will be referring to actual people, whether living or dead. For instance, you may be reporti a debate between Darwin and Huxley -- or showing how a film-star's latest divorce case illustrates a new legal rule. At other times, you may need to invent people to illustrate your argument. Either way, you may be able dramatize your teaching by including, for example:

or invented

Ways of dramatizing

- quoted remarks;
- complete conversations;
- narrative sequences; and
- case studies.

These can stimulate interest and help your readers relate your subject-matter to everyday life. Very often you can involve your reader as one of the "characters" in the dramatization. You can ask what the reader would say or do in the situation you describe. For examples, see Figures 7.3 and 7.4 (and also Figure 5.2D on page 98).

A role for reader

Figure 7.3:   Teaching with Conversation -- adapted from
Educational Technology in Curriculum Development by
D. Rowntree (Harper & Row, 1982)

> they can 'get by' without developing their methods. What I'm
> suggesting, really, is that the educational technology approach
> involves not just using scientific *knowledge*. . . .
>
> T: Which may be pretty thin on the ground?
> E: All right. . . but also using scientific *method*. By that I mean a hyp-
> othesis-testing method.
> T: Now how would you explain that?
> E: Well, educational technology would want the teacher – the
> 'professional' teacher, as you called him – to think of himself as a
> tester of hypotheses about teaching and learning. That is, he'd start
> with hypotheses, insights, about what purposes might be
> worthwhile, or about possible ways of achieving the purposes. . .
> T: From science?
>
> How would **you** answer T's question about the source
> of the teacher's hypotheses ?
>
> ....
> ....
> ....
>
> Now read on to see how E answered it.
>
> E: Maybe from science, maybe from philosophy, maybe from his
> experience or from that of his colleagues, very often from the
> suggestions of his students. But quite often his hypotheses would
> seem to come right out of the blue. After all, there's nothing in
> science itself to generate new hypotheses. Even Einstein once said
> they came from 'intuition, resting on sympathetic experience'.
> T: So you do allow for inspiration.
> E: But of course. Inspiration, intuition, wisdom, good judgement.
> These underlie all innovation and growth in education. Science itself
> doesn't produce the new ideas.
> T: Anyway, once you've got them . . .?
> E: Yes, though scientific method doesn't produce the hypotheses, it
> does enable you to evaluate them and elaborate on them once you've
> got them.
> T: I'm not sure I know what you mean by scientific method here.
>
> How would you reply, as E, to T's remark ?
>
> ....
> ....
> ....
>
> Now read E's reply.
>
> E: Simply that you regard your hypotheses experimentally. You try
> them out with learners, expecting to find that they work with some
> and not with others, and to different degrees. You'll be trying to
> account for these differences, using whatever scientific or practical
> knowledge seems relevant. And you'll expect to modify your

Figure 7.4: Part of a Case Study (from Open University

32   PUPILS

What do you do?

Your conscience as a governor is jolted. The school has always been a pleasant community and discipline has never been thought of as a problem. Yet here are signs of disruption. You must do something about it, you feel. But what?

▲Which of the following actions seem sensible at this stage?
○ Contact the girl's parents?
○ Contact the headteacher?
○ Contact the chairman of governors?
○ Contact the welfare services?

Contacting either the head or the chairman of governors would seem like a sensible first step. As a governor you should not contact the parents on your own initiative, or the welfare services.

As it happens, you decide to call on the chairman, who lives in the next street from you. It appears she has already heard about Rachel and shows you the following note she had from the head a couple of weeks ago:

> I think you ought to know we have a child here I really don't think we're going to be able to keep. Her father came to work on Blunt's farm in October. She is 8 years old and has been to six different schools already. She's in Mr Dean's class and is quite uncontrollable. I have taken her into my class for some of the time and she's been rude and insolent to me. Some of the other children are starting to copy her and parents have been complaining about bad language. The primary adviser came in to see Mr Dean (you remember he's a probationer) and she thinks Rachel does need special help. I've only three mornings' teaching help so I can't have Rachel on her own. I went to see her parents and they started rowing between themselves. They say that she's not badly behaved at home and that it's my job to deal with her. I'm going to ask if the educational psychologist will see her.

(Head to chairman of governors)

The chairman tells you that she has since been in touch both with the head and with the assistant education officer (AEO) at the education office. The head told her that Rachel has now been seen by the educational psychologist. The primary schools adviser has also seen Rachel in action and, according to the AEO, said:

> I don't think Rachel should be in Mr Dean's class. He hasn't the experience to deal with a child like that. I would suggest an additional part-time remedial teacher, but is there anyone available? And could anyone get out to that school? I don't suppose there any many buses. It would have to be someone with a car.

(Primary adviser to AEO)

The AEO has also given your chairman the gist of the educational psychologist's initial report, which is as follows:

> I've been to see Rachel. She showed signs of disturbance and she needs a lot of help. I am reluctant to suggest a change of school. She ought to have the chance to settle in one school and be helped to make progress. I have discussed a programme of remedial work with the head and I think Rachel could also be fitted in a couple of mornings a week at the special unit in Newton. If that fails, she may have to be considered for special education. I've seen the parents. There seem to be problems there. They were very aggressive and critical of the head. I will be sending you and the head a copy of my full report as soon as it is typed.
> *(Educational psychologist to AEO)*

Problems and treatment

So, Rachel appears to be presenting the school with problems.

▲Consider these two questions before reading on.
1 How would you sum up these problems from what you have heard so far?
2 What solutions (treatments) have been suggested by the three people whose reports you have read?

1 **The problems?**   Rachel is rude and uncontrollable, uses bad language and is influencing other children to their parents' displeasure and is not making satisfactory progress in her schoolwork.
2 **Solutions and treatments?**   The head is thinking of getting her moved elsewhere. The primary adviser suggests putting her in the class of a more experienced teacher and getting an additional part-time teacher to come in to give her remedial help. The educational psychologist is resisting the head's desire to get her moved, believing that she should be given a chance to settle in (after all, she's been at six schools already) and make some progress. To this end he has suggested a programme of remedial work and is also trying to get her a couple of mornings a week at Newton's special unit. However, he does consider, as a last resort, the possibility that, if she doesn't respond, she may need to be considered for transfer to a special school.

So, it seems that things are happening and, from what you know of the head, you have every confidence that he will be doing his best for Rachel – even if she is upsetting the peace and productivity of his hitherto trouble-free school.

Other voices. Another means of giving the learner a rest
from the sound of your voice, now and again, is to bring
in the voices of other people. This can be done by quoting
conversation, of course, as in Figure 7.3. The most
generally applicable way, however, is to bring in
quotations from other writers on your subject -- or
spoken comments from practioners. These may consist
simply of a few words or they may run to several paragraphs.

*Using
quotations*

If you are quoting another writer's words, don't take
more than you need. Occasionally you may want your
learners to read a whole article or a chapter from a book.
But usually you will do better to select from it -- perhaps
interspersing paragraphs of your own between the paragraphs
you quote. More than a couple of hundred words and the
tonic effect of a change in voice will begin to wane.   In
addition, you may be running into copyright problems.
Remember that all quotations must be credited to their
authors; and copyright permission must be sought (and
perhaps be paid for) if the amount quoted exceeds what is
normally accepted as reasonable (see pages 368-370).

...selectively

*Credits and
copyright*

Another way of bringing in some other expert's voice
is to get a colleague to comment on an early draft of your
material -- and then print his or her remarks in the
margins of your text or as footnotes. You could then do
the same for your colleague's lesson, if appropriate.
Figure 7.5 shows an extract from a lesson on management
-- in which the author presents her argument in the body
of the text but prints her colleagues' comments in the
margins. (The comments of learners on whom you try out
your draft materials can be used in a similar way -- or
in providing feedback on activities, as in Figure 6.2.)

*Printing
colleagues'
comments*

On page 134)

Finally, and most substantially, you may be able to
vary your voice in the literal sense -- from written voice
to **spoken** voice -- by recording some part of your lesson
on audio-cassette. Using audiotape opens up a whole new
world of learning stimuli which I discuss further in
Chapter 11.

*Using
audio-
cassette*

Figure 7.5:   Colleagues' Comments in the Margin of a Text
(An example from Open University course T243, Block 5)

Mechanistic attitudes to the design of work organizations had already had a long history before the popularization of the idea of scientific management in the United States at the beginning of this century. Scientific management embodied a refinement of the mechanistic view of the workforce which had flourished since the Industrial Revolution. It saw individuals as basically predictable, controllable and largely independent components. It advocated such practices as the division of work into small, easily-learnt tasks, which made workers more interchangeable and increased the scope for managerial control. It used the measurement of time and motion to high levels of precision to establish efficient work patterns which led to setting targets, measuring performance and comparing it with the targets set; it was a simple step to the linking of pay rates to the amount produced as a means of correcting the 'error-signal'.

> During the Industrial Revolution employers and others put a lot of time into attempts to structure attitudes – the obedient thrifty, and pious servant of the firm, and so on. *ER*

Scientific management has long since given way to succeeding managerial rationalities, but the kind of mechanistic thinking behind it did not die with the advent of new fashions in management. As Unit 5 points out, many years after Taylor, similar principles are still being used in the design of jobs on assembly lines. Some of these are the concentration of control functions, and setting of targets, in the hands of a single control unit; the division of tasks; and the attempt to correct deviations or error signals by means of remunerative controls.

> Not really. As a single coherent theory of management certainly, but people still talk a lot about scientific management in the West, USSR and China! *ML*
> But not just assembly lines – such principles have spread to all areas of work, including much white collar work through the use of various performance assessment or measurement techniques. *ER*

Control is more or less consciously embodied in the design of many production systems, but job designers have increasingly recognized that a variety of controls may be necessary to persuade the workforce to adopt the goals of management. For the greater variety of human behaviour, compared to the behaviour of machines, necessitates a greater variety of control mechanisms in people management systems than in mechanical ones. Managerial control strategies include not only remunerative control but coercive control (for example, by the mechanical pacing of the assembly line) and normative control (that is, control exercised through the granting or withholding of status, appreciation or respect). Each of these control strategies is perfectly compatible with the analogy of the control model, which specifies a particular *what* (the sequence of control procedures) not a particular *how*. But although managers may try to build an organization in which they *match* their control strategy to the expectations of type of involvement of the workforce (an interactive process, involving considerations such as the level of technology involved), this is a much more difficult process than in even quite complicated engineering systems. Not only do

> I'm not sure the slant of this passage is fair. A complicated process requires a very high degree of coordination. Achieving this requires a degree of uniformity (not all of which is necessarily unacceptable to the people involved). *JH*
>
> No. Normative control is essentially about trust relations and is therefore *much* more akin to open-loop control. *RP* (For a description of open- and closed-loop control, see Units 1/2.)

Vary the Activities

In Chapter 6, I suggest how learner-activities might
be varied. You can vary them in:

Ways of
varying
activities

- o *Level of difficulty*, e.g. you can begin with easy
  activities to build up the learner's confidence, but
  gradually make them more demanding.

- o *Type of activity*, e.g. reading, drawing, calculating,
  observing, imagining, discussing, making, etc.

- o *Manner of recording responses*, e.g. ticking boxes,
  providing a missing word or two, writing a sentence
  or more, drawing a chart, etc.

Within one lesson, and certainly from one lesson to
another, you should find need to give your readers variety
in all three ways. Sometimes, partly to encourage your
readers to get other people's reactions to what they are
studying, you may think it worth saying something like:
"Why don't you try this question on your family or some

*Family
activities ?*

friends, and see if they take a different line from you ?"

*Other
media*

Activities may be varied even further if you can bring
in other media, other ways of learning -- practical work,
audio-visual material, interaction with tutors and other
learners. I consider the use of other media in Chapter 11.

* * * * *

In this chapter, I have given you some basic ideas about
teaching at a distance. Clearly, this is more
problematical, and in many ways more demanding, than is
teaching face to face. In a written lesson, your approach

*No second
chances*

and examples and variety of stimulus just have to be
right first time.

```
*****************************************
*                                       *
*  BEING A DISTANCE TEACHER IS NEVER    *
*  BEING ABLE TO SAY: "I'M SORRY --     *
*  LET ME TRY TO PUT THAT ANOTHER WAY". *
*                                       *
*****************************************
```

8. EASING YOUR READER'S ACCESS

If your teaching is well-structured, readers stand a fair chance of learning from it. But their chances will be much improved if they can see what that structure is. If learners are to use your lesson intelligently, they'll need to get some idea of how it all hangs together. Otherwise, they will be reduced to hacking though it, page after page, in the hope that some grand design will eventually emerge. Unfortunately, they may get so bogged down in detail that they never see the wood for the trees.

evealing
our
tructure...

ACCESS DEVICES

Happily, there are a number of means by which you can make clear the structure of your teaching -- thus enabling readers to see what they are getting into. These are often called "access devices". They will help your readers to **access** your material -- that is, to find their way **into** the text and to find their way **about** in it.

hrough
access
evices"...

In the list below, I have grouped these access devices according to whether you would insert them before, during, or after the main body of your lesson:

n your
essons

Before
- o   Explanatory title
- o   Contents list
- o   Concept map/Flow diagram
- o   List of objectives
- o   Pre-test

During
- o   Introduction/Overview
- o   Links with other lessons
- o   Headings
- o   Numbering systems
- o   Instructions
- o   Verbal signposts
- o   Visual signposts
- o   Summaries

After
- o   Glossary
- o   Post-test
- o   Index

Now let us look at each of these devices in turn. Not
Not for   every lesson will need all of them. Some of them you may
every   choose to use for **groups** of lessons rather than for
lesson ?   individual lessons.

BEFORE THE LESSON

There are five access devices that might usefully appear
before the body of the lesson itself:

Explanatory Title

An obvious point, but one that's often neglected -- give
your lesson a title that tells the reader what it's about
Titles   Don't call it simply *Botany: Lesson 12* if it might, more
that tell   explicitly, be called *The Morphology of Flowering Plants*.
Similarly, *The Use and Abuse of Chisels* gives learners
more idea what to expect than would *Hand Tools: Module 4*.

Contents List

Present the learner with a list of the main topics in you
lesson, arranged in order of occurrence, with page number
Listing   Put this right at the beginning. If you are including
main topics   more than half a dozen topics in your list, indicate whic
are the most important ones. You can do this by underlin
indenting, using bolder type, and so on.

Such a structured list can provide a useful overview
of the lesson. One way of producing it is to list the
headings and sub-headings you have used in your text.

If **several** lessons are being bound together as a book
you'll need to decide where is the best place for the
contents lists. You could print them all together at the
beginning of the book. Or you could print each one at th
beginning of the appropriate lesson. Or you could
compromise -- putting a brief contents list, covering jus
Where to   the main ideas in each lesson, at the beginning of the bo
put them ?   and the full, detailed contents list in front of each
lesson. Remember, however, that wherever you put them,

*What will
most help
readers ?*
their purpose is to help your readers. They should help
them get a broad overview of the territory you are
covering in the lesson and, if only some areas are
relevant to their present needs, to locate them quickly.

Concept Maps/Flow Diagrams

A contents list can make clear the topics that are to be
dealt with -- but may reveal little or nothing about the
*Showing
connections*··· relationships between them. A concept map or flow diagram,
however, can show up the inter-connections. This can
help learners in their approach to the subject-matter.
Chapters 3 and 4 contain several examples of concept maps
and flow diagrams.

Figure 8.1A is an example from a course on systems
management, revealing to students how most of the sixteen
units of the course can each be classified in two different
ways. Each unit concerns either goals, information or
implementation & behaviour AND either operational, people-
management or socio-economic aspects. Thus, whatever
the learners are working on within this course, they can
relate it to this map of the main themes.

In fact, the diagram shown in Figure 8.1A is rather
generalized. It is typical of the kind you might want to
*between
or within
topics* present at the beginning of a **series** of lessons. It shows
the relationships between the main topics only. Lesson
by lesson, however, you might wish to offer more detailed
diagrams, like Figure 8.1B (and some in Chapters 3 and 4)
-- showing the relationships within each topic.

List of Objectives

*What will
they learn
to do ?*
Learners can find it helpful to be told what they might
expect to be able to do (or do better) as a result of
reading the lesson. A list of objectives near the beginning
may help them adopt a suitable approach to it. However,
a couple of reservations:

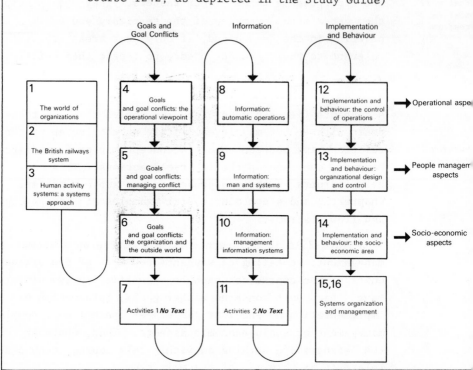

Figure 8.1A: A Course Structure (from Open University course T242, as depicted in the Study Guide)

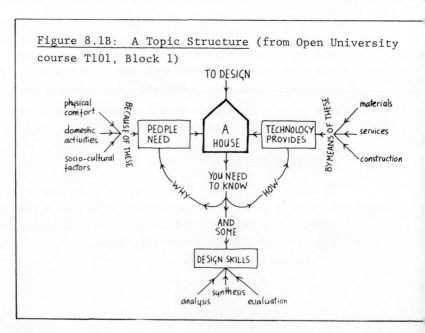

Figure 8.1B: A Topic Structure (from Open University course T101, Block 1)

o Don't include so many objectives that your learners
Don't swamp...   are overwhelmed by the apparent enormity of the
learning task ahead of them. Select the most
important.

o Don't couch the objectives in technical language
or blind with   that will mean nothing to learners until they have
science   completed the lesson. Find more familiar terms,
even if you have to be less precise. For instance,
"You will learn how to ungrunge the fedroonix" may
need to be expressed, more generally, as "You will
learn how to overcome the fault that occurs most
often in the equipment".

If the objectives can't be expressed non-technically, you
may like to put them at the **end** of the lesson rather than
at the beginning. In any case, you may wish to restate
your objectives at the end of the lesson. Instead of
saying, for example: "You will learn to distinguish
Self-   between...", say "Can you now distinguish between...?"
assessment   Thus you can provide a checklist against which your
readers can review what they have learned.

Whether you begin or end with the objectives (or both),
it can be helpful to mention the pages or sections where
each is dealt with in the text.

Pre-test

Pre-   Tell your learners what skills or knowledge you expect them
requisite   to have **before** they can benefit from your lesson. You may
abilities   deal with this by stipulating some previous lesson as a
pre-requisite. Alternatively, you may ask your readers
whether they can already define certain concepts, simplify
certain equations, or whatever it is you wish to assume
they can do already. You may even set them a pre-test --
Testing pre-   a set of questions which they'll need to be able to
requisites   answer satisfactorily if they are to cope with the work
in the lesson ahead.

DURING THE LESSON

Now for the access devices that belong in the body
of the lesson:

Introduction/Overview

*What an
introduction
might do*

An introduction can be very helpful, even if it takes
only a paragraph or two. It can fulfil any combination
of the following functions:

o Providing an overview of what is to come.

o Whetting the readers' appetite and convincing them
   that the lesson is worth spending time on.

o Dispelling any false expectations as to what the
   lesson might be about.

o Forging links between what readers know already
   and what you are expecting them to learn.

o Pointing out links with other lessons (or courses).

o Giving guidance on how to learn from the lesson.

You may sometimes find it appropriate to include in your
introduction a discussion of the concept map and/or
objectives. See Figure 8.2 for a sample introduction: how
many of the above functions does it embody ?

Links With Other Lessons

*Pointing out
the
connections*

Links with other lessons may have been pointed out in your
introduction, but they may be worth mentioning later as
well. Don't assume that readers will necessarily notice
such links for themselves. If your lesson is trying to:

- extend some ideas dealt with in earlier lessons; or
- blaze the trail for a later one; or
- offer a counterpoint to some other lesson,

then let your readers know, whenever and however often it
seems appropriate.

Figure 8.2: An Introduction (from Open University
course T101, Block 1)

Part Two What is a house?

4 Introduction

Imagine yourself going to view a house that your are considering buying. You would try consciously to 'view' the house from different viewpoints. Are the rooms large enough? Are they conveniently planned? Does the structure look sound? Is the house easy to keep warm? Is there noise from neighbours? Can you afford it? And so on. You try quite deliberately to make yourself very critical towards the house, so that you won't overlook any of its potential shortcomings.

However, back in your own old house (or once you have bought the new one) you quickly let your level of critical awareness drop. You learn to live with the house's shortcomings because they are outweighed by its advantages, or you adjust your patterns of living so as to manage within the house as it is, not as it ideally might be. Few of us ever manage to find, or to afford, our ideal dream house.

In Part Two of this block my aim is to help you to develop your critical awareness of a house from many different viewpoints. This is not simply to help you if you are buying a new house. Rather, it is to try to develop in you an awareness of a house as a designed artefact. I shall be trying to get you to develop a designer's view of a house, and this is a view that sees the house simultaneously in many separate ways and also *as a whole*, because the designer of any artefact sees his design as a combination, or synthesis, of many separate factors.

What better example of a house could I choose on which to base my teaching than your own house? Throughout this part of the block you will be asked to carry out study activities that are based on your own house. The purpose of these activities is not only to reinforce your learning from the text by applying the theoretical knowledge to a practical example, but also to provide you with practice in the design skills of analysing and evaluating. You will learn how to 'model' your house from different viewpoints and in ways that encourage and enable you to 'see' it more clearly from these various viewpoints.

Obviously, I am assuming that you do, in fact, have a house of your own that you can use

as the example in the activities. In some cases, the activities also assume that this house is a fairly conventional one: terraced, detached or semi-detached; probably two-storeyed, and so on. If you don't live in such a conventional house, then I'm afraid some of the activities will be impossible or irrelevant for you. The relevance of the activities will depend on what kind of 'house' you actually live in. If it's a family-sized flat, then most of them will still be relevant, but if it's only a small bed-sitter, then most of them probably won't be. If you find that you are stuck in this way, then you might consider using as your example someone else's house that you know well, such as your parents' or that of a friend.

In all the activities you will see that I have carried out the instructions myself, using my own house as the example, so that you can see exactly what the instructions mean, and what you have to do.

Exercise

What do you think was the purpose of the 'Introduction' you have just read? Look back over it and underline one sentence that seems to you to convey the purpose of the 'Introduction' most clearly. Write down in your own words what you think the purpose of the 'Introduction' was.

Discussion

The purposes of the 'Introduction' seem to have been to convey the author's main aims for Part Two of the block, and to give you some idea of what you will be doing in working through it. The first sentence of the third paragraph is a clear statement of an aim. You may have underlined another sentence, but check back to satisfy yourself that the sentence you chose

Headings

In theory, headings should be invaluable as an aid to learning from a text. They should help learners to:

o Find the parts of the text they wish to read.

o Recognize where one topic ends and the next begins.

o Appreciate which topics are grouped together as aspects of some large topic.

o Estimate (by noticing the number of pages devoted to each) which topics the author considers more important and which less.

I say invaluable "in theory" because I am not convinced that learners always know how to "read" the headings. Ma scarcely even notice them. It is true, also, that many authors don't know how to use headings helpfully. If you

suspect your learners might not otherwise be able to make good use of your headings, perhaps you'll think it worth explaining your system in the **introduction** to your lesson

In planning your headings, you may like to keep in min a hierarchical pattern such as the following:

Lesson title
Section headings
Sub-section ..
Sub-sub-section ..

Such a hierarchy of headings should reflect the structure of ideas you are developing in your lesson. In fact, thinking about the headings may help you sort out the structure for your own benefit while writing.

Certainly your learners may need to appreciate the hierarchy in order to grasp your structure. This may or may not be easy, since they will be meeting the headings one by one, in the order indicated by the numbers in the example above. You may consider revealing such a structu to your learners by presenting your contents list in hierarchical form. Alternatively, a separate concept map or flow diagram might serve the purpose.

w many
ades ?

Notice that the diagram above suggests three grades or levels of heading below the main title. Try not to use more than two or, at most, three grades. Otherwise, learners will find the system difficult to follow. Whether your text is to be typed or set in print, you'll have trouble making the headings visually distinct from one another if you use more than three grades. In this book, you'll notice, I have used three grades and have distinguished between them as follows;

o VARIETY OF STIMULUS

o Vary the Physical Format

o *Illustrations*. (Text continues on the same line.)

To use headings logically, follow this simple rule:

eping it
gical

```
*****************************************
*                                       *
*  A HEADING SHOULD REFER TO ALL THE    *
*                                       *
*  TEXT THAT OCCURS BETWEEN IT AND THE  *
*                                       *
*  NEXT HEADING OF THE SAME GRADE.      *
*                                       *
*****************************************
```

oss-
adings
in text

So far, I have been speaking about what are often called "cross-headings" -- headings in the main body of the text. There are two other types worth mentioning: side-headings and running headings.

uning
ds --
ong top

Running head(ing)s are so called because they run along the top (as in this book), or sometimes the bottom, of **every** page in the main text. With books, it is traditional for the running head on the left-hand page to mention the book-title while that on the right-hand page gives the chapter title. Since most readers actually do know what book they are reading, I would suggest that the running heads might more usefully state the chapter (or lesson)

titles and **section** headings. This can help your readers
both in locating the start of a particular section and,
when they are following the discussion in a lengthy secti
it keeps them aware of the heading that still covers what
they are reading.

Now, what about side-headings ? Unlike cross-headings
which break into the discussion, announcing a change of
topic, side-headings simply comment on it, allowing it to
flow on. They are written in the margins -- and can be
Side
headings   hand-written if you don't have a second typeface. They
-- in   are used less often, nowadays, than they might be. They
margins   can be useful in highlighting issues and in picking out
the main points of the argument for readers who want to
skim through quickly in order to preview or review. (Of
course their use needs to be planned. Use them too
sporadically and readers are likely to overlook them. Us
them too abundantly and there'll be little space left in
the margins for diagrams or for readers to write notes.)

Numbering Systems

Some writers number the sections and paragraphs within th
lessons. The first section would be 1.0; the first
sub-section within it, 1.1; the first paragraph within th
Numbering   would be 1.1.1; and so on. Such systems can be cumbersor
best   **and difficult** to keep logical. Hence they do not tell
avoided ?   readers much about the structure of your lesson. They ar
best avoided unless you have a frequent need to refer
readers to particular paragraphs by number.

Instructions

Remember that your readers are studying on their own. Th
need to know what you expect of them. They cannot read
your mind, and there is no-one else to tell them. All yo
Clear
expectations   expectations must be clearly written down -- or spoken if
you are providing an audiotape.

*nless you
ell them...*

If you want your readers to memorize something or write
it down in their notebooks, tell them so. If you want
them to think up examples of their own or relate a point
to their family or working lives, say so. Let them know
which bits of the text are vital and which they can skip
if they run short of time. Make sure they know whether
they are supposed to read the text/listen to tapes/perform
experiments, and so on, in a certain order, or whether
this doesn't matter. With activities, make clear that
some are meant to take only a few seconds while others
may occupy half an hour or more.

In general, keep your learners informed as to what
they are supposed to be doing. They may still choose to
do otherwise; but at least they shouldn't be able to say
they haven't been told.

*Keeping
readers
informed*

Notice that these are specific instructions, inserted
in the text wherever you think them relevant. They are
additional to whatever more general instructions you may
have given in your Introduction (about how to tackle this
lesson) or in a separate Study Guide (about learning from
all the lessons in the series).

Verbal Signposts

Similarly, you should keep your learners informed as to
what **you** are doing. Let them know where the argument is
going. Don't just tell them what you are telling them;
tell them **why** you are telling it. As you write, you

*Where are
you going ?*

should be able to help your readers with "verbal signposts"
like these:

> "On the other hand..."
>
> "In much the same way..."
>
> "Another example..."
>
> "But that's not the only way of..."
>
> "Now we come to an aspect that may surprise you..."
>
> "Let us turn aside for a moment to examine..."
>
> "Now we come to the really tough part of the argument..."

"What this all adds up to is..."

"But this no longer holds true when we look at..."

Floodlighting
your argument

Such phrases -- and countless others will occur to you
while you write -- seem to floodlight the structure of
an argument. They give your readers a glimpse into how
their author's mind is working, and help them read with
a sense of intelligent anticipation.

Visual Signposts

You will further help your reader if you can use visual
as well as verbal signposting. Where possible, let the
structure of your teaching be apparent at a glance.

Structure
at a glance

For instance, suppose you are learning from a text and
have just turned to the two pages shown in miniature belov

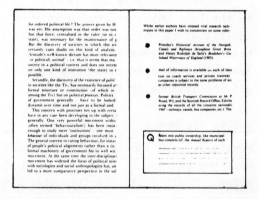

The left-hand page tells you nothing about the structure.
It is just a slab of prose. But the right-hand page tells
you -- at a glance -- that there are three main points and
a question to answer about them. Your mind has begun to
engage with the learning task before you've read a single
word of the page.

Learning
before
reading

Several of the layout features I mention in
Chapter 7 (page 154) can help with visual
signposting. So too can some of the graphic devices

her
gnposting
vices

I mention in Chapter 9. Different coloured paper for distinguishing between different sections (e.g. main text, project notes, tests, etc) would be another means of revealing structure at a glance.

Symbols in the margin are often a useful means of alerting readers to the kind of material that lies ahead. The symbols alongside might be used next to paragraphs that describe, or refer the reader to (in order):

- an activity (a question or exercise);
- practical work;
- video material;
- audio material;
- reading from another book;
- follow-up work; and
- an assignment to be sent to a tutor.

uter buffs
t call
e "ikons"

Some examples of such visual signposts can be seen in Figure 5.2F and G. Obviously, it doesn't matter what symbols you use so long as they are visually distinct from one another and are understood by your reader. As always, however, discretion is called for. If more than three or four kinds of material were being visually signposted within one text, the signals would be liable to shout each other down.

Summaries

al v
asional
maries

A summary reviews the main points that have been covered so far. The most obvious need for this device is at the end of a lesson. But you may sometimes want to summarize also at the end of sections within it.

ders' own
maries

Keep each summary as brief as possible. A common error (bringing confusion to the learner) is to introduce material that has not been previously discussed.

It can be worthwhile, as an activity, to ask your learners to attempt **their own** summaries, with or without

guidance from you. Then, as feedback, you can show them
your version. Such an activity can form a **post-test**, or
part of one, as shown in "SAQ 13" in Figure 8.3.

AFTER THE LESSON

There are three access devices you may want to deploy
after the body of the lesson:

Glossary

At the end of some lessons -- and almost certainly after
a **series** of lessons -- you will need a glossary. This
should contain working definitions of all the new concept
Refreshing   that have been introduced. These will normally be
definitions   definitions that refresh your readers' minds about what
they have learned -- rather than being so extensive that
they don't need to read the lesson at all.

Your glossary might usefully give references to the
pages in the text where each idea is discussed at length.
Again, compiling a glossary may seem to you an activity
Readers' own   worth setting your readers after some lessons. It could
glossaries ?   be one way of helping them summarize what has been taught

Post-test

What has been   This would consist of one or more questions that learners
learned ?   should be able to answer **after** having worked through the
lesson. Be careful not to over-do it. I have seen peopl
set post-tests that take longer to work through than the
lesson. This can be justified if the test is a learning
experience in its own right. For example, the activity
reauired may be one that learners find satisfying for its
own sake (e.g. building a working model), or it may be
How much   one that brings them personal feedback from a tutor.
time on a
post-test ?   But, with the majority of lessons -- where all you're
wanting to do is let learners check their grasp of the
main ideas -- I would suggest that a post-test should add

Figure 8.3: An End-of-lesson Post-test (from Open University course S101, Units 6-7)

Thus, by 1968, a wide variety of geological and geophysical observations had been integrated into one global theory, that of plate tectonics. In Section 5 of these Units we shall outline in more detail some of the processes that occur where plates are formed, and where they collide.

4.10.1   Objectives of Section 4.10

You should now be able to:

(a) Describe the plate tectonic hypothesis (this will be elaborated in Section 5.1). (SAQ 13)

(b) Describe the evidence that favours the plate tectonic hypothesis (SAQ 14):

(i)   seismic zones and first-motion studies of earthquakes;
(ii) geometry of spreading centres and transform faults;
(iii) poles of plate rotation and spreading.

Before reading on, complete SAQs 13 and 14.

SAQ 13 (*Objective (a)*) Complete the blanks in the following description of plate tectonics:

Ocean floor is envisaged as continuously accreting to a ..... (a) plate which is ..... (b) inactive, and which interacts with other plates along active zones of ..... (c) and seismicity. The movement of the plates over the surface of a ..... (d) can be described with reference to a ..... (e) of rotation. ...... (f) faults trend along the direction of ..... (g) circles about the ..... (e) of rotation, whereas oceanic ridges between these faults trend along ..... (h) circles passing through the ..... (e). There are three types of plate boundaries:

1 .... (i)   (do not worry if you list these in a

2 .... (j)   different order to those given in the

3 .... (k)   answer)

Along the first type, new ..... (l) is formed by ..... (m). Along the second type, oceanic crust and upper mantle is being ..... (n).

SAQ 14 (*Objective (b)*) Consider the list of topics we have considered in these Units:

A Deep-sea drilling results

B Palaeoclimatic data

C Palaeomagnetic data

D Ocean-floor magnetic anomalies

E Fit of the topography of continental margins

F Earthquake first-motion studies

G Magnetic polarity reversal timetable

Match these topics with those of the following concepts to which they contributed in a major way:

1 Continental drift (choose three items)

2 Sea-floor spreading (choose three items)

3 Transform faults (choose three items)

4 Plate tectonics (choose one item only)

*Lengthier
test after
several
lessons*

no more than, say, 20% to the time your learners have already spent on the lesson. This is not to say, however, that they would not appreciate a rather more extensive post-test after a **series** of lessons.

*The link with
objectives*

A post-test can help your learners read with a sense of purpose. Seeing it ahead, they know what they are working towards. In this respect, it works rather like objectives. Indeed, if you are printing objectives at the end of your lesson, you may follow them with related post-test questions (as shown in Figure 8.3).

*Post-tests
can also be
pre-tests*

By the way, if a prospective reader can answer your post-test questions **before** working through the lesson, you might want to consider advising that reader to skip it and go on to the next. (Provided your questions really have focussed on the essential issues.) You might also consider whether the post-test for one lesson could serve as the pre-test for the next.

Index

As with the glossary, an index may need to relate to a **set** of lessons rather than to each one individually. It can be invaluable to learners -- both to those trying to

*Checking up
and
checking back*

ascertain whether your lessons might have anything to say about topics of concern to them and to those who have already worked through your materials and are now trying to check back on a few points.

Key words

The index should consist of the key words (terms, name concepts) that readers are likely to look up. They should be in alphabetical order, with the numbers of the pages on which the associated idea is dealt with.

*Problems of
indexing*

So far, so obvious. But compiling an index is not a trivial task. For instance, it's no good just reading through your material and writing down only the key words and their page numbers. You need to be alert also for pages where the relevant idea is discussed but the key

word is not actually mentioned. There is also the danger
of getting lost in detail. List only the most important
ideas, or distinguish them from lesser ones by typography.
That is, print them in **bold type**, or CAPITALS, or <u>underline</u>
them if you are using a typewriter.

*   *   *   *   *

*ther
esson
omponents* Your tutorial-in-print may contain several other
components -- acknowledgements of help from colleagues,
thanks for copyright permissions, a bibliography of sources,
suggestions for further reading, etc.   But these do not
play a part in revealing the structure of your lesson,
so I have not dealt with them above.   (Nor have I talked
about the kind of Study Guide in which you might inform
learners about the structure of a whole course.)

SUMMARY

All the **access devices** mentioned in this chapter have
two functions:

*he functions
f
ccess devices*

o   They enable readers to find what they need within
the structure of your lesson; and

o   They make that structure more apparent to your
readers and so help them to learn.

Use access devices where appropriate and, if necessary,
tell your readers **how** you are using them.

```
*************************************************
*                                               *
*   CHECK TO SEE WHICH OF THE ACCESS            *
*   DEVICES I HAVE USED (AND HOW) IN THIS       *
*   BOOK.  DO LIKEWISE FOR OTHER MATERIALS      *
*   AS A GUIDE TO USING THEM YOURSELF.          *
*                                               *
*************************************************
```

9. TEACHING WITH PICTURES

Like most writers, and perhaps most teachers, I probably
rely too much on words. That is, I no doubt overlook
many occasions when pictures would teach better. For
instance, one could churn out who knows how many words
in an attempt to explain to the less numerate reader
why $(a + b)^2$ -- that is, $(a + b)$ multiplied by $(a + b)$ --
gives $a^2 + 2ab + b^2$. But the diagram below, with a side
measuring $a + b$, **shows** the truth of it directly:

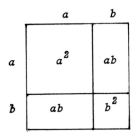

As Alice said, "What's the use of a book without pictures
or conversation ?". I've suggested elsewhere (page 7-19)
how conversation might usefully be brought into your
lesson. Now let us consider the role of pictures -- or,
more broadly, the **pictorial approach.**

GETTING AWAY FROM SOLID PROSE

What do I mean by a "pictorial approach" ? Obviously, I
include the use of such items as diagrams and graphs,
drawings and paintings, photographs and maps. But I want
to suggest a broader use of the term. I would say we
introduce a **pictorial** element into our teaching as soon as
we use the printed page to convey **something that could not
be spoken in words.** The "something" may appeal to the
reader's intellect, or emotions, or both at the same time.

Very often we launch into prose without even
considering that there might be other, perhaps better,

ways of saying what we might be able to say. For instance
Figures 9.1 - 9.4 show four different ways of talking abc

*Increasing
the pictorial
element*

soil classification. All use words, but the pictorial
element increases from 9.1 through 9.2 and 9.3 to 9.4.
In fact, 9.4 reveals the structure of the classification
in a way that is quite lost in 9.1. However, 9.2 and 9.3
may be quite practicable for the learner who just wants t
do quick classifications. Which one do you find easiest
to follow ?

So 9.2, 9.3 and 9.4 get away from conventional, solid
prose. Although they present words, they do not ask
readers to begin at the first word of a paragraph and rea

*Words
patterns*

on until they come to the last word. Instead, the prose
patterned so that one reader may use it differently from
others. Except with 9.3, all will probably start at the

*Readers'
choices*

first sentence, but where each goes after that will be up
to them. No-one will be expected to read all the words,
let alone the same words as every other reader.

*Photographs
would help...*

The patterned presentations in 9.2 - 9.4 could be made
more obviously pictorial by adding photographs of the
various soil types. What might be even more helpful

*though not
as much as
specimens*

(if not essential) in this case, however, would be
specimens of the soil types against which to check the
classification system.

Also, like most pictures used in teaching, all three
need some form of introduction or commentary **in words** --
to help the learner get the most out of them.

Figure 9.1:   Classifying Soils -- Prose Version

If your soil specimen feels gritty, like sand, and is
sticky, then if you can polish it between your fingers
so that it reflects light, it is a **sandy clay loam**.
If it does not polish, then it is a **sandy silt loam**.
If it is gritty but NOT sticky, and you can mould it
into a ball that holds together, it is a **sandy loam**.
If you can't mould it into such a ball, then it is a
sand. Furthermore, if it leaves a mark when you rub
it on a patch of clean skin, it is a **loamy sand**. If
your soil is NOT gritty but feels silky (creamy) and
you can polish it and change its shape it is a **clay
loam**. If you can change its shape easily, it is a
silty clay loam. If you can't change its shape it is
a **clay**. If the soil feels gritty and silky, but won't
polish, it is a **silt loam** (if clearly silky) or a
silty loam. If it is neither gritty nor silky, then it
it is just a **loam**.

Figure 9.2: Classifying Soils -- Directed Prose Version

1. Soil feels <u>gritty</u> (like sand) ... Go to 2.
   Soil does <u>not</u> feel gritty   ... Go to 4

2. Soil feels <u>sticky</u>   ... Go to 3
   Soil does <u>not</u> feel sticky   ... Go to 9

3. Soil will <u>polish</u> when rubbed
      between fingers   ... Sandy clay loam
   Soil will <u>not</u> polish   ... Sandy silt loam

4. Soil feels silky (creamy)   ... Go to 5
   Soil does <u>not</u> feel silky   ... Loam

5. Soil will <u>polish</u> when rubbed
      between fingers   ... Go to 6
   Soil will <u>not</u> polish   ... Go to 8

6. Soil's <u>shape</u> can be changed   ... Go to 7
   Soil's shape can <u>not</u> be changed.. Clay

7. The shape is <u>easily</u> changed   ... Silty clay loam
   The shape is <u>not</u> easily changed.. Clay loam

8. Soil is <u>clearly</u> silky   ... Silt loam
   Soil <u>not</u> clearly silky   ... Silty loam

9. Soil moulds into a <u>ball</u>   ... Sandy loam
   Soil does <u>not</u> mould into ball ... Go to 10

10. Soil leaves <u>mark</u> on clean skin... Loamy sand
    Soil does <u>not</u> leave mark   ... Sand

Figure 9.3: Classifying Soils -- Tabular Version

Ticks (✓) indicate the features shown by each soil type:

	Gritty	Sticky	Silky	very silky	Polishable	Forms ball	Mouldable	easily	Marks
Sand	✓								
Clay			✓		✓				
Loam									
Sandy clay loam	✓	✓			✓				
Sandy silt loam	✓	✓							
Sandy loam	✓					✓			
Loamy sand	✓								✓
Clay loam			✓		✓		✓		
Silty clay loam			✓		✓		✓	✓	
Silt loam			✓	✓					
Silty loam			✓						

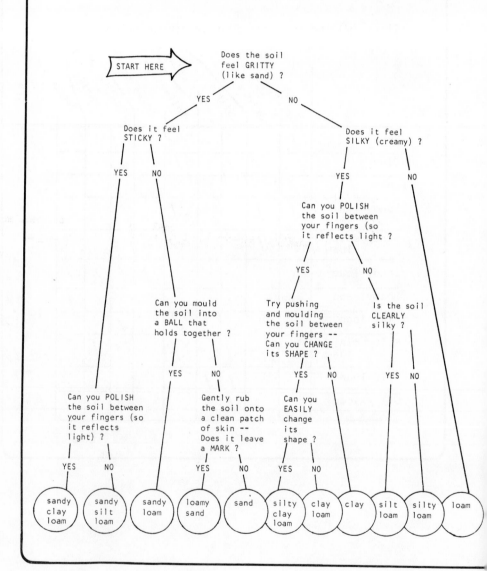

Figure 9.4:   Classifying Soils -- Algorithm Version

Roughly speaking, there are two ways of making your text more pictorial. You can use graphic devices (special layout, for example, as in Figures 9.1 - 9.4) or you can use pictures. Let's look at each of these in turn:

<u>Graphic Devices</u>

In this category I would include...

...prose set out in such a way as to emphasize a point or make sure the reader's attention is drawn to what is vital;

e.g. "Illustrations should be relevant, clear, accurate, and easy to use."

OR "Illustrations should be:
- relevant
- clear
- accurate
- easy to use."

... tables of words that highlight the relationships between ideas,

	Purpose	Context	Example
1	life purposes	the person as an individual	to enrich my experiences
2	role purposes	the person in a particular role	to do well at school
3	task purposes	the person in a role and a task situation	to write a project ev. the increase in world pop
4	specific purposes	a particular resource with- in a task	to obtain information or allon statistics of the U. the Registrar General's I

...and charts that do much the same thing,

...and tables that do it with figures;

TABLE 4 Mechanical properties of fibres

Material	Specific gravity	Tensile strength/kg cm⁻²	Young's modulus/kg cm⁻²
Tread rubber	1.1	200	70
Rayon	1.52	7000	190 000
Nylon-6,6	1.14	9000	50 000
Polyester (PET)	1.40	11 000	110 000
Glass	2.56	35 000	750 000
Steel	7.80	28 000	2 100 000
Aromatic nylon	1.50	29 000	1 360 000

...printers' symbols, which are also available on rub-down sheets for the do-it-yourselfer;

... as are textures
and shadings, and

... borders or "rules"
(lines of print)
which may be used as
"stoppers" or as
decorative borders
or boxes.

Pictures

All of the graphic devices I've mentioned above can be
useful in bringing pictorial relief or support to your
prose. Notice that none of them requires you to be able
to draw. If you **can** draw -- even if only a straight line
with help from a ruler -- your pictorial resources will
be that much richer. Similarly if you can take useable
photographs.

*Pictures
without
"drawing"*

If you can't create your own pictures, you will have
to brief someone else to do it for you -- or else make
best use you can of pictures that have already been
published elsewhere. However:

Almost certainly
you will be able
to draw your own
charts and graphs;

...simple maps;

.. perhaps some
rough-and-ready
cartoons;

... and possibly
recognizable objects,
provided they don't have
to look like any
particular specimen.

a flower

And, even if you can't
draw, you can perhaps
use a camera;

... or assemble
illustrations
from rub-down
sheets;

... or obtain
permission to
reprint someone
else's illustrations
(giving proper
credit);

Reproduced by kind permission of my son.

... or adapt
materials from the
many books of old
(and nicely out-
of-copyright)
engravings.

Who would believe
she was adapted?

Clearly, there are many ways of being pictorial. I have already suggested how graphic devices can help the reader's comprehension. But what about pictures ?

WHY USE PICTURES ?

The functions of pictures

Pictures can have any of several functions in a tutorial-in-print. They may have more than one at the same time. Indeed, you may include a picture for one purpose while your reader uses it for another. Here are ten possible functions for graphs, maps, drawings, photographs and the like:

Decoration

Pictures can be used (as can graphic devices) simply to relieve the monotony of solid print. Almost any kind of picture can serve to give your readers a visual break thus helping motivate them to carry on reading.

Amusement

Some pictures, cartoons in particular, can more deliberat motivate the readers by humanizing the subject and showin its lighter side. Here is one of a series of cartoons featuring a troubled dog with which one Open University t lightened the mood of its teaching about curriculum theor

'The complex nature of social reality only emerges when individuals are forced, through the pressures of interaction with one another, or in attempting to make sense of their world, to dive deeper and deeper for new or modified typifications to account for and make sense of their situation.'

Clearly, cartoons and other light-hearted pictures can
also teach. As in the cartoon above -- which presents a
far-fetched but thought-provoking example of the principle
being discussed -- they can high-light a key point and
make it memorable. (Another example of this kind of
exaggeration to make a point can be seen in Figure 5.2B.)

xample on
ge 94)

However, cartoon-type drawings do not necessarily have
to be funny as well. There is a long tradition of using
the "strip cartoon" to convey ideas in dramatized form.
(See Figure 5.2K for an example.)

xample on
ges 112-113)

Expression

Pictures can be used expressively -- to convey an emotion
or feeling. Thus, photographs might be used to suggest
the despair of unemployed workers; facsimiles of old
documents might be used to express the "actuality" of
some historic occasion; a strip cartoon (as in Figure 5.2K)
might be used to involve the reader in some situation of
conflict or confrontation.

xample on
ges 112-113)

A "montage" (as in Figure 9.5) can be useful in
conveying a variety of expressive images simultaneously.
In Figure 9.5, the montage is being used as a kind of
visual contents list for a tutorial-in-print.

Persuasion

Sometimes a picture
may be used not simply
to express or provoke
feelings, but also to
persuade the reader
towards a change of
attitude. The picture
alongside, from a
Russian anti-smoking
poster, is clearly of
this type.

Figure 9.5: A Montage (from Open University course E262)

Block 9
Language and Values

Illustration

This is a superior form of decoration. It involves
selecting some aspect of the text that does not absolutely
demand to be described pictorially, and picturing it
nonetheless -- perhaps with a pen-and-ink sketch or
photograph. For example, the learner who is reading
about Wordsworth's poetical philosophy may not actually
learn much from an eighteenth century print of Grasmere --
but is still likely to appreciate it as an adornment of
the page. (The notebook depicted in Figure 5.2K is
another example of illustration. See also Figure 7.4.)

amples
pages
2 and 158)

Description

Here the picture is meant to convey a necessary understanding
that could not be conveyed in words alone. It shows what
something looks like. As Bertrand Russell once said,
most of us can recognise a sparrow, but we'd be hard put
to describe its characteristics clearly enough for
someone else to recognise one. Far more sensible to show
them a picture. (The pictures in Figures 5.2G and J are
of this type.)

amples
pages
4 and 110)

Pictures can save us, by the way, from a danger I
mention in connection with analogies (page 144). That
is, it's no good, for example, describing a turtle by
reference to a tortoise if the reader has no idea what
a tortoise looks like. A picture avoids this problem.

Explanation

Some pictures do more than describe what things look like.
They show how they work, or how they can be operated. Such
visual explanations are often necessary to the teaching
of physical tasks. Imagine the difficulty of trying to
teach someone to tie a reef knot or play chords on a
guitar if you were denied the use of pictures -- and had
to rely on print (or a pre-recorded voice) alone.

(Figures on pages 100 and 102) Many physical processes, and the operation of much machinery or physical equipment, will also call for visual explanation. (See Figure 5.2E and perhaps even 5.2F.)

Notice, however, that a full explanation will usually need words **as well** as pictures. Figure 9.6 below shows a combination of:

- a photograph to **describe** what a thing looks like;

- a line drawing to **explain** how it works; and

- several lines of text to make clear what is not apparent in the pictures.

Figure 9.6: Two Uses of Pictures (from Open University course S236, Block 4)

(a)

(b)

path of main current
migration of meander
zone of erosion
point bar deposits

Figure 42 (a) A small meander in the River Ouzel, Bedfordshire. (b) The lateral migration of a meander caused by erosion of the outside bend and point bar accretion on the inside bend. Downstream migration also occurs, because maximum erosion occurs downstream of the mid-point in the meander.

So how does the amplitude of the meander increase? On the outside of a bend, water flows at a faster speed than on the inside. So while the outside bank of a meander is actively eroded, material is deposited on the inside bend of the next meander downstream. The sediment deposited accretes slowly sideways as a *point bar* at the same time as the outside bend is eroded further. The overall result is that lateral erosion is compensated by lateral deposition and the amplitude of the meander increases (Figure 42).

point bar

Simplification

Pictures offer us a means of simplifying reality, of making it more amenable to inspection. After all, reality may be:

problems
reality

- too big (e.g. the solar system);

- too small (e.g. the heart of a water-flea);

- too slow (e.g. the sequence of cloud types during the passage of an occluded depression);

- too fast (e.g. the wing movements of a humming bird);

- too inaccessible (e.g. the four stroke cycle in an internal combustion engine);

- too dangerous (e.g. defusing a bomb); or

- too cluttered up with confusing detail (e.g. the dissected body cavity of a frog.

Worse still, the reality may even be:

- invisible (e.g. the pattern of sound waves from an underwater echo device);

- extinct (e.g. dinosaurs); or

- not yet come into being (e.g. a "nuclear winter" scene).

In all such cases, pictures enable us to convey **something** of the reality. But it will be a simplification we convey -- satisfactory perhaps for our immediate purpose, but not to be confused with the real thing. A picture is

visual
analogies

like a visual analogy -- similar to the reality in some respects, but different in others.

Quantification

Many learners have trouble with numbers. So, when we need to consider quantities, compare sizes, recognize

number
pictures

changing proportions, and so on, it often helps the learner if we can present the data pictorially. Figure 9.7

shows some common ways of doing so. Such pictures work
by using differences in size between one part of the
picture and another to represent differences in size
between one number or quantity and another.

Figure 9.7: Common Ways of Picturing Quantities

1. PICTOGRAM -- Useful for giving a
    dramatic impression of data, but
    not precise enough for serious work.

2. BAR CHART -- Useful for showing up
    the differences between totals.
    Unless there is some logical order
    among the totals (e.g. successive
    years), the bars are arranged in
    descending order of size.

3. COMPOUND BAR CHART --
4. PIE CHART --
    Both are useful for comparing the
    contribution made by each of several
    categories of data to some overall
    total. The compound bar chart can
    cater for more categories and is
    easier to draw.

5. LINE GRAPH -- Used to show how a
    quantity changes over a period of
    time or how changes in one quantity
    relate to changes in another.

Tables as "pictures"

All such pictures of quantities would need an accompanying caption to enable the reader to interpret them. An alternative might be to show your data in a **table**. This is a less visual form of presentation -- but still better than burying your figures in a wodge of prose. In a table, there are no size differences to suggest numerical differences -- £9999 occupies no more space than £1000. But at least the figures can be made to stand out clearly.

Problem-posing

Figures 5.2J nd 5.2L are n pages 110 nd 116)

A picture can pose a problem or question to your learners. Or it can be the focus of a question you put to them verbally. Look at Figures 5.2J and L, and at Figure 9.8, for some examples. As you'll appreciate, many topics give rise to important questions that simply cannot be asked **without** using pictures.

At the very least, your learners may be asked what a picture represents. For instance, you might show them a photograph of a glaciated valley and ask them to point out evidence of glacial activity. Tables, graphs, charts and maps can be used to involve the learners in quite complex feats of analysis and interpretation.

```
*********************************************
*                                           *
*  REMEMBER THAT:                           *
*                                           *
*  o  PICTURES CAN SERVE MANY FUNCTIONS.    *
*                                           *
*  o  ONE PICTURE CAN SERVE SEVERAL FUNCTIONS *
*     AT THE SAME TIME.                     *
*                                           *
*  BE SURE YOU KNOW WHAT FUNCTION(S) YOU    *
*  INTEND EACH OF YOUR PICTURES TO SERVE.   *
*                                           *
*********************************************
```

GUIDELINES FOR USING PICTURES

Here are a few guidelines to bear in mind when using
pictures (including tables and graphs) in your
self-instructional materials:

Explain the Function

*What's
it for ?*

Consider whether you need to tell the learner why you have
included the picture. What function is it meant to serve
This should not be necessary with pictures that are meant
to be decorative, expressive or illustrative; but it may
be needed, let's say, with explanatory or problem-posing
pictures -- if the learner is to be persuaded not to
disregard them.

Balance the Functions

*Beware of
side-effects*

Try to make sure that some minor function of a picture
does not act against its major function. For example,
photographs of battered babies might produce too great
an emotional (expressive) effect for the learner to use
them easily as evidence of what the injuries actually
consist of.

Set Activities

*Making your
learners look*

Whenever you regard a certain picture as vital in
developing your learners' understanding, base an **activity**
upon it. This will require your learners to examine the
photograph, interpret the table, compare the graph with
those they have drawn themselves, or whatever. Without
such activities -- and especially if your text gives the
gist of what is in the pictures anyway -- many learners
will simply ignore most of your pictures.

Explain Conventions ?

*Will they
understand ?*

Ask yourself whether your learners will all understand th
graphic conventions you are using in your pictures. For
example, do they understand the purpose of shading or

hachuring on a map ? Do they appreciate the distinction
between solid lines and broken lines on a scale drawing
of a three-dimensional object ? Can they judge the size
of the objects shown in your photographs ?

ys and
ptions

If there is any doubt, you will need to provide a key
or a caption and/or describe the picture in the text.
Again, however, don't tell your readers so much that they
feel (correctly or otherwise) that they have no need to
consult the picture itself.

Print Picture Close to Text

As a general rule, try to print each picture as close as
possible to the piece of text that refers to it. Don't
expect your readers to hunt around for it. Any picture
on which an activity is based should certainly be on the
same page -- or at least on the same "double page spread"
-- as the instructions for that activity. You may even
need the "feedback" to be on the same page also.

nsider how
cture is
be used

What if the section of text referring to the picture
occurs near the bottom of a page, leaving no space for the
picture ? It might be tempting to fill in what space
remains with text relating to the next topic -- and put
the picture on the next page instead. Unfortunately, many
of your learners will read straight on , and will have
lost interest in the subject of the picture by the time
they come to it.

It would be better to put both picture and text on the
next page. This would, of course, leave a sizeable space
towards the bottom of the first page -- but there is no
law saying all the pages in a teaching text must have the
same number of lines. Indeed, some variety in page length
may even be a relief to your readers.

need to
l all
r pages

If a picture needs to be consulted repeatedly -- say
more than three times -- while working through the pages
of your text, consider presenting it as a **fold-out sheet.**

tures on
d-out
ets

Readers will then be able to keep it in sight throughout the lesson.

There are exceptions to the general rule discussed above. Some of your pictures -- especially decorations and perhaps some illustrations -- may not relate too closely to any specific piece of text. So you will have much more freedom as to where you insert them. You may use them wherever you think will afford most relief to the reader's eye.

Some pictures easier to place

Again, if your subject calls for colour photographs, technical considerations may demand that you print them all together -- and separately from the text commentary. A fold-out sheet might be useful here also.

Colour photographs

Graphic Emphasis

People learn best when they can easily see what point yo are trying to make. How can you help your learners to identify the important features of your pictures ? You may direct their attention verbally, in your text or in a separate caption. In addition, you may do it graphica within the picture itself. For instance:

Focussing learners' attention

o You may draw a box around the key area in a photograph, or use arrows or pointing hands to bri the reader's attention to various parts of a diagr

o You may print certain figures in a table in bold type or even in colour.

o You may number or letter various parts of a diagra to suggest the order in which you would like your reader to examine its parts.

There is an example of such graphic emphasis in a diagra on page 154. Figure 9.8 includes another example (and also shows a question being asked about the picture).

Figure 9.8: An Example of Graphic Emphasis (Adapted, with permission, from an Olivetti training manual)

Avoid Information Overload

Don't overload your pictures with information. For example, you may have a photograph that contains a good picture of the kind of fossil you are writing about. But many other fossils are in the picture also, and might distract the learners. Here you might consider cutting out the irrelevent parts of the photograph, and printing only the image that concerns your learners.

Removing superfluous details

    As another example, compare charts A and B below. Chart A may be readable, but chart B is too complex.

Chart A

Chart B

The visual spaghetti in Chart B above might be unravelled by making two or more charts out of it, as shown alongside.

Whenever a picture looks unduly complicated, ask yourself whether you really do need to present **all** the information Even if you do, ask whether you need to present it all at once. Perhaps you could present a little to start with getting your learners to note the main points -- before building up the complexity by offering further pictures,

Presenting one bit at a time

each of which contains further information.

Indeed, you might **build up to** a picture that contained all the information. And you could be confident that readers would understand it because they would have worked on it during its construction.

*Overload
in tables*
Tables of figures are often heavily overloaded. Excessive detail, together with unhelpful layout, can make it difficult for readers to pick out the important trends, patterns and relationships. If you are thinking of using tables produced by other people, you may well need to simplify or clarify them for your readers. Figure 9.9 shows ways of setting about this.

Pictures Don't Tell All

Pictures allow us to edit reality and get rid of all kinds of "superfluous detail". For instance, we might present our learners with a photograph or diagram of a fruit they are studying -- rather than a real specimen. Thus we would ensure they concentrated on what we regard as the "essential" features.

*Do pictures
over-edit
reality ?*
But we should not forget to ask whether the learners' concept of the fruit might thereby remain impoverished. Do they **also** need to experience the colour, smell, taste, texture, weight and three-dimensionality of some real specimens ? If so, pictures may be necessary, but they will not be enough.

Avoid Racism and Sexism

If you include pictures with people in them, take care to avoid charges of racism and sexism. Don't use picture that
*tereotypes
n pictures*
present racial or sexual stereotypes. Don't let your pictures suggest that blacks and asians are not encountered in the "developed" countries of the world -- except in low-status or subservient roles. Do not imply that women are essentially housewives and mothers, and are not to be

Figure 9.9: Clarifying a Table of Figures (Adapted from Open University course P670, Book 7, pages 33-35)

① THE RAW TABLE

Table 1 Central Government Expenditure by (selected) programme 1967-1977 (in million pounds).

Programme	1967	1970	1973	1977
Defence	2,427	2,465	3,481	6,854
Housing	1,129	1,319	2,328	5,111
Education	1,893	2,352	3,966	7,853
National Health Service	1,524	1,979	2,942	6,730
Social Security Benefits	2,899	3,921	5,534	13,213
Total General Govt. Expenditure	16,672	20,869	30,502	61,964

Source: National Income and Expenditure (1967-1977).

② THE PROBLEM

What conclusions can you draw from the table about the relative sizes of the programmes during the period 1967-1977?

How would you set about tidying the table so as to clarify its key features?

③ FIRST STEPS

Question
- Does the table appear to be just a jumble of figures?
- Is there any logic in the ordering of the rows or columns?
- Is it difficult to compare figures along a row?

Solution
→ Reduce the number of digits by either:
  • removing rows or columns
  • rounding each number to two significant figures.
  Use better spacing and layout.
→ The columns are ordered chronologically. Reorder the rows more logically – in decreasing size.
→ Interchange the rows and columns so that the years read down the side.

④ A CLEARER TABLE

LEAD TO...

Table 2, given below, is the result of applying these solutions to Table 1.

Table 2 Central Government Expenditure by (selected) programme 1967-1977 (in £000 (thousand) million pounds).

Year	Social Security Benefits	Defence	Education	National Health Service	Housing	Total General Government Expenditure
1967	2.9	2.4	1.9	1.5	1.1	16.7
1970	3.9	2.5	2.5	2.0	1.3	20.9
1973	5.5	3.5	4.0	2.9	2.3	30.1
1977	13.2	6.9	7.9	6.7	5.1	62.0

Source: National Income and Expenditure (1967-1977).

⑤ HOWEVER...

Laid out in this way, Table 2 permits easier interpretation. However, there are further refinements to the table which might aid a better understanding of this information. The second list of questions below will set you thinking about some of these possibilities.

Question	Solution
Would it help to find row or column averages?	→ Not particularly here.
Would it help to convert to percentages?	→ Yes. Because of inflation the relative size of each programme would be a more useful figure than the original absolute values.
Is the information internally consistent?	→ Note that the data for the five listed programmes do not add up to the stated total because not all Government Programmes are listed. Add an 'Other' column.
What other information is needed?	→ This depends on your purpose in analysing the data.

⑥ TAKING THE ANALYSIS FURTHER...

CAN PRODUCE...

The final adaptation is shown in Table 3. You will notice the addition (in brackets) of the percentage of Central Government Expenditure and the addition of an 'Other' column.

⑦ AN EVEN BETTER VERSION

Table 3 Central Government Expenditure by (selected) programme 1967-1977 (in £000 million pounds and as a percentage of Total Government Expenditure).

Year	Social Security Benefits	Defence	Education	National Health Service	Housing	Other	Total General Government Expenditure
1967	2.9 (17)	2.4 (14)	1.9 (11)	1.5 (9)	1.1 (7)	6.9 (41)	16.7 (100)
1970	3.9 (19)	2.5 (12)	2.5 (12)	2.0 (10)	1.3 (6)	9.3 (44)	21.9 (100)
1973	5.5 (19)	3.5 (11)	4.0 (13)	2.9 (10)	2.3 (8)	14.7 (48)	30.5 (100)
1977	13.2 (21)	6.9 (11)	7.9 (13)	6.7 (11)	5.1 (8)	22.2 (36)	62.0 (100)

It is possible to pick out some important features from the percentage figures in Table 3 which were not obvious before. For example, defence spending has fallen in relative terms, while spending on the NHS has increased.

⑧ BUT... MIGHT A GRAPH MAKE IT CLEARER STILL?

seen in responsible occupations -- except perhaps in a
role clearly subservient to men.

I can think of one distance course on child-rearing
whose authors were careful to show photographs of black
and asian mothers as well as white ones tending their
children. But it didn't occur to them to show fathers of
any colour sharing in these traditionally "female" concerns.
(This oversight was corrected, however, in the second
edition.)

*An
interesting
oversight*

Using Other People's Pictures

Sometimes you may wish to use tables, diagrams, photographs,
and other pictures that have appeared in other publications.
You may want to use the picture exactly as it is. Or you
may want to use just part of it. You may want to print a
section out of a photograph, or a couple of columns from
a table, or just one of several curves from a graph. You
may also want to add material -- e.g. verbal captions or
graphic emphasis -- to suit the particular needs of **your**
learners.

*With or
without
alterations*

If you intend to print the picture as it is -- or if
your alterations will still leave the picture (or part of
it) identical with the original -- **make sure you get
copyright permission** (see page 368).

*Getting
copyright
permission*

If you re-draw the picture (or take a new photograph) so
that it looks obviously different, you will not need
copyright permission. But it may be appropriate to mention
where the original of your picture appeared.

Testing Your Pictures

However careful you are in teaching with pictures, learners
may respond to them in unexpected ways. When you
developmentally test your lesson on a sample of learners
(see pages 338-350), find out how they respond to your
pictures.

*How do your
learners
respond ?*

Unexpected effects

Learners' responses will show up particularly where you have based activities on pictures. But other pictures, illustrations for instance, may also be having unexpected effects -- and perhaps ones that you are not too happy about. I remember one photograph showing two children sleeping in each of three beds crammed together in a tiny room. It was meant to describe over-crowding in slum houses. But, when the text was used in parts of the Third World, readers made remarks like: "They're lucky; they've got beds to sleep in" or "Look: only two to a bed".

However handsome a picture may be, learners may seem not to understand it -- or to understand it wrongly. In which case you'll need to replace it with a better one and/or give a better explanation of what the picture is trying to do.

Build Up a Stock of Pictures

Your own picture collection

All the time you are involved in preparing self-instruction you'll be running across pictures (or ideas for pictures) that may be relevant to one of your topics. Keep a folder or box-file in which to store such materials. They could save you hours of work later on. Remember to note the sources (where the pictures are from other people's work), so you'll know where to apply for copyright, and whom to acknowledge, if you use them.

Final thoughts:

```
*****************************************************************
*                                                             *
*   o  NOT EVERYTHING CAN BE SAID IN WORDS.                   *
*                                                             *
*   o  IF YOU CAN'T FIND THE WORDS TO SAY SOMETHING,          *
*      TRY PICTURING IT INSTEAD.                              *
*                                                             *
*   o  EVEN IF YOU CAN FIND WORDS,                            *
*      CONSIDER PICTURING IT AS WELL.                         *
*                                                             *
*****************************************************************
```

10. MAKING YOUR LESSON READABLE

As I hope you will agree, the tone of your lesson should
not be that of a textbook, nor of a lecture. Rather it
should be that of an enthusiastic teacher enjoying a
discussion of the subject with a responsive learner.
The tutorial tone Ideally, you should try to create in print the kind of
conversational style you might use in a one-to-one
tutorial.

Writing that speaks Somehow, in writing your tutorial-in-print, you need
to mentally conjure up your learner and imagine you are
talking with that individual. If you do this successfully,
your writing will be "readable". Your learner will "hear"
your voice reaching out from beyond the page.

There are two main components in developing a
readable style:

Two components
- writing conversationally; and
- writing plainly.

THE CONVERSATIONAL STYLE

The best way of getting across to the learner is to make
your writing friendly and informal. (By which I do **not**
mean chummy and careless.) Put down on paper what you
Friendly and informal might say to the learner if he or she were there in fromt
of you. To help in this, I offer four suggestions:

Use Personal Pronouns

You and I Speak to the learner directly. Call your learner "you" --
never "the reader" or "the learner". Speak of yourself
as "I" -- never as "the author" or "the present writer".
See what can happen if you ignore this advice:

> "The reader is reminded at this point that algorithms
> were brought to his or her attention by the author in
> the preceding chapter."

Those third-party references to "the reader" and "the
author" are alienating. The reader may well ask "Are they

talking to me ?" In fact, such authors are talking to
their typewriters rather than to another human being.

Being
direct

Notice the effect if, instead, we use personal pronouns
and speak to the reader directly. Not only does the tone
become conversational, but the excess verbiage floats away
also:

> "You'll remember I mentioned algorithms
>
> in the previous chapter."

Here are some more examples of this direct approach to
the learner:

Examples of
directness

> "Now try the problem below..."
>
> "Look at the diagram opposite..."
>
> "Compare your result with those I have listed below..."
>
> "If I had been asked the question, I would have said..."
>
> "You may disagree with me about some of the details, but..."

You may, on occasions, feel you want to say "we" instead
of "I". If so, make sure that both you and the learner
know to whom it refers, e.g.:

Who is "we" ?

> We = the author (royal/pompous plural); or
>
>   = the author and the reader together; or
>
>   = the author and his or her colleagues; or
>
>   = the author and other experts in the subject; or
>
>   = human beings in general.

Use Contractions

Contractions offer another means of making your writing
conversational. Don't feel it necessary, for instance,
to write "do not" in full every time you use that idea in
a sentence. According to the rhythm of the sentence,
and whether you'd have made the contraction in speaking
it, you may want to write "don't" -- as I did in the
previous sentence above.

When to
contract

Contractions can have a tonic effect. They help keep
the stuffiness out of your prose. Here are some that you
may want to use:

Examples of
contractions

- o   I'm – I've – I'll – I'd
- o   you're – you've – you'll – you'd
- o   he's – he'll – he'd
- o   she's – she'll – she'd
- o   we're – we've – we'll – we'd
- o   they're – they've – they'll – they'd
- o   isn't – aren't – wasn't – weren't
- o   hasn't – haven't – hadn't
- o   won't – wouldn't – shan't – shouldn't
- o   can't – couldn't – mustn't
- o   here's – there's – where's – how's – what's – who's – that's
- o   let's – it's (it is)

Write
as you'd
speak

But remember to use the contraction only if you'd have
used it in speech. Thus, you might properly have the
same pair of words repeated in one sentence, one pair
contracted and the other not. For example:

> "It is important that you should attempt the
> experiment, and you'll find it's not at all
> time-consuming."

Use Rhetorical Questions

Rhetorical questions can also help your conversational
flow. This is the kind of question you might pose without
expecting the reader to answer it. Indeed, you will often
ask such a question near the beginning of a paragraph --
and then go on to answer it yourself. Here is an example:

Questions
you answer

> "Now which of these averages is going to be most useful
> to us ? We've already seen that the median depends
> on the middle-sized observations only and ignores the
> extremes. The mode, on the other hand,..."

Encouraging
anticipation

Such an opening tends to grab your readers and engage their
interest. It encourages them to anticipate the answer
emerging in the rest of the paragraph. As a way of
presenting the teaching point, it can certainly be more
stimulating than the routine alternative:

"Now let us consider which of the averages will
be most useful to us..."

*Where
to use ?*

Of course, you can pose rhetorical questions anywhere in
your text. You do not have to confine them to the
beginning of paragraphs. For instance, you may sometimes
want to use one as a section **heading**. Again, they can
be useful in breaking up long and unwieldy sentences. For
instance, what can we do to improve the following
sentence ? :

"In order to distinguish between constant values and
variable values, lower-case letters are assigned to
the variables and upper-case letters to the constants."

Instead, we can start with a question:

"How shall we distinguish between constant values and
variable values ? Let's use lower-case letters for
the variables and upper-case letters for the constants."

*Don't
over-do it*

But always make clear that the question **is** rhetorical --
and not one that you are putting to the learner as part
of an activity. Also, don't over-do it. The tonic effect
of rhetorical questions would soon be lost if nearly
every paragraph had one.

Use a Light Touch

You may already have come across a mention of this
(page 156) -- but it is an aspect of the conversational
style, so I'll mention it again here. Be serious in your

*Avoid the
pedantic*

writing, of course -- but without being solemn. Be precise
be particular; be penetrating -- but don't be pedantic.

*Human
angle ?*

Exploit the "human angle" in whatever you are writing
about. That is, how does your topic impinge on your
reader as a person living in society -- not just as
someone studying your subject ? For instance:

"If you've trundled a trolley round your local supermarket
in recent months, you may have noticed the mysterious

patterns of parallel lines that have begun to appear on
all kinds of items from packets of cornflakes to
bottles of ketchup..."

If you see a "funny side" to the subject, let your reader
in on it. Don't drag in jokes for jokes' sake -- but
don't keep them out if they carry useful truths about the

*Don't
exclude
humour*

subject. For instance, in drawing the distinction between
short-term and long-term planning, I'm sure I'd want to
mention the man who fell from the top of the Empire State
Building and who, as he passed an open window on the
63rd floor, was heard to mutter "So far, so good".

But remember that your writing can still be friendly,
human and personal, without any striving after comic effect

*Don't
write for
posterity*

or attempts to be matey. The suggestions given above
should help you avoid the sterile "written for posterity"
source-book style.

Write as if you were **talking** to a learner with whom
you are **not too well** acquainted, and you will probably
succeed in being conversational without sounding

*Being
reader-
friendly*

over-familiar. Even computers, nowadays, try to be
"user-friendly". Can you afford to do otherwise ?

> *"He that will write well in any tongue, must
> follow this counsel of Aristotle: to speak as
> the common people do, to think as wise men do;
> and so should every man understand him..."*
>
> Roger Ascham (1515-1568)

WRITING PLAINLY

Plain talk

Any writer with objectives in mind -- and you have, haven't
you ? -- should warm to these words of H.G. Wells:

"I write as I walk, because I want to get
somewhere. And I write as straight as I can

just as I walk as straight as I can, because
that is the shortest way of getting there."

So, what is the secret of writing straight, clearly,

*Right words
in right
structures*

plainly ? I suggest it is a matter of choosing the righ
words and the right structures that will effectively car
your message. Let us begin by looking at words. Then
we'll consider the structures -- especially the sentence
in which those words will be carried.

*Familiar
words in
short
sentences*

The chief message that will emerge is that plain,
readable English depends on **short** sentences made up of
familiar words. To see what I mean, compare the old
nursery rhyme on the left below with the "committee-spea
(or gobbledygook) translation on the right:

Comparison

Traditional version	Gobbledygook version
Hey diddle diddle !	The amazing feline musicianship
The cat and the fiddle !	demonstrated in connection with
The cow jumped over the moon.	a rustic member of the violin
The little dog laughed	family occasioned among spectat
To see such sport,	a diversity of reactions includ
And the dish ran away	in the case of a female bovine
with the spoon.	quadruped, translunary saltatio
	of a diminutive canine,
	cachination; and of two article
	tableware, collusive flight.

Choosing Your Words

*Guidelines
for choice*

When writing, you will have a **choice** of words. Some wil
convey your message more plainly than others. Here are
some guidelines:

*Cut out
the surplus*

Use words, not phrases. Cut out surplus words. Don't l
yourself use several words where one will do. Watch out
particularly for elephantine phrases like "in the
approximate vicinity of" -- which can be replaced by
"about". Such phrases will be a drag on the action, and
can usually be replaced by one or two simple words. Here

are some examples of phrases to avoid, together with
their substitutes:

*Examples
of phrases
to cut*

- o   a large number of............................ many
- o   a certain amount of.......................... some
- o   at the present moment in time................. now
- o   for the reason that......................... because
- o   exhibits a tendency to...................... tends to
- o   in the event that........................... if
- o   in a satisfactory manner.................... satisfactorily
- o   having a value of........................... worth
- o   in the great majority of cases.............. usually
- o   of a serious nature......................... serious
- o   with a view to.............................. to
- o   on the grounds that, owing to the fact that....because

Gobbledygook

You'll run into many more such phrases -- committee-speak,
circumlocution, gobbledygook -- that can be simplified,
replaced or omitted altogether. Remember Alexander Pope's
telling couplet:

> *"Words are like leaves and where they most abound
> Much fruit of sense beneath is rarely found."*

Use familiar words. Use words your reader is likely to
understand. I don't know about you but, in that
gobbledygook version of the nursery rhyme, there were
at least two words I'd have had to look up in a dictionary.

*Shorter
words more
familiar ?*

    Psychologists have drawn up lists of the most-used
500 words in the English language, the most-used 1000,
and so on. There is no reason for you, as a writer, to
know exactly what words are on each list. But the idea
behind them is worth bearing in mind. Generally speaking,
the more syllables a word has, the less often it is
used. So, given a choice between two words, e.g. "count"
or "enumerate", you should be able to guess which is
likely to be more-used than the other.

Use everyday words

Try not to use words like "relinquish", "interment" and "exacerbate" when you might quite properly write "give up", "burial" or "worsen". Always look for the everyday word and, unless one of your objectives is to stretch the reader's vocabulary, use it in preference to the less familiar one. If you need help in finding everyday alternatives, consult a copy of *Roget's Thesaurus.*

Here are more examples: Notice that the less familiar word, usually of Greek or Latin origin, tends to be longer than the more homely alternative:

Examples

o reside   = live
o initiate = start
o utilize   = use
o locate   = find (or place)
o terminate = end

The fancy words are even more of a barrier when they gang up in phrases. For instance:

More examples

o endeavour to accelerate   = try to speed up
o tender assistance   = offer help
o capable of ambulatory locomotion   = able to walk
o cardiac arrest   = heart stopped
o nasal haemorrhage   = nose-bleed
o disseminate misinformation   = spread lies
o comprehensive cessation   = widespread stoppage
o employment terminations   = sackings
o aggravation of the redundancy situation = more sackings
o non-animate personal transportation system = bike/car

Not amusing

Such pompous gobbledygook just looks silly when you see it isolated like this. But it is not at all amusing when you find whole paragraphs are infested with the stuff. Look at this for instance:

"The provision of mathematical instruction for post-adolescent persons is a task the difficulty of which is of a considerabl larger order of magnitude, by virtue of the fact that their

Gobbledygook version

antecedent exposure to mathematics instruction of less than optimum effectiveness has resulted in attenuation of confidence. Their personal self-evaluation implies that mathematics is a field of human enquiry in which they are destined to suffer perpetual and irremediable lack of success, and it is a universal human prediliction to exhibit avoidance-behaviour in respect of pursuits deemed likely to augment the individual's initial self-perception of intrinsic ineffectiveness."

Translated, this seems to mean:

A translation

"It's much harder to teach adults about mathematics since poor teaching has already robbed them of confidence. They feel doomed to failure in mathematics -- and we all shrink from trying something at which we feel likely to fail."

The shorter the more emphatic

The long-winded phrases were not the only thing wrong with that paragraph, but you'll see how removing them has shortened its length and clarified its message. In general, try to do without multi-syllabled words and phrases, and your writing will become more emphatic and your meaning plainer. Don't say "the vegetation exhibited heliotropic inclination in the direction of the source of illumination" when you could say "the plants turned towards the light".

Avoid vague abstractions

Use precise words. Where possible, avoid using words that are general, abstract and vague. Any such word will be open to a variety of interpretations. So some of your readers will either form no clear understanding or will misinterpret it. To prevent this, choose words that are specific, concrete and precise. For instance:

Vague/Abstract	Precise/Specific
"Extreme danger is associated with the incorrect operation of this equipment."	"Keep the safety shield down or this machine may kill you."
"Appreciation was expressed in respect of the successful directorial intervention concerning research funding."	"The team clapped and cheered when they heard that Dr Jones had obtained the funds they needed to continue their research."

Analyzing waffle

Vague abstractions are responsible for much of the waffle that can clutter up our writing. Let us examine three examples, culled from self-instructional texts I have looked at recently:

Example 1

o "It has long been recognized that this model
    is not suitable."

By whom has it been recognized ? By the author ? By the general public ? By specialists ? And how long is "long" A few years or a century or two ? This statement says so much less than it appears to that its first six words might just as well be omitted.

Example 2

o "Society's attitude is still ambivalent to
    domestic violence."

What is meant by "society" ? Does the writer mean that some people in society feel one way about domestic violence while others feel differently ? Or does he mean that most of us (all of us ?) hold contradictory attitudes at the same time ? Or does he take "society's" attitudes to be those expressed in the law courts or the mass media ? One may well feel there is some kind of truth behind what he is saying. But what exactly **is** he saying ? Like the first statement we looked at, this one would have been acceptable as an introductory sentence which the author could then have gone on to explain. But neither author did so.

Example 3

o "There is an inverse relationship between socio-economic
    status and the importance of physical or functional
    incapacity as a factor in identifying someone as sick."

Let's assume readers know that "inverse relationship" means that one of two related things will grow as the other shrinks, and vice versa. "Socio-economic status" is abstract and vague; but let's assume readers know it has something to do with how well off a person is, and maybe something to do with the person's social class. This still leaves a yawning vaguess in the phrase "physical or functional incapacity". This shows up as

soon as we try to translate -- or rather, interpret --
the sentence, e.g. "Poor people are less likely than those
who are better-off to be thought of as sick [By whom ?
Doctors/friends/themselves ?] merely [This seems to be implied]
because [Because what ? The following is just a guess:] some limb
or organ is not working as well as it normally does or
they are no longer able to carry out their normal activities
activities".

Don't tease

The reader should never be put to such trouble in
trying to decide which of several possible meanings to
assign to a vague statement. Unless you really don't
know yourself -- in which case, admit as much to your
reader -- then say exactly **who** did **what** to **whom** with
which, and **where**, **when**, **how**, and with **what** consequences.
If your statement really does have several valid
interpretations, spell them out.

Be specific

The advice I've given in this section is related to
what I say in Chapter 7 about making plentiful use of
examples and case studies. Don't just generalize --
be specific.

Weasel-words and padding

Admittedly, it is not always easy to spot the vagueness
in our own writing -- especially if it reflects vagueness
in our thinking. But our use of certain "weasel-words"
and verbal "padding" **may** indicate that we are not being
as specific as we ought to be. Here are some expressions
to watch out for:

Examples

o cases – factors – fields – areas
o considerations – circumstances – respects
o may well – often – for the most part – by and large
o is affected by – tends to be associated with – relates to
o suggests to many people – is widely believed to
o position in regard to – has some connection with

Any one of the above may be enough to obscure the meaning
of a sentence. Put several of them together and the

result may be total inscrutability:

> "The position in regard to the employment situation
> is widely believed to be affected by balance of
> payments considerations."

*Deliberate
obscurity ?*

People who write like that either don't know what they are
talking about themselves or don't care for their readers
to know. Or so it would appear.

Use strong, active verbs. Of all the words in your
tutorial-in-print, it is the verbs that carry the weight
of the argument. Try to choose full-blooded verbs that
really tell what somebody or something **does**. Take an

*Active v
passive
verbs*

example: "Hamlet killed the King". In that sentence the
verb is **active**. It tells what someone did. What happens
if we make the verb passive, indicating what was done to
someone ?: "The King was killed by Hamlet". Because the
verb is passive, the punch has gone from the sentence.
The tone would be equally drab if the verb were active
but weak, e.g. "Hamlet occasioned the death of the King".

Here are some more examples of the contrast between
passive and active verb forms:

Examples

Passive	Active
"An experiment was performed".	"We performed an experiment".
"Calculators may be used".	"You may use a calculator".
"Errors in forecasting have been reduced owing to use of the new microcomputer".	"The new microcomputer has reduced errors in forecasting".
"The flask is to be held over a gas flame and heated until a colour change is observed in the liquid".	"Hold the flask over a gas flame and heat it until you see the liquid change colour'

*Pros
and cons*

Notice that the passive verb-forms usually involve
roundabout phrases; and the sentences are generally longer
than when the more direct, active verb is used. So the

active verb is likely to shorten a sentence as well as
give it punch.

*Passive
sometimes ?*

Naturally, you'll sometimes choose to use a passive
verb. This will happen if you want to put special emphasis
on the action rather than on the agent. For example,
"Free beer is provided by the management". Here, the
fact that beer is provided free seems to be more
significant than who makes it available. Otherwise, we
might write, "The management provides free beer".

*Strengthening
your verbs*

If your writing is to be forceful, your verbs will need
to be both active and strong. Too many textbook sentences
are merely agglomerations of gerunds and participles,
nouns and adjectives, strung together with a few
prepositions and bits of the verb "to be". Consider
the following example:

*Example for
treatment*

"The typical Equatorial day is of a fixed pattern. In
the morning it will be noted that the sky is in a clear,
calm condition. But with the daily accumulation of heat,
so the ascent of hot-air currents is begun, leading to
the formation of towering cumulus clouds and the regular
afternoon commencement of downpours of heavy rain."

There is not one strong or active verb in the whole paragraph.
Let's see if we can give it a little more zest by putting
some action and some strength into the verbs:

*Improved
version*

"The typical Equatorial day follows a fixed pattern. In
the morning the sky is clear and calm. But, as the earth
heats up, currents of hot air begin to rise, causing the
towering cumulus clouds to fill the sky. Regularly, every
afternoon, these clouds release downpours of heavy rain."

Apart from making it more forceful, the strong, active
verbs have led us to reduce the length of the paragraph.

*Inspect your
writing*

Make a habit of inspecting your own writing. Are
weak verbs silting up your prose ? Keep an eye on the

number of words that end in:

*Endings
to watch*

ed   (e.g. "noted)

tion (e.g. "formation")

ment (e.g. "commencement")

ing   (e.g. "leading")

*These examples are from
the first of the two
passages about the
Equatorial day.*

These weak endings usually go hand-in-hand with a weak verb like "to be", "to make" or "to have". The verbs "occur", "become", and "take place" can also rob a sentence of energy. For example:

*Examples for
comparison*

Weak	Strong
"A decline in enrolment was noted"	"Enrolment declined".
"To study for a higher degree is my intention".	"I intend to study for a higher degree".
"The briefing of new tutors took place last Thursday".	"We briefed new tutors last Thursday".
"Complaints from students become audible when delay in feedback occurs".	"You'll hear students complain if you delay their feedback".

*Not for
teachers*

Weak and passive verb forms can easily wrap one's meaning in cotton-wool. This is fine for people who are unwilling to be pinned down to a point of view. But it is no use to the teacher with objectives to reach.

Keep aware

Of course, you will need passive forms some of the time; and weak verbs also will have their place in your writing. My advice is simply that you should be aware of what kind of verbs you **are** using from paragraph to paragraph -- and be sensitive to the effect they are having on the tone of your prose.

*What is
jargon ?*

Use specialist vocabulary -- but with care. So far I have not mentioned the word "jargon". Some people use the term to refer to any abstract language that they find incomprehensible. Others use it for language they think pompous, snobbish, or trendily fashionable, whether they understand it or not. Such language I have discussed already under previous headings. Other people use the

word "jargon" to mean (indeed to castigate) specialist
vocabulary -- the "in-words" used by experts in a
particular subject to talk to one another about their
common interests.

The need
for jargon   Much as I would weigh in against jargon of the former
sorts -- especially abstract long-windedness -- I cannot
see that we can survive without our specialist vocabularies.
For the most part, the new terms we wish to teach the
learner relate to new **concepts**. Once the learner has
learned to attach meanings to the terms, we have an
invaluable shorthand that saves us having to spell out
the attributes of a concept each time we want to use it.
Imagine the bother, for instance, if we decided that
jargon like "triangle", "area" or "degrees" was not to be
used in a lesson on geometry.

How to use
jargon   If the technical terms you introduce into your lessons
are to avoid being derided as jargon, you'll need to take
care. Here are some basic DOs and DON'Ts:

o Don't use a technical term unless you are convinced that
   the learner needs it.

o Do explain a new term very carefully when you first
   introduce it, e.g. purpose, definition, examples of
   the concept.

o Do give reminders at appropriate points, e.g. when the
   term is being brought in again after not having been
   used for a while.

o Do give a guide to the pronunciation of new terms that
   are at all "difficult", e.g. "Pronounce it may-triss-ease".
   This will be so much easier, of course, if you intend
   providing an audiotape **as part of your** package.

o Do emphasize the introduction of a new term by use of
   typography -- e.g. underline it, **embolden** it, put it in
   CAPITALS, or print it in the margin also. This can be

How to use
jargon
(continued)

very helpful to the learner who is reviewing earlier
lessons in search of the first mention of key ideas.
(The traditional *italics* really don't give the
necessary amount of prominence to a word.)

o Do be especially careful in explaining technical terms
   that have a different meaning:
   - in everyday use, e.g. "significance" in statistics; or
   - in another subject your learners may be familiar with,
     e.g. "bonding" in chemistry and in sociology.

o Don't use too many new technical terms in the same
   paragraph. One new idea per paragraph is enough.

o Don't use alternative technical terms for the same
   concept (e.g. "microcomputer"/"personal computer")
   unless you are deliberately trying to habituate the
   learner to variety of useage and have mentioned this
   intention earlier in the text. An alternative strategy
   would be to mention all the variants early on, and then
   stick to one of them.

o Don't use a different technical term for the same
   concept in different lessons -- or not unless the
   reason for doing so is clear and spelled out to the
   learner, e.g. "Since this lesson is based around a
   chapter from Bloggs and Moggs in which they use the
   term "grundlefink" for what we have so far called
   "skewdop", we too will use their term in our
   accompanying commentary". Here, you will need to
   compare useage with colleagues writing other lessons.

o Don't revert to an everyday term once you have
   introduced the technical word.

And finally:

o Don't use everyday terms or personal figures-of-speech
   (e.g. "tutorial-in-print") in such a way as to suggest
   that they are generally-accepted technical terms.

Now for the second aspect of writing plainly. Even

From words
well-chosen words can lose their effect if they are
embedded in poor structures. So how can you write

...to
structures
sentences and paragraphs, and use punctuation, so as to
carry your message plainly and readably ? Here are
my suggestions:

Simplify Your Sentences

Write like
you talk
One of the underlying suggestions of this chapter is that
you should write like you would talk to a learner. If you
do, your sentences will be short and simple; for long,
convoluted sentences just don't occur in ordinary
conversation -- even among subject-specialists.

Long
sentences
difficult
to read ?
In academic prose, however, they occur with depressing
frequency. It is all too easy to pick up a textbook or
academic journal most of whose sentences meander over
three lines or more. Such sentences tend to be too crammed
with ideas, relationships and qualifications to allow
of easy reading. You often have to read them two or
three times over before you can be sure you've understood
them. For instance:

Example
"Pellagra, a slow-developing disease which used to be very
widespread among rural dwellers in warm, sunny climates where
maize was the staple food, and which is a disease characterised
by skin rash, diarrhoea and, in later stages, by deterioration
of mental faculties, sometimes to the point of imbecility, is,
however (as proved scientifically by Goldberger and his
colleagues who, in 1916, in the United States, studied the
incidence of the disease in seven textile mill communities,
proving indeed that it can be produced, prevented or cured by
changes in diet), a nutritional disorder."

Why
prefer
short ?
Keep them short. The shorter your sentences, the more
vigorous they will be. The fewer the words, the more
emphatic. The more often you use the full stop, the more
often your readers can pause for thought. And it is
during those pauses that your meaning will seep through.

*20 words
enough ?*

As a general rule, try to prevent your sentences from exceeding 20 words. (That's about two lines of typewriting Some must unavoidably be a little longer. A few may even contain 30 or 40 words -- so long as you have a good ear for the rhythms of prose and a firm grasp of the ideas you wish to convey. But if you need several longish sentences in any one paragraph, you'd do well to balance them with some very short ones -- of 10 words or less.

*But vary
lengths*

Indeed it is important that you do vary your sentence length. If they were all short, they would make for a choppy, breathless read. To some extent, the length of a sentence may be influenced by its position in the paragraph. You may feel your readers will be able to digest a longish sentence in the middle of a paragraph -- provided you have enticed them in with a couple of short, snappy ones. Likewise, you may sometimes want to punch home the point of the paragraph in a brief final sentence.

*Splitting
complex
sentences*

Whenever you read through a piece of your writing, look for places where you can split the complex sentences. Look out for the "ands", the "buts", the "howevers", the "furthermores", and all such words that introduce phrases and clauses that might practicably be broken off to make separate sentences. See how we might thus re-write the paragraph about pellagra that I showed you earlier:

*Rewritten
example*

"Pellagra is a slow-developing disease characterised by a skin rash, by diarrhoea and, in the later stages, by deterioration of mental faculties, sometimes to the point of imbecility. It used to be very widespread among rural dwellers in warm, sunny climates where maize was the staple food. However, pellagra is a nutritional disorder. It can be produced, prevented or cured by changes in diet. This was scientifically proved by Goldberger and his collegues who studied the incidence of the disease in seven textile mill communities in the United States in 1916."

Keep the pattern simple. Actually, if you keep your sentences short, you'll probably find they stay simple in pattern. That is to say, they will not contain so many clauses and phrases that the learner is confused by the number of relationships involved. Here is a sentence that has too much going on it to allow easy comprehension:

Short = simple

> "The fact that the molecules in a liquid are closer together and thus the attractive forces between them are very much greater than the very minute forces between the molecules of a gas, is responsible for the greater resistance by a liquid to compression."

Example

But we can make this message easier to read and comprehend if we re-package it into shorter sentences. In doing so, we also simplify the sentence patterns:

> "The molecules in a liquid are closer together then they are in a gas. As a result, the attractive forces between the liquid molecules are much greater than the very minute forces between the gas molecules. Hence, liquids are more resistant to compression than are gases."

Rewritten example

Be careful with negatives. Many learners find negative constructions difficult to handle. The very sight of phrases like "not unsuitable" may send them back to the beginning of the sentence to re-read. Do try to avoid double negatives. For one thing, you may say the opposite of what you mean, e.g.:

Negatives confuse

> "There is no reason to doubt that the evidence is not devoid of significance."

But even if you get it right -- and you really are trying to say that the evidence has some significance -- you give your reader too much trouble in working out what you are saying and in wondering whether that is also what you mean. Usually, such a sentence can be expressed more positively, e.g.:

Express positively

> "There is no reason to doubt that the evidence is significant."

Or, better still: "The evidence is significant."

Here is a negative construction that gave me trouble
recently:

Troublesome
example

> "The use of force should not be seen to be the
> prelude to any concession which was not acceptable
> to the islanders before the occupation."

The sentence is not helped by its use of "which" instead
of "that". But the main difficulty comes from its two
negatives; this can be eased somewhat by replacing "not
acceptable" by "unacceptable".

Watch your word order. Pay some attention to the order

Placing
your words

words in your sentences. This advice is sometimes
illustrated by showing how the placing of a word like
"even" or "only" can totally transform the meaning of
a sentence. For example:

Examples

o "Only the cat sat on the mat." *(None of the other animals did*

o "The only cat sat on the mat." *(Other creatures were present -*
least two from another species; they may or may not have been
sitting on the mat also.)

o "The cat only sat on the mat." *(It didn't stand or lie down.)*

o "The cat sat only on the mat." *(It sat nowhere else.)*

o "The cat sat on the only mat." *(There was just one mat -- the*
one the cat sat on.)

More generally, however, word-order does make a difference

Emphasis ?

to the rhythm and emphasis of your sentences. Compare
these two examples:

Comparison

> "We say a current flows
> when electrons move in
> the same general
> direction for a period
> of time."

> "When electrons move in
> the same general
> direction for a period
> of time we say a
> current flows."

Explanation

Usually, the emphasis comes at the end of a sentence.
the sentence on the left above might be defining a term
("current") that learners have already met; while the
sentence on the right is presenting them with a term
to attach to an already familiar concept.

Need for variation

Vary your patterns. Try to avoid a monotonous repetition of sentence structure. Notice the tiring rhythm of the sentences in this next paragraph:

Example

> "Railway lines expand in hot weather. So they are laid in separate lengths. There is a gap between each length and the next. The lengths are bolted together by fish-plates. The fish-plates are drilled with oval holes. These oval holes allow the bolts to slide when the rail expands."

These sentences look as if they have all been poured from the same mould. They are all virtually the same length -- between six and twelve words; and they all have a similar structure. Furthermore, the flow of the paragraph is so staccato that it is difficult to see how the various ideas link together. To cure the resulting tedium, it's forgiveable even to increase the average sentence length:

Rewritten example

> "Since railway lines expand in hot weather, they are laid in separate lengths with a gap between one length and the next. Fish-plates are used to bolt the lengths together. Each fish-plate is drilled with oval holes which allow the bolts to slide as the line expands."

Clearer relation-ships

This revised version varies the length and pattern of its sentences, and the relationship among the various ideas emerges more clearly. Even though the average sentence length has increased from 8½ words per sentence, none is longer than 22 words and the average is still quite acceptable at 16 words per sentence.

Watch Your Paragraph Length

Remember that each paragraph you write should be elaborating on or leading up to a key sentence. That key sentence contains the main idea of the paragraph. If your

Too many main ideas ?

paragraphs tend to ramble on indefinitely, there's more than a chance that each contains more than its fair load of main ideas. If so, some of them are likely to get overlooked by your reader.

Split over-loaded paragraphs

Inspect your paragraphs. If you see more than one main idea being expressed, make each the subject of a separate paragraph -- even if you need to add more words. For instance, the paragraph about pellagra (page 224) should really have been two paragraphs -- the first describing its general characteristics and the second identifying it as a nutritional disorder. Notice the key sentence for the "second" paragraph stuck in the middle of the extract.

What is reader used to ?

In most popular newspapers, the paragraph is just about extinct. In the interests of layout and "white space", practically every sentence is its own paragraph. Yet this risks falling into another trap -- of failing to show how the ideas in separate sentences link up to form a coherent argument. All the same, if your learners are *Daily Tabloi* readers, don't give them too many paragraphs that are longer than this one. Too solid a block of print will weary their eyes and confirm all their worst anxieties about learning.

Pausing for thought

And, remember, the breaks between paragraphs -- just like those between sentences -- provide your readers with "thought pauses". They may or may not want to use every one, but it's wise to make them available.

Other forms of layout

Remember also, as I mention in Chapters 7 and 9, you can break from paragraphs altogether, where appropriate. You can create breathing space on the page by using, e.g.

- lists (like this one);
- boxed items;
- tables (of words or figures);
- flow diagrams; and so on.

Punctuating for Meaning

Avoiding punctuation problems

Punctuation does play a part in readability; but if you use short sentences and active verbs, you'll probably ha' few problems with it. The more frequently you use the full stop, the less use you'll have for any of the other punctuation marks.

Pauses   The purpose of punctuation is to help the reader grasp
and   your meaning. It substitutes for the pauses and emphasis
emphasis   you would use if you were speaking to the learner. If you
                 ever do have trouble punctuating, try reading your

                 sentences aloud. Notice where you pause briefly; notice
Read   where you read as if in amplification of what you've just
aloud ?   said; notice where you try to read two consecutive
                 sentences as if they were more closely connected than
                 usual; notice where you want to give particular emphasis
                 to a word or phrase:

How to   o If you want the reader to pause only briefly,
punctuate ?   insert a comma.

                 o A full stop gives a longer pause.

                 o If you want to insert a comment (not too lengthy a one)
                    on what you've just written, enclose it in brackets.

                 o Alternatively -- perhaps to make your writing more
                    open in texture -- you can set off the comment by
                    a pair of dashes.

                 o If you want two short sentences to be linked together,
                    use a semi-colon; this gives a longer pause than a comma
                    but shorter than a full-stop.

                 o If you want to give particular emphasis to a word,
                    <u>underline</u> it (if your copy is typed), or have it printed
                    bold or in CAPITALS.

                 o If you must emphasise a complete statement, use the
                    exclamation mark ! (But one only, and not too often !!!)

                 o Notice the use of "blobs" as a punctuation mark -- to
                    tell your readers they are approaching a list of
                    related items.

                 MEASURING READABILITY

hat makes   By this time you should be clear about some of the factors
or   on which readability depends: Friendly, conversational
eadability ?   tone. Human interest. Well-chosen words, preferably

short ones. Specific, concrete references. Strong, active
verbs. Short, simple sentences.

*Measuring
readability*

A number of people have used such factors to develop
ways of measuring readability. One of the most practical
is that described by Robert Gunning in *The Technique of
Effective Writing* (1952). He calls it the Fog Index.
This judges the "fogginess" or heaviness of a piece of
writing by the average length of its sentences and the
proportion of multi-syllabled words it contains.

The Fog Index

Here is how to calculate the Fog Index of a piece
of writing:

*Calculating
the Fog Index*

1. Take a random sample of about 100 words.

2. Count the number of complete sentences, stopping
    your sentence count with which ever sentence ends
    nearest the 100 word target.

3. Divide the number of words by the number of sentences
    to arrive at the **average sentence length** in the passag

4. Count all the words that have **three** syllables or more.

5. To get the Fog Index, apply the following formula:

$$\frac{2\left(\begin{array}{l}\text{Average}\\\text{sentence}\\\text{length}\end{array} + \begin{array}{l}\text{Number of}\\\text{long words}\end{array}\right)}{5}$$

Example

Thus, if the average sentence length in a certain passage
were 17 words and the passage contained 8 words of three
syllables or more, the Fog Index would be:

$$\frac{2(17 + 8)}{5} = \frac{50}{5} = 10$$

*The
danger
point*

Clearly, the more you use long sentences and long words,
the higher will be your Fog Index. Gunning suggests
that 12 is the danger point. Of all the successful autho
whose prose Gunning tested, none came out with a Fog Inde

above 11. Of the popular American magazines he tested, *Reader's Digest* had a Fog Index of 9 and *Time* had one of 10. I leave you to calculate the index yourself for some of the publications you believe to be typical of your learners' preferred reading. I doubt if many of them will exceed 12.

Calculate your own

If the Fog Index looks too tedious to calculate, here is a short-cut cousin you might try instead: Simply work out the **average number of long words per sentence.** (Again, take a "long" word to be one of three syllables or more.) If your average exceeds 3, your prose will be more difficult than that of most novelists and, indeed, of most top-selling authors writing for non-specialists. You may like to check this figure for the kinds of material you know your learners do find readable.

A short-cut method

Such measures are rough-and-ready tools. They offer a useful check on material that looks difficult. If you apply one a few times, you'll probably develop an eye for prose that would over-tax your readers -- without even having to do any calculations. You'll see at a glance that no amount of human interest and conversational tone will help unless you cut out the long words and break up the long sentences.

Developing your "eye"

SUMMARY

To produce effective, readable writing:

o   Write in a friendly, conversational style:

- Use personal pronouns
- Use contractions
- Use rhetorical questions
- Use a light touch
- Exploit the "human angle"

o   Write plainly:

- Cut out surplus words
- Use short, familiar words

- Use precise words
- Use strong, active verbs
- Use specialist vocabulary -- but with care
- Write short, simple sentences

And, as a check on how well you have done so:

```
*****************************************
*                                       *
* READ YOUR WORK ALOUD.                  *
* ANYTHING YOU FIND TEDIOUS OR AWKWARD   *
* TO SPEAK MAY BE EQUALLY SO FOR YOUR    *
* LEARNERS TO READ.                      *
*                                       *
*****************************************
```

11.   INTRODUCING OTHER MEDIA

In Chapter 4 I discussed the issues involved in choosing
appropriate teaching media. The chief of these is:

*See the
list of
media on
page 73*

To which media do you and your learner have access ?

Multi-media Packages

*The printed
page*

Throughout this book I have assumed that PRINT will be
your most accessible medium. That is, your learners will
spend **most** of their time, I imagine, considering words and
pictures on the printed page.

*Need for
other media*

But it is both possible and desirable that they should
use other media as well. For one thing, the additional
media may enable certain kinds of understanding that would
not otherwise be possible. Furthermore, the variety -- the
change of stimulus itself -- may refresh and invigorate
the learner.

*Multi-media
courses*

Hence you might aim to make each course, and to some
extent each lesson, a **multi-media** experience -- even if
one medium is used more than all the others put together.
Which media might **you** be able to use in addition to print ?
How far will you be limited by the fact that your learners
may have little or no regular contact with one another,
or with a teacher ? How will you choose and use media ?

Basic Requirements

*The demands
on a medium*

There are seven requirements that must be met by a medium
if it is to make an effective contribution within a course:

o You must have the know-how that enables you to
   exploit the unique educational qualities of
   that medium.

o Your teaching in that medium should be clearly
   related to that in the rest of the course material --
   i.e. not be "tacked on" as an optional extra.

o Learners should recognize that the medium has something special to teach them.

o They should be able to use the medium conveniently.

o They should have appropriate expectations about the medium -- and the study skills necessary for using it

o They should have some control over the timing and rate of presentation.

o They should be provided with printed support material

Five media

Consider how these conditions might be met as you read about the five media I discuss in the rest of this chapter

- Practical work
- Audio material
- Video material
- Computers
- Human media.

PRACTICAL WORK

Practical work is essential for many subjects, especially when our objectives relate to skills as well as knowledge. Even knowledge, however, may sometimes be acquired more easily and with deeper understanding and interest if the learner can carry out suitable practical work. Such work

Types of practical work

may vary from observing the behaviour of patients in a doctor's waiting room, to interviewing fellow-apprentices to cutting up a sheep's brain, to compiling a weather reco: and so on.

Practical work in S-I ?

Self-instruction does not rule out practical work. In some cases, learners may be able to carry it out without moving from their chairs. See Figure 11.1 (and 5.2H). Certainly, much practical work, especially in the arts and social sciences needs no very special equipment. (Se Figure 11.2.) For example, even distance learners could easily carry out an interview or census, make a musical instrument, or collect plant specimens.

Figure 11.1: <u>Practical Work</u> (from Open University course S101, Unit 1, page 22)

Home Experiment 2   Pendulum

Take a piece of thin string about 1 metre long and make a simple pendulum by tying some small, compact object to one end—a normal-sized key would do. Place a watch with a seconds-hand in front of you so that you can see your pendulum and the watch at the same time. (Alternatively you can, of course, use a stop-watch in one hand while holding the pendulum with the other hand.) Hold the free end of the string, or better still tie it up to a hook or any other suitable support. Count how many times within 10 seconds your pendulum has gone through the complete sequence of one swing. Or, alternatively, measure the time it takes the pendulum to complete 5 or 10 swings. Try to answer the following questions.

ITQ 3   Does it matter whether you count as one swing the sequence of motion from one extreme position to the opposite extreme and back, or the sequence starting from the vertical position to one extreme through to the opposite extreme and back to vertical?

ITQ 4   How does the number of swings completed in 10 seconds (or the time taken to complete 5 or 10 swings) change when you shorten the length of the pendulum by holding or suspending the string at a point nearer to the swinging object?

ITQ 5   Can you find, by trial and error, the lengths at which the pendulum will complete 5, 8 and 10 swings within approximately 10 seconds?

ITQ 6   What are the periods of the swinging for the three cases described in ITQ 5?

Figure 11.2: <u>Practical Work</u> (from Open University course TAD292, Unit 3, page 15)

7   AN 'OVEN GONG'

Try the following.

Take a metal rack from an oven and attach to each of two adjacent corners a piece of string about three feet long. Wrap the free ends of the pieces of string around the index fingers of your hands, and plug your ears with these fingers, the rack suspended below. Now get a friend gently to play the rack as a metallic gong, with a spoon, a pencil, and perhaps another small object made from a different material. Ask the friend to vary the point of striking, the strength of blow, the density of the sounds, as much as possible. Allow long periods for listening to the resonance. *You have tapped yourself in to a remarkably intricate vibrating structure which previously was virtually inaccessible.* Even your partner can now hardly hear the sounds he is making for you.

Can you find further objects with a virtually self-enclosed vibrating system, that can be tapped in a similar way, to reveal their hidden sound world?

FIGURE 11.3: Use of Home Experiment Kit

(from Open University course S101, Unit 14)

Home Experiment 2

To do the experiment you will need the following items from your Home Experiment Kit, Part 2:

Apparatus*

100 cm³ beaker

100 cm³ measuring cylinder

rack of test-tubes

5 cm³ syringe

2 dosing pipettes†

wash-bottle containing distilled water

spatula

Chemicals

sodium hydroxide

dilute hydrochloric acid (8.9%)

ferric nitrate (iron(III) nitrate)

potassium thiocyanate

Part 1

(a) Using your measuring cylinder, measure 50 cm³ of distilled water into a beaker and add five pellets of sodium hydroxide, NaOH. Allow to dissolve.

(b) Add enough ferric nitrate, $Fe(NO_3)_3$, to a test-tube until the rounded bottom is full. Add enough distilled water to half-fill the test-tube, and shake until the solid dissolves.

(c) Add *one* crystal of potassium thiocyanate, KSCN, to a test-tube and add enough distilled water to half-fill it. Again shake to dissolve.

All three solutions are ionic. Note the colour of each solution and try to decide which ions are present: record these in Table 2.

TABLE 2   Observations for part 1 of Home Experiment 2

Solid	Colour of solution	Ions present
sodium hydroxide, NaOH		
ferric nitrate, $Fe(NO_3)_3$		
potassium thiocyanate, KSCN		

Now listen to the first part of the tape.

EXTRACT FROM TAPE:

"*Now that you've prepared the three solutions, check your entries in Table 2. First, the columns: Both the sodium hydroxide and the potassium thiocyanate solutions are colourless. But the ferric nitrate solution should be yellow. If you found any marked difference from these colours, you should make up that solution again, taking care that the test tube or flask is really clean -- wash it well with distilled water before adding the chemical, and don't forget to wash and dry your spatula before using it.*

Now what about the ions in these solutions? Well, you've already met sodium hydroxide, so I expect . . . "

Making Facilities Available

Sometimes, however, practical work is impossible unless
the learners can get their hands on special materials or
equipment. In such cases, either the learner must be
brought to these facilities, or the facilities must be
sent to the learner.

*Special
needs*

Face-to-face. If learners are studying on-site, then
laboratory or workshop facilities can perhaps be scheduled
at suitable times. There may well be difficulties, of
course -- in that learners studying at their own pace may
be ready to carry out a given piece of practical work on
quite different days (or even weeks) from one another.

*On-site
learners*

If learners are studying at a distance, it may not be
easy to bring them to a centre for practical work at the
most opportune time -- if at all. But the possibility is
worth exploring, e.g. as a "one-day school" or a "summer
session" in a local college.

*Distance
learners*

Another possibility, with some distance courses, will
be to arrange for someone connected with the learner's job
to provide practical experience -- perhaps as part of a
wider tutorial role.

Help at job

Home experiment kits. Otherwise, or maybe additionally,
we need to consider the second alternative -- sending the
equipment to the learner. Some Open University courses
send a treasure chest of equipment to students in the form
of a "home experiment kit". Students may be sent chemicals,
glassware, microscopes, rock specimens, seeds, and so on --
even extending to an electric reed organ and a helium
neon-laser for producing holograms.

*Sending
equipment*

At the other end of the scale, I know of one college
whose home experiment kit for an elementary physics course
includes household items like a duster, a comb, and a reel
of cotton thread. You might suppose that such items would
be easily obtainable by the learners anyway. But the

What to send ?

course developers were presumably unwilling to take the
risk that they might not bother. If you suspect that your
learners might be at all disinclined to carry out practical
work that you believe to be essential, then you will need
to anticipate any difficulties or inconveniences that might
serve as excuses for avoiding it.

The benefits available...

With the necessary equipment -- and the guidance and
feedback from printed worksheets or an audio-cassette (see
Figure 11.3) -- learners can obtain a wide variety of
experimental experience. Nevertheless, the value of such
experience (in terms of attaining the course objectives)
must be weighed against the problems of:

and the problems

- costs;
- safety;
- warehousing ;
- insurance;
- distribution and recovery of equipment, and so on,

that the system might entail.

Learning from models

Models. Sometimes, practical work may be based not on rea
objects but on **models.** This was essential with one Open
University course in which students needed to understand
how the Greek astronomer, Ptolemy, contrived to "explain"
the seemingly irregular motion of the planets while under
the illusion that they revolved around the earth. The
course materials provided a "do-it-yourself Ptolemaic
universe kit" -- two sheets of card on which were printed
various shapes which learners could cut out and manipulate
on the turntable of a record player. By this means, the
ingenuity of Ptolemy's thinking was made physical for
the learners.

Another example

Another course, on geology, provided similar sheets of
printed card from which the learners can make
three-dimensional models of faulted blocks of rock.
Figure 11.4 shows the instructions given to learners. By
moving the model blocks around in relation to one another

Figure 11.4: Using Cardboard Models (from Open University course S23, Block 2)

Faults do not simply go up and down, nor are fault surfaces simply vertical planes of movement. The 'downthrow' we have been looking at so far is merely the simplest, most conspicuous effect of a fault movement and serves only to introduce us to the topic. To familiarize yourself with the sort of displacement that can happen on a fault, build Models 8a and b. They represent two blocks separated by a fault plane which is the inclined plane (Fig. 63a). The first thing to notice is that steeply dipping beds are involved, and that the *same* sequence of beds dipping in the *same* direction is represented on both Models. Move the models about to find out how you can bring the beds into concordance on either side of the fault. You should find that you can do this by moving the block either vertically (Fig. 63b), or horizontally (Fig. 63c). Thus a movement straight up and down the fault plane can produce a lateral offset of the beds exposed at the surface (Fig. 63d).

Vertical movement only brings grit bed together on both sides of fault. Horizontal movement only brings grit bed together on opposite sides of fault.

Figure 63   Models 8a and 8b which represent two parts of a faulted block (a and d) and can be moved either vertically (b) or laterally (c) to bring the beds on either side into concordance.

This is an important point to grasp and you should study the models until you understand it fully. Maps record the distribution of rocks only at the surface, so faults on maps will only show an *apparent* movement, and much of the terminology of faults is concerned with their apparent movement. The actual amount and direction of movement, however, is much more important, and much more difficult to determine. It is only when one can recognize a particular point on each side of the fault that the true displacement can be measured. On the Models 8a and b, an ancient wash-out channel has been located in a thick grit band on both sides of the fault, to provide a marker point on each side of the fault.

learners can come to understand how the surface-
distribution of rock types (as shown on a geological map)
relates to what might be under the surface.

Different
understandings

Such physical manipulations -- whether of the earth's
crust or the solar system -- provide for a different
route to understanding than would reading about the
movements or even watching someone else perform them.

Observed Experiments

All the same, it may be impossible, or inappropriate to
provide the learner with facilities for carrying out **all**
the practical activities that might conceivably be of
interest within your course. Some experiments or
manipulations may be too dangerous, too costly, too
time-consuming, too demanding of skills irrelevant to the
course, and so on. In such cases, you may revert to a
method common enough in "conventional" courses, and let

Demonstrations

the learner **observe** a demonstration.

You, however, are less likely than conventional teacher
to have an opportunity to demonstrate "in the flesh". If
you were producing videotapes, practical demonstrations
could be shown in moving pictures, with accompanying sound
track. Without videotape (or film), you would have to
make do with "still" pictures, together with either a

Moving
or still
pictures ?

printed commentary or an audiotape. In some cases, such
a series of still photographs or drawings -- like a
strip cartoon -- may serve perfectly well to demonstrate
successive stages within an experiment or other practical
manipulation. See Figure 11.6 (page 254) for an example.

Activate your learners. You will, of course, be at pains
to ensure that your learners are not passive observers.

Involving
the learners

You will need to engage them in critical and constructive
activity. Prior to the experiment or demonstration, you
might ask them to suggest how it might be designed. Or
you might ask them to point out weaknesses in designs that

you have suggested. During the experiment or demonstration
you might get them to record their observations, according
to some specified criteria. Afterwards, you might get them
to explain what they have seen -- or even to come up with
hypotheses based on their observations and design a further
experiment to test these hypotheses.

The learners' roles

Such observed demonstrations need by no means be a waste
of time. They are certainly preferable to the "cookbook
science" so many of us did at school -- following a recipe
like robots and "adjusting" our results to fit what we knew
was expected. That was rarely an enlightening activity.
Practical work of the "hands on" variety can sometimes
inhibit thinking. There are times when learners can learn
more by observing -- so long as we lead them to do so
thoughtfully, anticipating, explaining, and criticizing
the demonstrator's actions and results.

Observation sometimes better than manipulation

Summary

It is clearly quite feasible for self-instructional courses
to include practical work -- especially in the arts and
social sciences where it often takes the form of working
with other people or with documents. Even in scientific
and technical subjects, much can be done with cheap and
easily available materials and equipment, or with models.
Where necessary practical work requires more specialized
apparatus, ways must be found of getting it to the
learners, or them to it -- or of enabling them to observe
(and mentally participate in) a demonstration.

Practical work is feasible in S-I

```
*****************************************************
*                                                   *
*   SOME SELF-INSTRUCTIONAL COURSES INCLUDE          *
*   A PROJECT -- MAYBE SEVERAL WEEKS OF              *
*   LARGELY SELF-DIRECTED PRACTICAL WORK ON          *
*   A TOPIC AGREED BETWEEN LEARNER AND TUTOR.        *
*                                                   *
*****************************************************
```

AUDIO MATERIAL

Presenting recorded sound

Here we are talking chiefly about **recorded sound**. This can be presented in several different ways:

- o Audio-cassettes (audiotape)
- o Gramophone records
- o Radio broadcasts
- o Television (or film) "sound track".

In this section I shall concentrate on audio-cassette and radio. Gramophone records I shall mention in passing when dealing with audio-cassettes; sound tracks I shall assume (but not discuss) in the later section concerned with "video material".

Radio

When Open University courses began in 1971, each had a half-hour radio programme broadcast twice each week by the BBC. But few courses make much use of radio today. The reasons for this lie among the conditions listed at the beginning of this chapter. Radio has the following drawbacks (as does broadcast television):

The drawbacks of radio...

- o Learners must tune in at a **fixed time**, regardless of whether that time is convenient and whether they have completed any necessary preparatory work.

- o Learners **cannot replay** the broadcast at will (unless they have taped it).

- o Learners must learn at the **fixed pace** of the broadcast. (No opportunities to pause for thought.)

- o Learners may not be used to paying attention and **learning** from broadcasts -- as opposed to using them casually for entertainment or news.

compared with a book

The burden of these disadvantages can be judged by comparing listening to a broadcast with reading a book. With a book the learner has control -- and probably possesses more of

the necessary learning skills and expectations as well.
Fortunately, the solution is at hand in the shape of a
tape-player. Cheap audio-cassette players are now easily
available, and broadcast radio can do little that cannot
be done better by an audio-cassette. In the Open
University, the use of audio-cassettes has grown as that
of radio has declined.

*Audio-
cassettes
preferred*

This is not to dismiss radio altogether. If, for
example, a local radio station were interested in
broadcasting programmes associated with your course, the
possibilities might be worth discussing. Such "air time"
might be useful for general "familiarization" material,
where no great concentration is required from listeners.
For example, you might broadcast discussions between tutors
and learners, or "phone ins" with learners quizzing a panel
of experts, or even a "magazine" covering a variety of
talking points related to the course.

*Using
local
radio...*

*for keeping
in touch...*

Such programmes would have the advantage over audio-
cassettes (pre-recorded before the course begins) of being
able to exploit **current** issues. They could even be
broadcast "live". You would probably find, however, that
learners listened only sporadically to such programmes --
unless they expected the content to be crucial to what they
wanted from the course. And you might well feel that any
such crucial material would have been better deployed on
audiotape or in print.

*and for
current
issues*

Audio-cassettes

With audio-cassettes you can avoid the inflexibilities of
radio. In particular, they enable your learners to:

*he benefits
f audio-
assettes*

- use the material at any time they choose;
- stop and start the sound at will;
- replay a passage as often as they wish; and
- skip over any material they do not need.

Three uses for audio-cassettes

In what follows, I discuss three ways of using audio-cassettes:

- for presenting aural source material;
- for lecturing; and
- for tutoring.

Naturally, more than one of these may be used within a single learning session. And if you can think of yet other uses, so much the better.

The sounds of your subject

Source material. Clearly, you can use audiotape to present the "raw sounds" of your subject -- e.g. the call of the coot, the grinding of the gears, the magic of Mozart. In that last case, gramophone records might provide superior sound, and make it easier for the learner to locate separate sections of the recording. But such records would be very expensive if you had to compile and produce them specially for the course.

Types of audio source material

Here are some further types of source material that might be presented on audio-cassette:

o Foreign language dialogues.

o Spoken glossaries of "hard-to-pronounce" terms.

o Conversations to be analysed -- e.g. between doctor and patient, architect and client, teacher and pupil.

o Discussions or interviews with practitioners of the subject -- e.g. police officers and criminals talking about their way of life.

Print cannot substitute

Some of the above items, e.g. the conversations, could be transcribed into print. But to do so would lose the nuance of speech (and the telling silences) which might be vital to understanding, not to mention sympathy and involvement. Non-verbal sounds could not be transcribed at all.

Additional guidance needed

Needless to say, a tape of source material would not be much use on its own. Learners would need guidance, either in printed form or on the tape itself, as to how to approa

it and how to use it in their learning. You may sometimes
want your learners to listen to source material at intervals
while reading a tutorial-in-print. For example:

*Listening
within a
tutorial-
in-print*

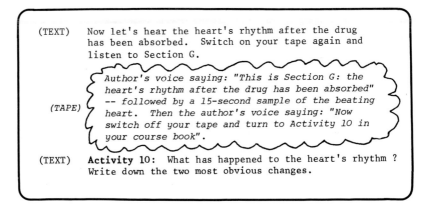

(TEXT) Now let's hear the heart's rhythm after the drug
        has been absorbed. Switch on your tape again and
        listen to Section G.

(TAPE) *Author's voice saying: "This is Section G: the
        heart's rhythm after the drug has been absorbed"
        -- followed by a 15-second sample of the beating
        heart. Then the author's voice saying: "Now
        switch off your tape and turn to Activity 10 in
        your course book".*

(TEXT) **Activity 10:** What has happened to the heart's rhythm ?
        Write down the two most obvious changes.

Another example of this way of using source material is
to be found in Figure 5.2F.

(On page 102)

Lecturing. This is a straightforward if pedestrian way of
using the medium. Some distance learning institutions
began by basing their distance courses on recordings of the
lectures that were first presented to on-site students.
These would be supplemented by printed notes, which might
reproduce any chalkboard drawings of slides that the
lecturer may have shown.

*Useful but
limited*

Such material has little to commend it over the printed
word. If the lecturer is a world authority and/or has a
particularly memorable delivery, then learners may enjoy
the opportunity to hear what he or she sounds like.
(Perhaps this is really another kind of "source material" ?)

*Why not
in print ?*

But the lecturing voice is likely to sound too elevated
for easy listening when it's coming from a plastic box on
the learner's bedside table. A more personal, intimate
tone is required if you are to make best possible use of
the very "user friendly" audio-cassette player.

*More intimate
one needed*

Speaking to
individual

Tutoring.   To use the medium in this way, you need to be conscious of speaking to the individual learner. What might you be saying ? One thing you might do is guide the individual through some task or exercise. For instance, you might talk the learner through:

Guiding
through
some task

- operating a machine;
- assembling a model;
- handling soil specimens;
- completing a form or questionnaire;
- studying a series of photographs;
- following a sequence of printed calculations;
- setting up an experiment;
- consulting tables of statistics;
- examining a map or blueprint; and so on.

Printed
instructions
can distract

Giving such guidance by your spoken voice would be particularly beneficial in situations where your learners need to keep their eyes on what they are doing -- and **not** keep turning back to a printed page for instructions.

An example

The most striking example I have come across was in an Open University course in which the learner needs to inspect a number of stereoscopic photographs of geological structures, using a 3-D viewer. In practice, it takes the eyes a few seconds to achieve the full 3-D effect, because one must force oneself to focus "through" the photograph rather than on it. It would be literally nauseating, as well as time-wasting, if one had to keep re-focussing on a printed page (and then back on the photograph again) in order to find out what features to look for next in the photograph. Thanks to the "talk-through" provided by the audio-cassette, one can maintain the difficult focus without interruption once one has attained it.

"Walkabout"
tapes ?

Such guidance or talk-through tapes can even be used away from the desk. In many of the world's big art museums it is possible to stroll around looking at exhibits with the recorded voice of an expert burbling into one's

ear through headphones. If your learners are willing to
wear lightweight headphones out of doors, and carry a
cassette-player, your recorded commentary could accompany
them on nature trails, town walks, visits to exhibitions
and building sites, tours of architectural edifices, or
whatever is appropriate to your subject.

ooking
s well as
istening --
audiovision"

Notice that the medium in the examples mentioned so
far is not just recorded sound. The learners are not
merely listening. They also have to **look** -- at pictures,
at real objects, even at print. This mixture of media, a
planned combination, is often called "audiovision".

udio
ithin
rint

As with audio source material, audio tutoring also can
be used within a tutorial-in-print. Figure 11.3 shows an
example where the instructions for performing an experiment
are given in print, and learners are asked to write their
observations in a printed table -- but the author **speaks**
her comments on this activity on the audiotape. (This
makes it less likely that learners will run across the
feedback accidentally before trying the experiment
themselves.) Once the author has finished commenting, she
asks learners to switch off the tape and perform the next
experiment.

oken
torials

You can, of course, shift the balance of your teaching
from print towards tape -- and aim for the **spoken**
equivalent of a tutorial-in-print. However, learners will
still need to look at things as well as use their ears --
so it will be an audiovisual tutorial. In this kind of
sequence:

w to do it

1. You talk to your learners rather than expressing
    your teaching points in writing.

2. While they listen, you may be getting them to turn
    the pages of a booklet, which you have laid out with
    text and pictures.

3. Every so often you will ask them (on the audiotape)
    to answer a question or carry out some exercise

(like an ITQ or SAQ) -- perhaps writing their answers in the booklet.

4. Each time you set such an activity, you will say "Stop the tape now, and start it again when you have finished..." You may record a few seconds' of music at this point, as another signal for the learner to switch off.

5. When learners switch on again, they hear your feedback and comments on the activity. You will talk about the kind of answers they should have come up with. Or, if they're not the kind of answers that can be spoken (e.g. diagrams or complex calculations), you may direct your learners to a page in the booklet where the answers have been printed.

6. Having finished commenting on the previous activity, you go on to the next teaching point you want to talk about, as in 1 and 2 above.

Audiovision frames

Figure 11.5 shows an extract from an audiovision booklet. It contains a number of "frames" which carry the material that the teacher is discussing and asking questions about on the audio-cassette. The blank boxes are for the learner to write answers before getting feedback from the tape.

Teachers like audiovision

Audiovision tapes have become increasingly popular in the Open University -- both with teachers and learners. Teachers comment favourably on the fact that they can speak naturally to the learner, exploiting informal examples and minor asides. They can also use tone of voice to suggest what is important and what is less so, in a way that would not be possible in print. (Everything I say in Chapter 10 about writing **conversationally** applies with even greater urgency when you are writing a script for an audiovision cassette.)

Figure 11.5: Audiovision Notes (Adapted from Open University course D210)

NOTE 11   SHIFTS IN DEMAND AND SUPPLY CURVES

Question
Which of the shifts 1–4 are increases and which are decreases?

	Shift	Increase or decrease
Demand	1	
	2	
Supply	3	
	4	

NOTE 12   WHAT WOULD BE THE INITIAL EFFECT OF THE FOLLOWING CHANGES IN CONDITIONS?

Change in conditions	On demand	On supply	Increase	Decrease
1 A product suddenly becoming fashionable	✓		✓	
2 Frost affecting much of Brazilian coffee crop				
3 Sudden fall in incomes affecting sales of a product				
4 Bumper grain harvest				
5 New and cheaper system for extracting oil/gas				
6 Rise in the costs of transport of a product				

NOTE 13   FOUR BASIC DEMAND AND SUPPLY SEQUENCES

What happens after:
1   An increase in demand?
2   A decrease in demand?
3   An increase in supply?
4   A decrease in supply?

Learners like it too

Learners, for their part, speak of the satisfaction of hearing their teacher's voice: "It's just like having your own tutor in the room with you". And if you have any learners who are not too adept at reading, they may be even more appreciative.

Easy for do-it-yourself

Fortunately, audiovision lessons are cheap and easy to prepare. Most teachers can record perfectly useable lessons in their own homes without help (or interference) from professionals. And they are equally cheap and convenient for learners to use.

One final thing to remember: Because the learner carries on working, under the tape's guidance, even when the cassette player is switched off:

```
***********************************************
*                                             *
*   20 MINUTES OF TAPE TIME MIGHT PROVIDE     *
*   FOR AN HOUR OR MORE OF LEARNING TIME.     *
*                                             *
***********************************************
```

VIDEO MATERIAL

Moving pictures

Here I am talking about **moving pictures,** with or without accompanying sound. Television is now the most typical means of presenting moving pictures in education and training (though film is far from defunct). It can take three main forms:

Three ways of using television

1. *Television programmes.* The typical television programme is around half an hour in length and is meant for viewing from beginning to end without a

Straight-through viewing

break. It is heavily influenced by professional broadcast standards and formats (e.g. documentary or drama). Some teachers will make use of broadcast programmes or of "off air" recordings (copyright requirements permitting), while others will make their own.

2. *Video segments.* Here, the videotape contains a
number of separate clips, sequences, segments.
Each lasts no more than six or seven minutes and
is designed to trigger some kind of activity from

Stop-go viewing
with activities

the learner. Viewers are meant to stop the tape
after each segment to answer questions about it
(perhaps rewinding to view it again first) -- or,
if they are viewing in a group, to discuss it with
their colleagues. The video viewing may well be
interspersed with reading or learning from
audio-cassette and there is no necessity for the
video segments to make up a continuous "storyline"
as in video material of Type 1.

3. *Interactive video.* Clearly, Type 2 video is already
more interactive than is Type 1. But the label has
been captured by a form of presentation in which
Type 2 video segments (on video-cassette or video-
disk) are called on to the screen by the learner's

Computer-controlled
pictures

interaction with a personal computer. Such a system
allows you to run a tutorial-in-print on the
computer screen (interspersed with appropriate
moving pictures and sound) -- but in such a way that
your teaching really does vary according to the
learner's responses, and different learners may be
branched into different teaching sequences.

Production Problems

Unlike audio, the production of video material is no

costs and
conflicts

do-it-yourself operation for the teacher with a couple of
weekends to spare. It demands access to very costly
production equipment and considerable amounts of time for
planning. Furthermore, if you are to produce video
material of respectable quality, you will need the help
of professionals. This opens up the possibility of
conflict between what they consider "good television" and
what you consider "good teaching".

With interactive video, the production costs are
particularly horrendous. There you would have to work with
computer experts as well as television experts. Current
experience suggests that many months of highly expensive
professional time are needed to produce material that will
keep the learner busy for perhaps half an hour. For this
reason, interactive video seems of research and
experimental interest only for the time being -- and not

*Little
relevance
just yet ?*

likely to be of immediate relevance to most developers of
self-instructional courses. So I disregard it in the
discussion that follows.

Presentation Problems

Presenting video material to self-instructional learners
can also be both difficult and costly. On-site learners
and distance learners pose different problems:

On-site learners may either be:

*Presenting
video
on-site*

- brought together periodically for **group** viewing of
    material appropriate to the part of the course they
    are **supposed** to have reached; or

- given **individual** access to a video-cassette player
    whenever each learner is ready to view the material.

*Group
viewing*

Group viewing has the advantage that learners (and tutors
if they are present) can **discuss** the video material. It
may also economize on equipment. The disadvantage,
however, is that some learners may have fallen behind in
the course, and some may have pushed on further than most
So the single showing of the video might come too early
for some, too late for others -- unless it is designed to
be independent of the sequence in the rest of the course
materials.

*Individual
viewing*

Individual viewing offers the learner more **control**. He
or she can choose the most pertinent time at which to wor
on the video material. And, as with audiovision, the
learner can stop it and think about it, and replay bits

of it, as often as he or she likes -- or as often as the video lesson itself suggests. However, the individual will be one of several; so a number of copies of the video material, and a number of playback machines, may need to be available. Furthermore, there will be the expense of providing accommodation, security, supervision, maintenance and, perhaps, an appointments system.

Presenting video to distance learners

Distance learners, on the other hand, are impossible to reach with moving pictures -- except at even greater expense. In the Open University we have been lucky to have access to the BBC's facilities, both for producing television programmes and for broadcasting them nationwide to students in their own homes. Notice, though, that this combines the disadvantages of fixed viewing times and lack of easy opportunity to discuss the material with others -- besides inhibiting the "video segments" approach.

Video-players to be widespread ?

Maybe within ten years, video-cassette players will be as widespread in people's homes as audio-cassette players are today. Even so, it might be prohibitively expensive to produce and keep track of multiple copies of videotapes -- especially if learners were numerous, and too geographically distant from one another to share. One alternative might be to arrange occasional viewing sessions at local centres, but that would raise all the problems I've already mentioned in connection with on-site learners.

Is Your Motion Really Necessary ?

Would still pictures suffice ?

In view of the great expense involved in planning, producing and presenting moving pictures, we clearly need to ask this question. Is **motion** really essential in the pictures you want to show your learners ? Or would a printed set of "still" pictures, perhaps with audio-cassette commentary, serve just about as well ? (Figure 11.6, to which I referred earlier, shows how a series of such pictures can even illustrate change over time.) Could you

Figure 11.6: Showing Change with Still Pictures
(Adapted from Open University course T352, Unit 10)

The Development of Grain Structure during
Solidification of a Simple Casting

① Liquid poured into a cold mould causes a layer of chill crystals to form on the mould walls.

② The chill crystal layer releases heat during formation and heats up the wall of the mould. As a result, the temperature gradient in the liquid is less steep.

③ The innermost chill crystals grow towards the axis as the temperature falls below T_m giving rise to columnar growth. No further nucleation is necessary.

④ Columnar growth continues until opposite sets of crystals meet, if there is no nucleation in the centre of the liquid.

Alternatively:

Under certain conditions, nucleation may occur in the centre of the liquid before columnar crystals meet. This gives rise to course equiaxed crystals.

justify the additional expense, and maybe inconvenience --
for both teachers and learners -- of using video ?

You will need to weigh your own decision in the light
of your own special circumstances. Below you will see my
suggestions for sample applications in which video might
be justifiable -- provided your time and resources could
not be expected to produce **greater** dividends of
understanding and satisfaction by being invested in less
voracious media:

Sample applications. Each of these possible applications
for video assumes that **motion** is essential. I have not
tried to avoid overlap, and my list is meant to be
suggestive rather than exhaustive. Video might be worth
using:

o To demonstrate the use of tools or equipment.

o To demonstrate activities that learners are to carry
out, e.g. interviewing or car-driving.

o To present experiments in which the processes (rather
than, or as well as, the results) must be observed.

o To present a dramatic performance (e.g. a play or a
ballet) or a musical performance -- if it is
important to see as well as hear the performers.

o To analyse change over time, using animation,
stop-frame, slow-motion or speeded-up pictures, e.g.
the movements of an animal or of the atmospheric
belts on Jupiter.

o To suggest the spatial, three-dimensional qualities
of a still object -- e.g. a building or a piece of
sculpture -- by moving the camera around it, thus
giving the viewer a sense of sharing space with
the object.

o To show a discussion or interaction between two or
more people in which "body language" is important --

and/or in which it is necessary (and would otherwise be difficult) for the learner to identify who is speaking at any one time.

o   To take the learners into situations -- e.g. down a copper-mine or into the cockpit of a jet plane making its landing -- which they might not otherwise be able to enter (and which they could not properly experience through the medium of still pictures).

o   To provide primary source material for the learner t explore or analyse, using principles or techniques developed in the course -- e.g. archive film of historical events or video recordings of naturally occurring situations (like classroom exchanges between teachers and children, or animal courtship behaviour).

Summary

This section has not been encouraging of the use of moving pictures in self-instruction. If you are thinking seriously about using video material, here are four cruci questions to ask yourself:

Four questions to ask avout video

1.   For this particular course/lesson, could video material provide worthwhile learning experience that could not be provided more cheaply using other media ?

2.   Can I make it possible for my learners to view the video material ?

3.   Can I make my own video material, or obtain suitab material made by other people ?

4.   In view of the costs -- both to me and to the learners -- can we use video without having to economize on more essential media or neglect more worthwhile opportunities ?

eo
ments
ally
ferable ?

If you do decide that video is essential and justifiable, don't be persuaded that you must therefore make "television programmes". Most of the applications I listed above would have been served as well or better by the "video segments" approach.

and furthermore:

```
************************************************
*                                              *
*   MUCH OF WHAT IS NOW TAUGHT ON TELEVISION   *
*   COULD BE TAUGHT AT LEAST AS WELL IN        *
*   PRINT (TEXT PLUS STILL PICTURES) --        *
*   WITH OR WITHOUT AUDIO SUPPORT.             *
*                                              *
************************************************
```

MEDIA NOTES

nted
port
erials

This seems a good point to emphasize the need for **printed** support materials. Let's call them "media notes". I mentioned such materials more than once while discussing practical work and audio-cassette teaching. If you want the audio-cassette learning to be closely integrated with the study of a tutorial-in-print, your audiovision notes might be anything from a few scattered paragraphs to a substantial section within the text of the tutorial-in-print. Alternatively, your audio-cassette lessons may be free-standing and the associated print materials may make up a separate booklet.

al with
media

However, media notes are equally vital for serious study using radio, video, or computers. In fact, it may be the media notes that reveal to learners how the media lesson is meant to tie in with the rest of the course -- and thus persuade them to spend some time on it. In general, media notes might perform any of the following functions:

ctions for
ia notes

o Describing the content of the media "experience".

o Explaining its purpose, e.g. in terms of aims and objectives.

Functions of
media notes

o   Showing how it links with ideas and methods taught in other parts of the course.

o   Explaining how to use any special equipment or materials involved -- especially any safety aspects.

o   Giving guidance on how to learn from the experience.

o   Providing questions or activities for the learner to tackle before, during or after the experience.

o   Providing feedback to these questions or activities.

o   Reproducing "stills" from a video sequence or computer lesson to help the learner recall the experience afterwards -- or providing pictorial (and text) material for study during an audio-cassette or radio lesson.

o   Summarizing the main points.

o   Suggesting follow-up activities.

Not too
little...
not too much

If you give too little information in such media notes, your learners may neither see the point of using the medium nor be adequately equipped to make the most of it if they do. Yet if you give too much, learners may either neglect to read the notes before using the medium or else read the notes **instead of** using the medium.

Examples

With the exception of Figure 11.6, every figure so far in this chapter shows an extract from media notes. For two final complete examples, look at Figures 11.7 and 11. Figure 11.7 relates to a geological field trip, Figure 11.8 to a television programme. (If the latter notes had been for a "video segments" tape, they would have mentior several points at which learners should stop the videotap and the questions they should tackle at those points.)

Figure 11.7: Media Notes for a Geological Field Trip
(from Open University course S236)

THURSDAY Fossils and sediments, Staithes and Quarrington

Start 0830

Equipment required

These notes
Field notebook
Clipboard
Compass clinometer
Staithes field sheets
HARD HATS ARE VITAL
Hammers and goggles are useful for Quarrington.

Aims of the day

Staithes

1 Identify the sedimentary rock types, sedimentary structures, trace fossils and body fossils exposed in some Lower Jurassic strata.

2 Record the occurrence of these features in a sequence of strata on a partially completed graphic log, and complete the log.

3 Measure the orientations of palaeocurrent indicators in the strata examined.

4 Infer environments of deposition of the sequences and, in the case of that in the graphic log, how these changed over time.

Quarrington

1 Interpret the lithologies and sedimentary structures in the Permian strata.

2 Comment on the depositional environments, and the palaeoclimate at the time of deposition.

The route

The route leaves Durham on the A177, past the Science Site, passing over Coal Measures, hidden under drift deposits, to Bowburn and to Quarrington.

From Quarrington the route follows minor roads eastwards across the Permian strata to join the east coast trunk road, the A19, which is followed south through the Teesside industrial complex. Note the ICI Billingham works, which were originally developed to exploit anhydrite in the Upper Permian. Reserves are now exhausted and the mines closed. In the distance will be seen the British Steel complex at Grangetown and the ICI Petro-chemicals Division at Wilton. This area contains the biggest acreage of petrochemical works in the country.

South of Middlesbrough the route follows the A174 and the A171 through the town of Guisborough. The route skirts the foot of the scarp forming the northern edge of the Cleveland

Hills formed of Lower Jurassic (Lias) beds capped by sandstones of the Lower Deltaic Series. Skelton, Brotton and Loftus were centres of the now defunct Cleveland Ironstone mining district. Boulby is a deep mine from which potash salts from the Upper Permian Evaporite Series are extracted.

Staithes

Introduction

Staithes is situated some 12 km north-west of Whitby on the coast of County Cleveland. You will leave the coach at the top of the hill leading down to the harbour. *Please take all your essential equipment including your lunch as you will be away from the coach for the rest of the day.*

The visit consists of two exercises, both along the sea cliffs that flank Staithes harbour (Figure 4). You will be walking over the wave-cut shale platform, which in places is fairly slippery; so stout boots and care are necessary.

SAFETY NOTE

You must not linger on any part of the shore when your tutor asks you to return to Staithes. Timing is crucial since the incoming tide covers most of the platform, and can easily cut off stragglers. Do not go further than Old Nab when doing the graphic log exercise, and if you are unsure about your mobility along this stretch of shore, your tutor will show you the limits within which you should stay. Please keep within sight of your tutor at all times. You must wear your helmet when approaching the cliffs, since fine fragments drop down even in fine weather.

For the same reason you are advised not to hang around unnecessarily under the cliffs. Neither of the exercises at Staithes requires a hammer. Indeed, please refrain from hammering any part of the section, so that it can remain unspoilt for later students and also because loosening of the cliff wall by hammering may provoke rock falls.

In some weeks during the summer school period the tides may make this exercise impossible and an alternative exercise (described on separate sheets) will be done.

General stratigraphy

The section along the shore on both sides of Staithes harbour exposes strata of the Lower Jurassic (Lias), dipping gently to the south-east. Along this section four distinctive units can be seen; they are:

1 the Jet Rock Formation (youngest),

2 the Grey Shales Formation,

3 the Cleveland Ironstone Formation and

4 the Staithes Formation (oldest).

Figure 4 Map of the Staithes area.

Figure 11.8:   Media Notes for a Television Programme

(from Open University course D102, Unit 8)

12   TV STUDY GUIDE

TV8   THE END OF THE LINE

This programme looks at different explanations of the causes of economic crises – the explanations that arise in everyday conversations – and places them in the context of the theories that have been discussed in this unit. We again use the drama format of a dialogue between Steve and John: Steve is made redundant, and they argue over why their particular factory is being closed; but it becomes clear that the argument is, inevitably, about why the economy as a whole was in a crisis.

Before the programme

Try to ensure that you have reached this point in the unit. If you have not been able to find the time to get this far, you will still find the programme useful, but try to read Sections 4 and 7 quickly before it starts. Make sure you are familiar with the distinction between basic and immediate causes of crisis: it is elaborated in those sections.

During the programme

The programme is concerned with the causes of crisis, but while watching it you should look for the different levels of causes that are discussed. On the one hand, there is the question of whether John's or Steve's actions should be blamed for causing their particular firm to close or whether it resulted from structural causes beyond anyone's control. On the other hand, there is the problem of what causes crises in the economy as a whole: how do factors such as a collapse of demand, falling profits and conflict between labour and capital interact?

After the programme

Write down, briefly, your answers to the following questions. They are not meant to be a test, but instead a means to help you check your understanding of some of the points in the unit and programme.

1 Think of the argument between Steve and John. In the course of it several explanations for the factory's closure were put forward. Here is a list of some of them – try to complete the missing words with either 'much' or 'little':

    Demand for the product was too . . .

    The capitalist installed too . . . new machinery.

    The workers put up too . . . resistance to the scrapping of traditional methods of working.

2(a)

Q How might higher wages in John and Steve's factory have *increased* its difficulties?

A By intensifying the fall in its . . . (fill in the relevant word).

2(b)

Q How might higher wages in factories have helped to *ease* the difficulties of the economy as a whole at least temporarily?

A By leading to an increase in workers' . . . for . . . goods and thereby weakening the . . . cause of crises. (Fill in the three words).

(If you found question 2(b) difficult, read through Section 8 and try again).

The answers are given at the end of the unit text (p 47 below).

COMPUTER TEACHING

This section will be no more encouraging than that on
video. In one form or another -- like Computer Assisted

CAL and CBT

Learning (CAL) or Computer Based Training (CBT) --
computer teaching has been around for some time. For two
decades or more, cynics have remarked that "Computer
assisted learning is the medium of the future -- and it
always will be."

That future may be closer now, thanks to miniaturization,
mass production, and the diminishing cost of powerful

*Enormous
costs*

equipment. But the costs remain enormous -- especially
the labour costs of designing suitably interactive learning
materials -- and seem likely to severely restrict the
worthwhile use of computers in education.

*Software
development
time*

Experience in the Open University suggests that between
two and four **months** of professional time are needed to
produce a CAL exercise that will engage learners of varied
ability for one **hour**. Similar estimates have been heard
from commercial computer organizations. (Producing
computer-based interactive video is even more time-
consuming.)

*Delivery
costs*

The delivery system is also very expensive. Even
assuming your institution can allow your students access
to a suitable mainframe computer, or at least a powerful
minicomputer, there will be the costs of terminals,
telephone bills, and all the servicing and administrative
costs I mentioned earlier in connection with **on-site video.**

*Distance
learners*

As with video, the costs of equipping and administering
a computer teaching system may become huge if your learners
are studying at a distance and have to travel to a number
of CAL centres to use terminals. Many of your learners
will nowadays have microcomputers in their own homes, of
course. But there are so many different models, each

refusing to run programs written for other machines; and,
in any case, most home computers are too underpowered to
do anything very sophisticated, educationally.

Forms of Computer Assisted Learning

Despite the problems, some institutions can justify using
computers for some courses. The Open University, for
example, operates a national network of some 250 computer
terminals linked to its mainframe computer. It also has

*What can
a computer
do for S-I ?*

several courses on which computers are **sent** to students
for use in their homes. So what can computers do for
self-instruction ?

In theory, a powerful computer should be rather
proficient as an instructor. After all, it can:

*Its basic
abilities*

- store considerable amounts of information;
- select from it at great speed;
- present the learner with print and animated diagrams;
- respond to contributions typed in by the learner;
- give immediate feedback to the individual learner; an
- deal differently with different learners.

Again in theory, computers can be programmed to use their
teaching potential in three main ways:

*Three possible
contributions
to teaching*

1. *Tuition*. Here the program requires the computer to
act as a patient, personal tutor. It leads the learner
through a sequence of material which they are expected
to master. The computer can discover in what areas ea
learner has difficulties -- then explain the ideas

*Tutoring the
individual*

involved, using appropriate examples and exercises --
and test the learners at each step to check how well
they have understood.

Different learners may be presented with different
examples and test exercises, according to their earlie
responses. And the program may "branch" different

learners into different kinds of material according
to the particular difficulties or interests they reveal.

2. *Simulation.*   The second form of computer teaching
uses the computer to simulate a particular situation
or system with which the learner can interact.   Thus
the learner will be able to "experiment" in total

Safe
experiments...   safety with, let's say, a nuclear reactor, an ailing
hospital patient, the processes of mountain-building,
or the economic structure of the EEC.

Learners can call up the information that will enable
them to run the reactor, treat the patient, and so on,
as they think fit, trying out their interpretaion of
the underlying principles.   The computer will tell them
what effects their decisions are having -- especially

with
individual   if the reactor is about to go critical or the patient
feedback   expire.   (See Figure 11.9 for an extract from a
simulation exercise.)

3. *Data-crunching.*   Here the computer is used as a means
of searching large amounts of data and/or of
manipulating it at high speed.   Thus the learner might
ask the computer to search for certain figures or
patterns in hundreds of census returns or to produce
complex charts and graphs.

In seconds or minutes, the computer may be able to
provide learners with data that might otherwise have

Relieving
drudgery   taken them hours or days to work out.   Relieved of this
drudgery and delay, learners can get on with the more
important task of making sense of the data.

So much for the theory.   In practice, much that is offered

The humbler   in the name of CAL and CBT seems to concentrate on telling
reality   and testing (especially testing) rather than on teaching.
Too often it makes little or no use of the computer's

Figure 11.9: CAL Simulation -- Extracts from an On-screen
Discussion between Computer (C) and Student (S) (from
(from W. Feurzig's "Decision Making", in *Computer Assisted
Learning in the Health Professions,* Harvard Medical School,
1970, edited by L.M. Stolurow, et al)

```
            AFTER DISCUSSING THE PHYSICAL APPEARANCE OF A
            CASE-STUDY PATIENT, THE STUDENT (S) AND COMPUTER (C)
            CONTINUE THEIR ON-SCREEN DISCUSSION AS FOLLOWS:
    S   Laboratory reports ?
    C   Fine.  Which lab tests would you like to have done ?
    S   X-ray.
    C   X-ray will be taken.  Results will be sent to you
        as soon as possible.
    S   Urine exam.
    C   The analysis will be done.
    S   Rectal exam.
    C   You're not being careful.  The patient is too
        acutely ill for a rectal examination.
    S   WBC
    C   The white count will be taken.
    S   Pulse ?
    C   Unchanged.
        Some of the first series of lab reports have just come in.
        Urine exam:  Insufficient fluid for analysis.
        RBC:  5 million.
        WBC:  15500.
        Differential:  Shift to left.
        When the other reports are in you'll be notified.

            (PART OF DIALOGUE OMITTED)

    C   Perhaps you think it too early too arrive at any definitive
        conclusion.  On the other hand, you may be prepared to
        make the diagnosis now.  Are you ?
    S   No.
    C   Fine.  Nevertheless we've got a fair amount of information
        -- at least enough to raise some, perhaps several,
        diagnostic possibilities.  Have you any in mind ?
    S   Acute pyelonephritis.
    C   Unexplained fever, chills, malaise, and flank pain are
        certainly consistent with acute pyelonephritis.  Do you
        think that the absence of dysuria reinforces the diagnosis ?
    S   No.
    C   Right.  And isn't the white count somewhat high for
        this diagnosis ?
    S   No.
    C   You're wrong.  The white count is high, though a later
        reading is indicated for substantiation.

            (PART OF DIALOGUE OMITTED)

    C   Any other thoughts as to diagnosis ?
    S   Pneumococcal pneumonia.
    C   I see you're still interested in this diagnosis.
        Are you absolutely sure ?
    S   No.
    C   What would help you nail down the diagnosis ?
    S   Evidence from X-ray findings.
    C   Good.  Anything else ?
    S   Evidence from blood culture.
    C   What you really need is evidence from the sputum smear
        and culture.  Anyway, continue with your investigation
        and we'll see what happens.
```

The program was designed by Dr Preston K Munter of Harvard University

Any better than print ?
unique capabilities. Too often it could be done just as well (if it is worth doing at all) in the pages of a book.

```
**************************************
*                                    *
*  COMPUTERS ARE TOO EXPENSIVE TO    *
*  USE AS ELECTRONIC PAGE-TURNERS.   *
*                                    *
**************************************
```

If you believe you can put computers to better use in your subject, here are some questions to ask yourself:

Some questions to ask

CAL Checklist

o Will CAL provide a learning experience that is both essential and incapable of being provided by a cheaper medium ?

o Do we have the ability and the time to think out and produce quality teaching programs -- perhaps at the rate of 2-4 months per hour of learner time ?

o If not, can we be sure of obtaining relevant programs of quality from outside sources ?

o Where, when, and at whose expense will learners use CAL ?

o How can we ensure that learners do take up the opportunity to use CAL ? (For example, by basing assessment activities on it.)

o Can we do enough teaching with CAL to make it worthwhile for learners to acquire the necessary skills ?

o Can learners be given any form of human help -- e.g. by tutors -- if they get into difficulties ?

o How will tutors or other helpers be chosen and prepared for their role ?

o What printed back-up material (media notes) might learners need to help them get the most out of the learning experience ?

o What arrangements can we make for evaluating and
   improving each CAL package in the light of learners'
   experience with it ?

*A non-
teaching
role*

Administrative footnote. Even if you decide not to use
CAL, if your institution has a computer, you may appreciate
its help in the **administration** of your course -- especially
if you are dealing with large numbers of learners. For
instance, you might use it to keep records -- e.g. How many
of your learners are falling behind schedule ? How many
of your tutors are marking with undue severity ? -- and to
mark objective tests.

HUMAN MEDIA

*Human beings
are "media"*

This may seem an odd heading, especially in a book about
self-instruction. But people can have their learning
"mediated" -- that is, deliberately conveyed or at least
influenced -- by contact with other human beings, even
when they are studying at a distance. This contact may
or may not be face-to-face. Learners may be in touch with
tutors (or other learners):

*Forms of
human contact*

   - by writing to one another;
   - by telephone;
   - by exchange of audio-cassettes; or
   - by face-to-face contact.

*Is face-to-
face contact
possible ?*

Face-to-face contact is, of course, easier for on-site
learners. But all four types of contact may be possible
for distance learners also. They may, for example, be
encouraged to meet together regularly, with a tutor, to
pursue group discussion or practical work based on their
individual preliminary studies. Even very occasional
contacts with other learners and/or with tutors may be
invaluable to your learners and are worth considering in
your course planning where possible.

Roles for Human Contact

We can identify a number of roles for human encounters in
and around a self-instructional course. Not all of them
demand the services of trained, paid tutors:

Encouragement and support. Self-instructional learners
(especially those learning at a distance) may be prone to
anxieties. They may worry about whether their approach to
learning is appropriate; about whether they are reaching
satisfactory standards; about how to reconcile their
studying with the demands of family life and friends;
about whether it will all be worthwhile for their career
or other aspirations -- and so on.

*Personal
anxieties*

The necessary encouragement and support can best be
provide through "live" contact with another human being.
At the very least, such a person can enable "sufferers" to
get it off their chests and talk through their problems.
Trained counsellors may be needed for serious cases,
especially where specialized knowledge is required. But
even the learners themselves -- in "self-help groups" --
can help dissipate one another's routine anxieties.

*Help from
others*

Remedial tuition. However thoughtfully you prepare your
materials, some learners are going to have difficulties
with them. You may be able to arrange for learners to
discuss such difficulties with a tutor. (But don't be
like some course developers who assume they can therefore
take less trouble with their materials and leave it to
tutors to "tie up the loose ends".)

*Discussing
learning
difficulties*

Inspirational teaching. Occasional face-to-face seminars
can refresh the learner's spirits. Before each new stage
of the course, learners might be brought together for a
session at which the tutor sums up the course so far and
sets the scene for what is to follow. Learners might

Motivation

thereby feel gratified at having covered so much ground already and heartened for the work that still lies ahead.

It is generally easier to stimulate your learners' motivation face-to-face than it is in print, or even on audiotape. Though, as with all these roles, an inept tutor could do your learners more harm than good.

Can go wrong

Practical teaching. You may have been able to build all necessary practical work into your self-instructional materials. But, in some subjects, learners will need face-to-face demonstrations, and they will need to carry out their lion-taming or their open-heart surgery under the guidance of an expert who can give them immediate feedback while observing their performance.

Guided practical work

Advice on options. Not all courses require every learner to follow exactly the same path. Some give learners considerable freedom to decide which areas they will concentrate on. Others have a substantial "project" component, in which -- perhaps after the first part of the course has given a grounding in the subject -- learners are expected to select and explore a topic of their own choice.

Choices

In such cases, the learners may benefit from access to a tutor who can help them not just with choosing topics but also with organizing their personal researches. Learners may also need advice on which bits of the course they can safely neglect if they start running out of time.

Study methods

Marking and commenting. Marking and commenting upon learners' written work seems to me an essential feature that distinguishes self-instructional teaching from publishing. For one thing, the obligation to present their work at frequent intervals helps pace the learners' endeavours. Even more importantly, commenting helps shape the learners' learning. Without personal feedback

Personal feedback

on what they have accomplished, they might just as well be reading teach-yourself books.

Tuition by correspond-ence

Written comments can be seen as **tuition by correspondence** and will be especially valuable to distance learners, who are so much less likely than on-site learners to get any face-to-face discussion of their work. (More about the role of commenting in Chapter 13.)

Tutors and Other Human Contacts

You and others ?

If you are running just one course, for a small group of learners, you may be able to perform all the above roles single-handed. Otherwise, you will need to think about how other colleagues might be recruited and briefed to play their parts as tutors, advisers, or whatever.

Keeping colleagues informed

Communication with tutors. Getting other tutors to work effectively with learners -- at least as effectively as you would do yourself -- depends on good communication. You will need to provide tutors with a full set of course materials and to make sure, perhaps at a briefing meeting, that they are familiar with the content and rationale of the course. They will also need written information ("Tutor Notes") concerning any specific instructions or general guidelines you wish them to follow. (See Figure 13.4 on page 324 for an example.)

Getting reports

Once tutors have begun their work, you may ask them for regular reports about the good, bad and curious aspects of the course that they encounter in dealing with learners. Conversely, you will need a mechanism -- perhaps a regular meeting or a newsletter -- for sharing new information with them, and for passing on any revised instructions.

Maintaining colleagues' interest

Teaching to other people's (your) course materials may not seem a very creative task. So how do you help maintain your tutors' interest ? Human tuition is a rare and

precious resource in a system that has set out to be
self-instructional. Tutors need to know exactly what is

Knowing and
caring

expected of them -- and to care that it is done well --
or this resource may be squandered.

Other human contacts. Let us not forget the other "human
media" that might help our learners. In particular,

Learners
can help
each other

learners can get help from one another. Socially, they
may support one another through times of self-doubt. And
they will help one another sniff out the limits of the
system, identifying what the "hidden curriculum" really
requires of them.

They can also help one another with course work. Each
may understand points that fox another. And even if both

Can even
learn from
one another

are flummoxed, at least each may be reassured to find that
he or she is not alone in confusion. With vocational or
professional education in particular -- e.g. where farmers
or teachers or zoo-keepers are studying together -- the
learners' diverse experiences, when fed into discussion,
may actually form part of the subject-matter of the course
Each learner may see his or her own experience differently
as a result.

Bringing about such collaboration may not be easy,
especially if learners are studying at a distance. One

Facilitating
contacts

thing you might do is provide names, addresses and
telephone numbers of all learners in an area who agree to
being on the list. Learners who have recently completed
the course might also be named as contacts. If you could
also arrange an informal gathering for learners to meet o
another, this might overcome the reservation many learner
might feel about making "cold contacts" with mere names o
a printed list.

"Self-help groups" might begin to evolve from such

Self-help
groups

informal gatherings, or indeed in the social after-glow c
more formal tutor-led sessions. If your learners are

studying on-site, then self-help groups may arise
spontaneously. Even so, especially if learners rarely
need to study in the same place at the same time as one
another, you may need to give each learner a list of all
the learners on the course.

Proctors

With some on-site courses, the helping of learners by
other learners is built into the system. The "Keller
Plan", for instance, uses more advanced learners -- under
the general supervision of a tutor -- to act as "proctors".
In this role, they administer and mark the periodic tests
on which the progress of the new learners depends, and at
the same time give considerable informal tuition.

*Practical
teaching*

Another role for the more advanced learners would be to
demonstrate practical activities and supervise the learner
learners' own practical work. This might both take some
pressure off the tutors and appear to learners as less
threatening than the same close attention might seem if
exercised by the tutors.

*ooking after
he proctors*

You may, however, ask "What's in it for the proctors ?"
Some institutions give course credit to learners providing
such help; others may offer financial rewards. It is also
necessary to consider the same issues of briefing and
training that I mentioned in connection with tutors.
Proctors and "demonstrators" will be even less experienced
than tutors, and it could be disastrous to leave them to
"sink or swim".

*t other
man
ntacts*

Finally, in thinking about other human contacts, let us
not forget family, friends and workmates. Clearly, they
can have a negative effect on the learner's studies if they
are not supportive, or at least sympathetic. But they can
actively help with learning also. In teaching some topics,
you may give your learner certain questions to discuss with
colleagues in order to gather a variety of experiences and
viewpoints. In a more general way, learners might be
encouraged to discuss their studies with anyone who seems

at all interested. Even if the other person doesn't
contribute much, the efforts to articulate and put across
the main ideas will help sharpen up their own understanding

Checklist for "Human Media"

*Questions
about using
human media*

Finally, here are some basic questions to ask about the
human media:

1. Does the course need tutors and/or proctors ?

2. What roles must they perform ?

3. Where can suitable people be found ?

4. How can they be recruited and rewarded ?

5. How can they be informed (and kept informed)
    as to what is expected of them ?

6. How can they be kept motivated ?

7. How can their work be monitored ?

8. What other "human media" might learners usefully
    make contact with ?

9. How can we facilitate such contacts ?

Remember:

```
*************************************
*                                   *
*   SELF-INSTRUCTION DOES NOT MEAN  *
*   ALWAYS LEARNING ON YOUR OWN.    *
*                                   *
*************************************
```

FINAL MEDIA CHECKLIST

To help you make sense of this chapter as a whole, let
me repeat a set of key questions which I introduce in
Chapter 4. You need to ask these questions about the
whole course and about each individual lesson within it:

*So which
media shall
you use ?*

o Which media are available to me **and** to the learner

o Do any of our learning objectives imply particular

types of stimuli and particular media ?

o If so, how and to what extent -- e.g. for what proportion of the learner's time -- would I wish to use each of the preferred media ?

o What would it cost me **and** the learner (in money, time and convenience) to use those preferred media ?

o Would less expensive media be **acceptably** effective ?

o Do the chosen media offer the learner sufficient **variety** of stimulus and activity ?

o How can I **combine** media (e.g. print and audiotape) for maximum interest and effectiveness ?

Finally, my own personal opinion:

```
******************************************
*                                        *
*  OF ALL THE MEDIA WE HAVE DISCUSSED    *
*  IN THIS CHAPTER, THE ONE WITH THE     *
*  MOST UNDER-USED POTENTIAL FOR         *
*  SELF-INSTRUCTION IS AUDIOVISION.      *
*                                        *
******************************************
```

12. THE PHYSICAL FORMAT OF YOUR LESSONS

In what physical form is your lesson to be presented to
the learner ? This may be entirely your own decision.
For all I know, you are not only writing but also
illustrating, typing, reprographing and packaging the
whole thing yourself. But that seems unlikely. Your
material will probably be "processed" by a typist and a
Other
specialists reprographics expert, and you may also be dealing with a
graphic designer and even an editor.

Each of these specialists will contribute his or her own
ideas as to how your lesson might be presented. And each
Constraints may identify several constraints on what is possible. Some
such constraints may arise from the physical limitations of
the resources available. Others may be "house rules"
imposed on all authors. Yet others may turn out to be
simply the personal preferences of the specialist.

This chapter is meant to help you understand what might
be possible for your lessons, and to decide what you would
regard as desirable. In it, I discuss:

Sections
in this
chapter o How your lessons might be packaged.

o How the text might be reproduced.

o How your pages might be laid out.

o How typography might be used.

PACKAGING YOUR LESSONS

How is your teaching material to be packaged ? If you have
any choice in the matter, there are at least five factors
to bear in mind:

Five
factors 1. How many different **kinds** of material are involved ?

2. By what means are the materials to be **delivered** to
your learners ?

3. In what variety of **contexts** might learners wish to use the materials ?

4. Might learners wish to **add** materials of their own ?

5. How long might they wish to store and **re-use** the materials ?

Considering the Questions

Your answers

Let us consider those five basic questions, one by one. In the process, I'll raise a number of new ones. But I must leave you to answer them as best befits your own needs and circumstances.

Variety of materials ? Your learner may be getting not only your tutorial-in-print but also, say, textbooks or collections of readings, audio-cassettes, specimens, home experiment kit, filmstrips and viewer, and so on. If so, you will need to think out a way of putting the items *Coherence* together in a reasonably coherent and manageable fashion. You can't hand them all over separately, but nor can you simply throw them together in a paper bag.

Possibilities

Can you at least reduce the number of separate items ? Can a number of separate lessons be bound together ? Can audio-cassettes (and perhaps filmstrips and viewer) be fastened to a flat sheet of plastic or cardboard of the same size as your text ? Do you need to provide a plastic wallet to hold certain items -- and/or a cardboard box to contain all of them ?

How and when ?

Delivery ? You may be handing the materials to your learners personally. Or they may have to go to one or more other people to collect them. Or you may be sending them through the mail. Is the learner to get all the materials for the course at the outset ? Or are they doled out, bit by bit, as he or she progresses ?

Each of these delivery methods imposes different packaging restrictions. If you give learners a great pile

of materials, they may have trouble carting it away. If a
variety of separate bits and pieces have to be distributed
to learners by other people, components of the course may
easily get lost. If you are frequently mailing material
to learners, they may find themselves unpopular with their
postman (or have materials stolen from their doorstep) if
many of your packages are too big to go through the normal
letterbox.

Receiving all the course materials at once may be
daunting to some learners (though helpful to others).
But getting them separately may make it difficult to
provide for coherent storage -- and increases the risk
that some learners will fail to get some of the components.

Contexts of use ? In what variety of contexts might
learners want/need to use your materials ? How might this
affect the packaging ? For instance, learners who want to
do some of their studying on the bus to work will not thank
you for giving them a thousand-page volume to hump around.

Should each lesson be detachable from the rest, e.g. in
a slip-case or ring-binder ? Again, if learners might
want to use "other media" -- e.g. audiotapes, practical
work, video -- somewhere other than where they keep their
course material, should the media notes be detachable ?

Adding material ? You might expect learners to add
material of their own to the course -- either during it or
afterwards. They might add their own extensive notes,
calculations, designs or essays. Or they might add
up-to-date articles, photographs, newspaper reports,
photocopies from books, and so on. Do you care how they
store these ? If you wanted learners to interleave such
additions with the relevant sections of your text, then
you could help by presenting your material in loose leaf
form for a ring binder.

Storage and re-use ? You will also need to think of how
your learners might store the course materials. Unless

Margin notes:
Possible snags
And more
How will learners use ?
Detachability
How store additions ?

*Storing
materials*

you provide storage boxes or files -- or can rely on the
learners doing so -- the more separate bits and pieces you
provide, the more likely they are to mislay some of them.

*Binder or
binding*

Furthermore, if the materials are to be in long-term
use, paper for a ring binder needs to be heavy enough not
to tear where the holes are punched. If, instead, you are
providing bound booklets, the binding must be strong enough
to stand repeated opening and closing. Yet: booklets with
glued spines (laughingly called "perfect binding") often
fall apart; stapled pages may prevent the book being opened
flat; comb-bound books can be awkward to store and may not
allow for an identifying title to be shown on the spine; a
stitching is expensive.

Your Answers

*No
ready-made
answers*

There are, of course, no ready-made answers to the questi
above. You will need to decide what is **desirable**, and
listen to advice about what is **possible**, within your own
institution. The over-riding question to bear in mind is

```
*************************************
*                                   *
*  HOW DO I ENVISAGE MY LEARNERS     *
*  USING THE COURSE MATERIALS ?      *
*                                   *
*************************************
```

FOUR METHODS OF TEXT PRODUCTION

Here I want to draw attention to four different methods o
getting your lessons reproduced. Each has its own
advantages and disadvantages. It is worth your knowing
about them, even if they are not all available to you at

*The four
methods*

present. The four methods are:

o Photocopying
o Stencil duplicating
o Offset litho printing
o Letterpress printing

Photocopying

If you are producing materials for a small number of
learners, you may well consider using a photocopier. The
best known trade name is Xerox, but there are now numerous
makers, between them offering a wide range of equipment of
good quality.

Photocopiers will give good reproduction of typing,
handwriting, line drawings, and facsimile pages from books.
Some photocopiers can also give acceptable reproduction of
photographs, and some may perform other useful tricks like
over-printing in colour, copying on both sides of a sheet
of paper, and producing copies that are smaller or larger
than your original.

Photocopying is a process you can easily carry out
yourself, without needing to rely on a technician. But, if
you want more than a certain number of copies, it may be
expensive compared with other methods.

Stencil Duplicating

With this form of reproduction, a typewriter is used to cut
your text into a waxed stencil "master", and copies are
made by a machine that presses ink through the master onto
sheets of paper. The basic equipment is rather limited.
Drawings and line diagrams have to be cut directly into the
master with a stylus. Furthermore, although the stencil
master should be able to produce as many good copies as you
might want in one run, the quality of subsequent runs may
be less and less satisfactory.

It is possible to use a thermal copier to make a master
without having to type or draw directly onto a wax stencil.
Indeed, the machine will make a stencil by copying any
typewriting or print (text or line drawings) that contains
print -- from an ordinary sheet of paper. The method is
quick and easy, but the masters produce rather fuzzy copies.

*Many
makes*

*Many
tricks*

*Do-it-
yourself*

*Cutting
stencils*

*Thermal
stencils*

Fuzzy

*Electronic
stencils*

An electronic scanner -- a more expensive machine -- allows you to cut stencils incorporating photographs and even full colour. The print quality is better than that obtainable from the first two types of stencil mentioned above; and, using special masters, you can print thousands of good masters.

Offset Litho Printing

*What offset
can do*

The offset litho machine reproduces from a paper, plastic or metal plate onto which your text and pictures have been transferred by any of a number of different photographic or electrostatic processes. Your "original" can be typed or handwritten. It can incorporate printed text from other sources. Line drawings, charts, and special headings of rub-down lettering can be stuck on the page wherever you need them. And it can even incorporate photographs after they have been "screened" (a process in which the shades of grey are converted to dots of varying sizes) using separate equipment.

Freedom

In short, offset litho gives you enormous freedom in preparing your original -- often called "artwork" or "camera-ready copy". You can stick whatever you like on your page -- provided you make a clean job of it -- and alterations are easily made. Furthermore, the print quality will be good for thousands of copies and (at least if you use metal plates) later reprints should be no less good. Many commercial books, including this one, are now produced by offset litho.

*...and
quality*

Letterpress Printing

*Traditional
method*

This is the traditional method that most people think of when "printing" is mentioned. It is done by a machine that prints directly from raised metal letters, each of which has been put in place, manually or mechanically, by a skilled technician known as a compositor. The machine can

print thousands of excellent copies, with no deterioration
in a later reprint.

But compositors are extremely well-paid, and the labour
costs make letterpress too expensive for print runs of less

Expensive

than a thousand or so copies. Furthermore, illustrations
have to be prepared separately from the text, and the
additional costs involved are likely to limit the number
you can afford to use.

Which to Use ?

You may or may not have a choice of method. If given a
choice, I would usually opt for offset litho. It allows
you so much scope in composing your own pages -- especially

ffset is
y choice

if you want to make frequent use of pictures and other
visual devices. Letterpress might produce a more
prestigious-looking text; but learners might not find it
markedly more attractive, and it would certainly not be
more legible. Yet you and/or they would pay dearly for it.

My general remarks above, however, are clearly not a
sufficient basis for choosing. Find out what methods are

1at is
1urs ?

available in your institution. Look at examples of the
kinds of material they can produce. Discuss the pros and
cons with colleagues who have used them and with any
technicians whose help you would need. Then decide which
of the available methods best suits your needs at a price
both you and the learners can afford.

LAYOUT

In this section I invite you to consider how you might want
the pages of your tutorial-in-print to look. How might
your material be laid out ? For instance:

2stions
layout

o   What page size and format to use ?

o   How many columns ?

o   How to use the margins ?

o   How might pictures be placed ?

o   Should colour be used ?

*House
rules ?*

Again, your institution may have its own "house rules", giving you little choice in these matters.

Page Size and Format

Page size.   Ideally, this should depend on the kind of material you are presenting. Generally speaking, a tutorial-in-print can benefit from having pages even larger than this book -- allowing flexibility in arranging the frequent activities and pictures. If, on the other hand, you were presenting little but continuous text, a page smaller than this might suffice.

*How to
choose*

The A-series

In the UK and the rest of Europe, the A-series of pape sizes (promoted by the International Organization for Standardization) is now widely used.   The system is pictured in Figure 12.1 below:

Figure 12.1:   International A-series Paper Sizes

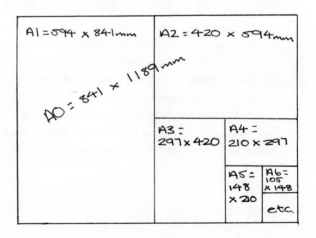

*Constant
shape*

Each numbered size has one side in common with the prev: side, but halves the other side.   Thus it keeps the same shape but has half the area.

A4 is a very popular paper size for self-instructional course materials. It allows plenty of space in which to lay out text, activities and pictures for maximum effect. Furthermore, ring-binders, files and wallets are all readily available in this size. So are pads of paper for the learners themselves to write on and insert in the package if they so wish.

If you cut A4 in half across its long side, you get A5. This sheet has the same proportions as A4 but, of course, has only half the area. It would therefore restrict you in your layout and would still be a shade too large to enjoy the possible advantage of being "pocket-size".

Format. By this I simply mean which way up will you use the page ? You may print with the short edge of the page uppermost ("portrait" format) or with the long edge uppermost ("landscape" format).

Portrait

Landscape

Even if you use the conventional "portrait" format, you may well include a "landscape" page from time to time. They can be useful if you wish to display a large photograph or table. If you want your learners to read some text along with the picture, however, you'd be wise to print both at the same angle lest they twist their heads off.

Columns and Margins

*How many
columns ?*

An A4 "portrait" page may be printed in one, two or even
three columns. A "landscape" page can take three or four.
Using more columns, with a smaller type-size, enables you
to get more words on a page. The consequent saving in
paper, however, is offset by the fact that readers may be
put off by pages that are too heavy with print. Apart fr
being more difficult to read, densely-printed pages can b
dispiriting to learners in that they may feel themselves
be making very slow progress through the book.

*Single v
double*

Columns. The simplest approach (if you are not using
letterpress) is to use a single column, typing directly
onto the page. Double column, on the other hand, would
require you to type the columns separately, perhaps reduc
them in size on a photocopier, and then paste them side b
side on a new sheet of paper.

*Width of
column*

If you use a single column, its width should ideally t
no more than three quarters of the width of the page if
you are using type of this size. With smaller type, don'
let the column exceed two thirds of the width of the page

*60 (max)
characters
per line*

If a line of type is too wide, reading becomes diffict
because the reader's eyes are constantly delayed in
locating the beginning of the next line, especially if t
are printed close together. Research suggests that 60
characters (letters and/or spaces) is about the maximum
line-width that can be read comfortably. That is about
dozen words.

*Wide
margin*

Margins. If you keep your single column of print to abc
two thirds of the page, you will have room for a wide
margin on one side. The wide margin can be used for:

*Uses for
margin*

- side headings;

- paragraph numbers;

- material that would otherwise be "footnotes";

Figure 12.2:   Varying Line Widths and Spacing

Key: *The long lines in A are more difficult to*
       read than the shorter ones in B. However,
       extra space between the longer lines, as in
       C and D, may somewhat improve on A's
       legibility. With a larger type-size (E),
       the spacing and line width of D is even
       more legible.

A   Using more columns, with a smaller type-size, enables you to get more
       words on a page. The consequent saving in paper, however, is offset
       by the fact that readers may be put off by pages that are too heavy
       with print. Apart from being more difficult to read, densely-printed

B   Using more columns, with a smaller type-size, enables you
       to get more words on a page. The consequent saving in
       paper, however, is offset by the fact that readers may be
       put off by pages that are too heavy with print. Apart from

C   Using more columns, with a smaller type-size, enables you to get more

       words on a page. The consequent saving in paper, however, is offset

       by the fact that readers may be put off by pages that are too heavy

       with print. Apart from being more difficult to read, densely-printed

D   Using more columns, with a smaller type-size, enables you to get more

       words on a page. The consequent saving in paper, however, is offset

       by the fact that readers may be put off by pages that are too heavy

       with print. Apart from being more difficult to read, densely-printed

E   Using more columns, with a smaller type-size, enables you

       to get more words on a page. The consequent saving in

       paper, however, is offset by the fact that readers may be

       put off by pages that are too heavy with print. Apart from

- repetition of a technical term that is being newly introduced in the text alongside;

- small illustrations;

- larger illustrations that occupy the full width of the page;

- captions for pictures that are set within the area of the block of print;

- visual signposts (see page 175);

- verbal instructions to the reader;

- the reader's own notes or comments; and so on.

Restraint

Obviously, some restraint is called for. Any one margin that contained all these types of information would be an eye-sore. And even if some margins display side-headings, for example, while others display technical terms or captions, how will you enable readers to tell at a glance what kind of information you are offering them ?

Margin either side

Your wide margin can be on either side of the column of type. Perhaps your choice will be determined by whether you want your reader to look at marginal items before or after reading the text. In the former case, your wide margin ought to be on the left; in the latter case, on the right. If you expect readers to do much writing in the margin, most would prefer the wide margin to be on the ri

Justify edges ?

Incidentally, although the left-hand edge of your bloc of type will form a straight vertical line ("justified" a the technical term has it), there is no need for the right-hand edge to do so. An unjustified, ragged edge, a on this page, may look rather less professional to you -- but readers are unlikely to notice, and it will not imped their reading. On the contrary, the ragged edge helps in distinguishing one line from another and thus aids the reader's eye in locating where it wants to be in the paragraph. The reader will also be saved from the peculi

spacings and frequent hyphenations that can result from
justification. Even with a two-column layout, an
unjustified right-hand edge is quite acceptable.

Placing Your Pictures

*Picture
near words*

When a paragraph refers to a picture, try to place the
picture as close to it as possible. Try to ensure that
your reader can see both the picture and the words
referring to it at the same time, without having to turn a
page. The reader should certainly not be given another
paragraph to read on through before the picture comes into
sight.

Examples

Small pictures can be placed alongside the paragraph in
the margin, if it is wide enough. Larger ones will go into
the body of the text. Try not to leave just one or two stray
lines below a picture at the bottom of a page. The reader
is likely to overlook them. Better to give the picture more
space and move those lines to the next page.

If you have a two or three-column format, you can run a
picture across one, two or three columns. If you run it
across more than one column, you would do well to move it
right to the top or bottom of the page, or the reader may
lose the downward flow of the columns.

Ideally, you should design pairs of adjacent pages
together as a "double-page spread". Thus, for example, you
would be able to prevent two over-dense pages from falling
opposite one another; but you might allow one fairly dense
page if the opposite one were largely pictorial:

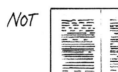

Double-page Spreads

Colour

There are three ways in which you might want to use colour in a lesson:

*Three forms
of colour*

o   Coloured print or line drawings.

o   Coloured photographs.

o   Coloured pages.

*What
colour
ink ?*

Print.   Black ink is easier to read than any other colours and should always be used for the bulk of any lesson. A second colour (contrasting with black but not so pale as to be invisible in artificial light) can be both attractive and useful in distinguishing one kind of text from another. However, a second colour adds to the expense, and its signalling role can usually be fulfilled in cheaper ways. If you must use it in illustrations, however, (e.g. in graphs or maps), then you may be able to use it for print as well, without extra cost. You may also introduce occasional blocks of solid colour, e.g. as a background to certain sections of the text.

A simple
hand-viewer

Photographs.   Colour photographs are especially expensive to print. If you are producing only a few dozen copies of your tutorial-in-print, it would be considerably cheaper to take colour prints and stick them in by hand. Alternatively, colour filmstrips can be provided cheaply together with a simple hand-viewer costing next to nothing.

*Coloured
paper*

Tinted pages.   You may feel that certain sections within a lesson might be presented on coloured paper. For instance test questions might be on blue-tinted paper; media notes green; and instructions for practical work on pink. This can be quite effective, provided you don't make your book too much of a bewildering rainbow. Restrict yourself to pastel tints, and preferably no more than two or three of them. Inserting occasional coloured pages will not, howe

Costs

be possible with letterpress printing -- and even with other methods it will add something, if only a little, to the costs of production.

TYPOGRAPHY

You've now given thought to the overall shape of your pages and the text that will be on them. But, in printing your text, you will need to decide how to use:

Four
aspects

- typeface (style of type);
- spacing of type;
- headings; and
- rules and borders.

Let's look at each of these in turn.

Basic Typefaces

Your choice of typeface (if you have any choice) will depend on what equipment you will be using. For example:

What
equipment ?

o An ordinary typewriter.

o A "golfball" or "daisywheel" typewriter (or a word processing printer) offering a limited range of typefaces.

o A printers' letterpress composer, offering an enormous range of typefaces.

rdinary
ypewriter

Obviously, an ordinary typewriter will be the most limited, but there is still much that you can do with it. Such a typewriter usually offers one or other of the first two faces illustrated below -- either "pica" or "elite". . Some typewriters may have, instead, a "sans serif" typeface, or even "italic" or "script". Obviously, all of these will give you both upper case (capital) letters and lower case letters.

Figure 12.3: Comparing Typefaces

This is typed in PICA, a large face giving only 10 characters per inch.

This is typed in ELITE, which is smaller and gives 12 characters to the inch.

This is an ITALIC typeface (like ELITE, but sloping) with 12 characters per inch.

This is SCRIPT typeface with 12 characters per inch and meant to resemble handwriting.

This is a SAN SERIF typeface (no little tails) -- again 12 characters to the inch.

Your main typeface

Either of the first two or the last of the typefaces above (or their letterpress equivalents) would be suitab for the main body of your text. Italic or script, howev can become tiresome to read if they run over more than a paragraph or two now and again for special effect. Your learners are likely to be most accustomed to an upright typeface with serifs; of the two shown above, Elite is probably to be preferred. It is closer to the size of print most often found in books ("10 or 11 point") and allows you to get more words on a page without it looking any more dense.

Contrasting typefaces

Occasional special typefaces. Whatever typeface you us the body of your text, you may occasionally want someth different. You may want to use more than one typeface, as to distinguish between different kinds of items in y lesson. You may, for instance, want to print instructi for activities in a different face from the main text, and the feedback comments in yet another face.

Special effects

A few "special effects" are obtainable with an ordinary typewriter. You can use <u>underlining</u> and CAPITALS. You can widen your S P A C I N G. You can even **embolden** a word or phrase -- either by inserting a thin piece of paper between type and ribbon or by backspacing and typing over the same letters several times. Such devices are adequate for picking out the odd word or phrase, or heading. But they would make for uncomfortable reading if allowed to occupy more than a couple of lines of print.

Extended contrast

What if you want to distinguish between more **extended** sections of text -- e.g. feedback on activities, or guidance on how to study a section ? There seem to be four possibilities:

Four approaches

o Keep a second typewriter with a different
   face, e.g. italic.

o Use coloured type (discussed under "Layout" above).

o Use indentation -- and/or boxes -- and/or put a
   lot of space around the special item.

o *Write the section in your own fair hand .*
   (Handwritten self-instructional books are not
   uncommon nowadays -- like Mr Wainwright's celebrated
   fell-walking guides, Figure 12.4.)

Golfballs and daisywheels

In producing this text, I have used a "golfball" typewriter. Such machines, like "daisywheel" typewriters and some word processors, make it possible to switch between pica, elite, san serif, bold, italic, and so on. You may also be able to use a photocopier to vary the **size** of your type in order to distinguish one kind of material from another.

Restraint again

However, such versatility can be a dubious blessing. It is easy to over-complicate a text with too much typographic razamataz. Few people ever fully exploit the potential of an ordinary (but imaginatively used) typewriter.

Figure 12.4:   A Handwritten Text (from *The Southern Fells* by A. Wainwright, Westmorland Gazette, 1960)

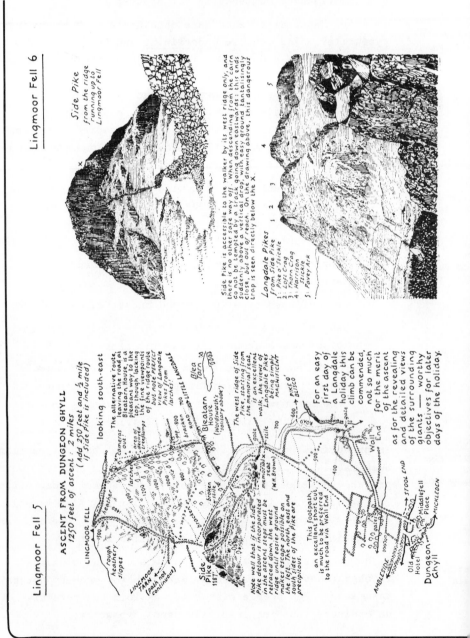

Spacing Your Type

Legibility
& structure

Here we are concerned both with legibility and with how to make clear the structure of your lesson:

Legibility. Whatever form of type you choose, its spacing on the page strongly affects its legibility. The main problem is how to keep your reader's eyes moving smoothly from left to right, and yet be able easily to locate the beginning of the next line. As I have already shown, the longer the lines, the more difficult this becomes -- especially if there is too little space **between** lines. (See Figure 12.2.)

Space
between
lines

Revealing structure. The spacing of your type can also help reveal the structure of your teaching. Thus it acts as an "access device" (see Chapter 8). It can help your reader make appropriate approaches to different sections of the text. For instance, how will you use space to indicate the beginning of a new paragraph ? You may leave an extra half line-space between paragraphs, or indent the first line, or do both. (I prefer to do both.)

Spacing
as
access
device

Example

Example

To distinguish an activity from the preceding text, you may wish to leave more space than you do between ordinary paragraphs. And, between the activity instructions and the feedback, you may wish to leave an even greater space -- to act as, or perhaps to accommodate, a "stopper".

xample

You **will also** need to decide how much space to **leave** around headings. You will notice that my headings are close to the block of text that follows them than to that precedir them. The latter space is the same as that between paragraphs. First and second level headings have space belc them; but third level headings I have run directly into the first line of the text they relate to.

*Indenting
blocks*

You may want to indent whole blocks of text, e.g.
quotations from other authors. Lists too may need space
around them, as may text that you put in a box. After an
indented section, it is better not to indent the paragraph
that follows. Just make sure it has at least the normal
line-space you are using between paragraphs.

Headings

Three basic grades. In Chapter 8, I suggest three grades of
headings as the maximum that either you or the reader will

*How many
grades ?*

be able to keep track of. These are fairly easily
distinguished typographically, even using an ordinary
typewriter. In this chapter, for example, examples of the
three grades are as follows:

Examples

o   "TYPOGRAPHY
         You've now given thought to the overall shape..."

o   "Basic Typefaces
         Your choice of typeface (if you have any choice)..

o   "*Revealing structure*. The spacing of your type can
         also help reveal the structure..."

*Heading
after
heading ?*

Designers often advise against allowing one heading to
follow directly below another, without any text between
them. Notice at the beginning of this section, for
instance, how "HEADINGS" is followed at once by "Three
Basic Grades". Designers might suggest inserting a line
or two of text under the first heading to introduce the
material covered under the following sub-headings -- e.g
"In this section we shall look both at the basic grades
heading and at special display headings that we need only
occasionally. Such an overview can sometimes seem

heavy-handed, however -- especially if the ensuing section is short.

For big headings ?

Display headings. For major "display" headings -- e.g. the titles of your lessons or groups of lessons -- even letterpress might not produce lettering large enough to make a powerful impression. A typewriter certainly would not.

Headlining

One alternative is to use a **headlining machine**. With some such machines you can impress letters onto sticky tape from a variety of typefaces; the type can then be cut up and stuck on your page. Other headlining machines work photographically.

Here is a sample of lettering
on HEADLINING TAPE

Rub-down lettering

The other alternative is to use a sheet of rub-down lettering -- Letraset is the best-known brand. These are available in a wide range of typefaces and sizes. See Figure 12.5 for samples.

Using rub-down

Such lettering (and other graphic devices) is easy enough to apply to a sheet of paper. But it needs to be done slowly and carefully and requires a good eye for spacing -- even if one has taken the trouble to draw faint pencil guide-lines first. However, if you do apply one letter too close or too far from its neighbour (or too high or low), you can easily rub it off and try again. For occasional use it's worth the trouble. San serif typeface is easier to use, e.g. Univers or Helvetica (bold or extra bold). The title-page of this book is embellished with Univers bold (24 point).

Figure 12.5:   Samples of Rub-down Lettering (Letraset)

Futura Black ● Bauer

abcdefghijklmnopqrstuvwxyz
ABCDEFGHIJKLMNOPQRSTUVWXYZ
1234567890 ß &?!£$[.,;:]

Gallia ●

AABCDEEFGHIJKLMNOPQRRS
STTUVWXYZ
1234567890 ÆØ &?!£$(.,;:)

Helvetica Medium Condensed ● Letraset © 1977

abcdefghijklmnopqrstuvwxyz
ABCDEFGHIJKLMNOPQRSTUVWXYZ
1234567890 æøßÆØ &?!£$(.,;:)

Sapphire ● Stempel

ABCDEFGHIJKLMNOPQ
RSTUVWXYZ
1234567890 &?!£$[.,;:]

Schneidler Old Style ●

abcdefghijklmnopqrstuvwxyz
ABCDEFGHIJKLMNOPQRSTUVWXYZ
1234567890 æøßÆØ &?!£$%(.,;:)

Univers 65 ●○ Deberny & Peignot

abcdefghijklmnopqrstuvwxyz
ABCDEFGHIJKLMNOPQRSTUVWXYZ
1234567890 æøßÆØ &&?!£$(.,;:)

Univers 66 ● Deberny & Peignot

abcdefghijklmnopqrstuvwxyz
ABCDEFGHIJKLMNOPQRSTUVWXYZ
1234567890 ß &&?!£$(.,;:)

Rules and Borders

*Useful
devices*

Rules (straight lines of various thickness) and decorative
borders are a useful typographic device. They are available
both on rub-down sheets for the do-it-yourselfer and in the
"toolkit" of a letterpress printer. They can even be
created on an ordinary typewriter. For example:

Examples

Some rub-down rules and borders (Letraset)

Rub-down

Some typewritten rules and borders:

ypewritten

*re
amples*

You will notice that a rule has been used at the top of
each page of this book -- just to separate the running
headings from the rest of the text. Heavier rules have
been used to enclose material presented as "Figures".

The more elaborate decorative borders can have a
special role in a tutorial-in-print where they make useful

Stoppers
& boxes

"stoppers" for activities. (See Figure 5.2I on page 108, for example.) They can also be used, as in this book, to box certain kinds of recurring text. In both cases, restraint is necessary. Don't use a border so florid that it dominates the page. And don't make frequent use of more than two or three different borders or their dramatic effect will be lost.

Restraint

FIVE FINAL POINTS

Condi
Consider
format
early

o Don't leave thoughts about the physical format of your lesson(s) until after you have finished writing. Even if you have no choice of format, or have to reach agreement with colleagues, the sooner you know what possibilities and limitations await you the better. That way you may be able to write in such a manner as to make the best of them.

Other
materials ?

o Don't forget to apply the same standards of layout and typography to any materials you offer aside from the main text -- e.g. course guide, tutor notes, and so on. Also, if you want to include articles or book chapters written by other authors, would their layout and typography be acceptable if you printed facsimile copies ? Might it even be desirable, both in giving your reader a change of visual style and in marking the out as different from your text ? Or do you need to have them retyped in the same format as your own material ?

Look
critically

o Do look critically at other people's layout and typography as well as your own. No book is perfect in that respect (not even this one). You can learn from other people's errors as well as from their successes. For a start, you might look again at the sample pages shown in Figures 5.2A-L -- and note the varied ways in which they do or do not embody the ideas discussed in this chapter.

(On pages
92-117)

o   Do try to ensure -- if you have any influence at all in
    the matter -- that materials are **not** produced in so

Yet more
restraint

    glossy (expensive) a version, or in such large
    quantities (several years' worth), that you cannot
    afford to dump some of them and rewrite if they later
    prove unsatisfactory in use.

o   Above all, remember that:

```
****************************************
*                                      *
*  EDUCATIONAL DESIGN IS TOO IMPORTANT  *
*  TO BE LEFT TO THE DESIGNERS.         *
*                                      *
****************************************
```

13. ASSESSING YOUR LEARNERS

Assessment needs planning

In this chapter, we are concerned with how your learners' learning might be assessed. Thoughts of assessment should be with you as soon as you start planning your self-instructional teaching. Whatever kind of assessment you go in for, it can easily determine your learners' whole approach to their studies. So it is important to use the kind of assessment appropriate to the kind of learning you want to encourage.

Extra care needed with assessment in S-I

Of course, you may say: "But I've been teaching -- and assessing -- for years. What's new ?" The vital difference is that self-instructional learners are working on their own. Your learners may be anxious about what the assessment task requires of them -- but they may be unable to question you about it, or negotiate how they would like to tackle it. They may not even know other learners with whom they might discuss it. Furthermore, **you** may not know until too late about how your learners' learning is being affected by your assessment demands -- and you may be unable to do much about it, even if you do know. Hence, with self-instruction, assessment needs to be thought out more carefully, and spelled out more explicitly, than is usually the case with face-to-face teaching.

THE NATURE OF ASSESSMENT

at is sessment ?

What is assessment ? I hope we can agree on one thing from the start:

```
************************
*                      *
*  ASSESSMENT ≠ GRADING  *
*                      *
************************
```

Assessment is not to be confused with grading and marking. While you can't grade or mark a learner's work without first assessing it, it is quite feasible (and will sometimes be more appropriate) to assess without going on to award grades or marks.

Gaining knowledge of the learner

Assessment is an attempt to gain knowledge of the learner's response to your teaching. In particular, what is the nature and quality of your learner's learning ? What are each learner's strengths and weaknesses, interests and aversions, fresh achievements and lingering blind spots ?

THE PURPOSES OF ASSESSMENT

Two uses of assessment

Why might we want to gain knowledge about the nature and quality of the learner's learning ? I would identify two main purposes for assessment -- according to the use that is to be made of the results:

1. To aid the learners in their subsequent learning.

2. To report on what they have already learned -- e.g. as a grade or as a written report on each learner.

The first use of assessment is sometimes called **formative**. because it is meant to help form the learner's learning. The second is called **summative** because it sums up what each has achieved.

Formative Assessment

Helping learners to learn

Formative assessment is involved every time you use what you have learned about a learner in order to decide what to say to that learner next. Similarly, your learner may assess his or her own understandings and difficulties in order to decide where next to put his or her efforts. Such **self**-assessment is an essential part of the kind of "pre-recorded" teaching we are discussing in this book. We make use of "activities" (SAQs and ITQs) in order to help the learners monitor and develop their own learning.

Tutors' comments

We may also require the learner to tackle occasional tests and examinations; and these will be assessed by a tutor. Again, the tutor may provide comments that may help the learner to learner. One of the functions of

these more formal exercises may be to let the learners
know how closely their work approximates the standard

*External
expectations*

expected by some **external** examining or qualifying body
that they hope to satisfy.

Summative Assessment

*Reporting
on learners*

The purpose of summative assessment is to report, or put
on record, what is known of the learners' learning. What
did they study ? Did they pass or fail ? What grades
did they get ? Are they now competent to work without
supervision ? Such reports are usually for the benefit of
other teachers, of professional bodies, or of potential
employers.

*Exams and
tests*

The clearest example of summative assessment is the
end-of-course examination. Here, the prime purpose is to
establish what the learners have achieved -- not to give
them feedback that will help them develop their learning.
Mid-course tests and assignments can also be used
summatively, however, if they contribute to the learners'
final grades or reports.

Three General Points

*formative
nd summative
ompared*

o Any one act of assessment can be used **both** formatively
   and summatively.

o Some courses may have **no** summative assessment -- e.g.
   "hobby" or "interest" courses on subjects like amateur
   bee-keeping or managing your household finances.

o **All** courses need formative assessment, preferably
   carried out by someone else in addition to the learner
   -- e.g. by a tutor.

The Timing of Assessment

*en to
sess ?*

**When shall learners be assessed ? As we have noted, their
work can be assessed during the course, lesson by lesson,
and/or at the end of the course. If any of the in-course**

*Continuous
assessment*
assessment is used summatively, it is often called
"continuous assessment". In some courses, the learner's
overall course "result" depends on a combination of
continuous assessment and end-of-course examination.

You will know what kind of assessment will be possible
for your course. What I am talking about in this chapter
will be applicable to any kind. My examples, however,

*Tests for
tutor checking*
will be related specifically to the kind of test or
assignment you might set the learner for checking by a
tutor at the end of a lesson or series of lessons within
a course. (The self-assessment activities you might set
within a lesson are thoroughly discussed in Chapter 6.)

Thus, at the end of every hour or so's study, you might
set your learners a little test on what they have covered

*How long
per test ?*
so far. As a very rough rule of thumb, you might think
5-10 minutes of testing would be about right for an
hour of studying. Of course, you could save these up and
set your learners, say, a half-hour test after three hours
-- or even have them spend a couple of hours on an
assignment for their tutor after about 12 hours of study.
Even if they were to tackle a number of smaller tests, you
might require them to wait until several were completed
before sending them to their tutor for comment.

WHAT TO ASSESS ?

What aspects of the learners' learning will you expect to
assess in your occasional tests or assignments ? Surely
you will wish to assess their attainment of **lesson**

*Test the
objectives*
objectives and their progress towards attainment of the
course objectives. Indeed, in presenting your tests and
assignments, you may wish to remind your learner of which
objective each item relates to. (See Figure 8.3, on
page 177, for an example of this.)

For many teachers, it is only at this stage -- when the
start thinking seriously about how to assess -- that talk
of aims and objectives really begins to make sense. In a

*Test = the
objectives ?*

way, at least from the learner's viewpoint, the assessment
tasks **are** the lesson objectives. For instance, whatever
the lofty aims and objectives you may have in mind, if
learners are eventually assessed merely on how well they
have memorized certain details from the lesson, then
recalling those facts is the **real** objective as far as the
learners are concerned.

True tests

So, when you come to assess what learners have got from
a lesson, it is essential to use methods that truly relate
to **your** aims and objectives (and not to some other possible
aims and objectives). For example, it is all too easy to
set out to teach people, say, how to repair a punctured
tyre -- and yet end up by asking them not to do it but to
write an essay about how to do it !

*sk the
ppropriate
uestion*

More subtle mistakes can be made by assessing a
closely-related (but different) objective. If, for
for instance, our objective were to have the learners
interpret a certain kind of graph, it would be an
innappropriate form of assessment to ask them merely to
draw the graph instead. We cannot necessarily infer the
possession of one ability from seeing the demonstration
of another.

```
******************************************
*                                        *
*   THE QUESTIONS THAT ARE EASIEST        *
*   TO ASK MAY NOT BE THE ONES            *
*   YOU MOST NEED TO HAVE ANSWERED.       *
*                                        *
******************************************
```

METHODS OF ASSESSMENT

*at should
arners do ?*

What will you get the learners to **do** in order to show what
they have learned from your lessons ? Don't put the
finishing touches to the first draft of a lesson before
you've thought about this question. Some writers would
say don't even start the first draft until you have.

For the sake of this discussion, I shall divide
assessment exercises into two broad categories:

*Product v
process
assessment*

o *"Paper-and-pencil exercises"* -- like essays, worked
calculations, multiple-choice tests, project reports;
where there is a physical **product** to assess.

"Situational exercises" -- like discussions,
interviews, performances or displays of learners'
practical skills; where what is assessed is an
activity or **process** that may or may not result in
any physical product.

Paper-and pencil Exercises

The paper-and-pencil test is the most familiar assessment
device, in conventional as well as self-instructional
teaching. It may take the form of a so-called **objective
test**, consisting of various types of multiple-choice
question. Or it may require learners to construct their
own answers -- e.g. in the form of a few words, a
paragraph, an essay, or a report of several thousand words
perhaps with diagrams and calculations.

*Objective and
"own answer"
tests*

"Own answer" tests. The most basic kind of "own answer"
question requires only words or brief phrases as answers.
For example, to draw on the subject of Diet and Nutrition
(as I shall throughout this section):

*Short
answers*

Q. What is the name of the disease affecting
children who eat insufficient protein ?

A. *Kwashiorkor.*

Q. Why is meat considered high quality protein ?

A. *Because it contains amino acids in similar
proportions to human tissue.*

Longer answers can be called for:

Longer
answers

Q. Write a paragraph (not more than 200 words)
    explaining the importance of a balanced diet.

Q. Use your table of Average Energy Requirements
    to calculate the dietary needs of each of the two
    people whose daily activities are listed below. Then
    Then, using the Food Composition tables, evaluate
    the adequacies of their daily diets as given below.

And even
longer

The "own answer" required can be longer still. Learners
might be set an essay of several thousand words on world
food supplies. Or they might be asked to report at similar
length on their own field study of how a group of people
exposed to advice about nutrition have altered their diets.

To present
an argument

Questions requiring such extended answers will usually
be asked when we want the learner to present an **argument** --
an analysis, interpretation or evaluation, reviewing the
relevant facts and coming to some sort of conclusion about
them. Such arguments need not be restricted to essays and
reports. If the situation seemed appropriate, learners
could, for example, be asked to write a letter as if to
the editor of a newspaper, or a review of a book on the
subject, or the script for a television programme about
it, and so on.

markers
may disagree

"Objective tests". One of the problems with "own answer"
exercises is that teachers cannot always agree as to the
quality of the learners' answers. Thus, the same essay,
or even mathematical exercise, might get a different grade
from different teachers -- because they happen to value
different aspects of the learner's performance.

deskilling
the marking

With objective tests, however, the markers' subjective
preferences cannot affect the grades. (That's why they're
called "objective" tests.) Marking could be done by people
quite ignorant of the subject -- or even by a computer.

Multiple-choice questions

Objective tests are composed of multiple-choice questions of one form or another -- e.g. "one from several", "true-false", or "matching".

The "one-from several" question

The most widely useful type of question (or "item") is the "one from several". Here, the item is made up of a question or an incomplete statement, followed by several alternative answers -- one of which answers the question or completes the statement correctly. The learner may be asked to ring or underline the correct answer. For

Two forms

example, here are two ways of asking the same question:

> o Children whose diet is deficient in protein
>   are liable to a disease known as:
>
>   A.   Beri-beri
>   B.   Marasmus
>   C.   Rickets
>   D.   Kwashiorkor
>   E.   Scurvy
>
> o What is the name of the disease to which children
>   are liable if their diet is deficient in protein ?
>
>   A.   Beri-beri
>   B.   Marasmus
>   C.   Rickets
>   D.   Kwashiorkor
>   E.   Scurvy

Which is easier to read ?

Notice that the incomplete statement in the first version above has been replaced by a straightforward question in the second. Often this will be easier for learners to read, especially when the alternative answers are long one

Two-from-several

A variation on this type of question is to let **two** of the answers be correct. In such cases, it is best to offer at least seven alternatives from which the two are to be chosen. (Otherwise, guessing is just too likely to be rewarded.)

Use enough distractors

Even with "one answer from several", it is unwise to use fewer than four "distractors" (as the **incorrect** answer are called). This rule is broken, for instance, by items that merely ask the learner to agree or disagree with a series of statements, e.g.:

   o Children whose diet is deficient in protein
      are liable to Kwashiorkor. TRUE or FALSE ?

Avoid 50/50
questions

Such true/false, yes/no, agree/disagree questions are best
avoided in objective testing. After all, the learner has
a 50-50 chance of guessing the correct answer. There are
other drawbacks. It can be difficult to think up relevant
statements that are indisputably right or indisputably
wrong. In any case, you may think that directing your
learner's attention to statements that are false is rather
a dubious teaching technique.

he
matching"
uestion

The "matching" question is another type of item
occasionally used in objective tests. Here the learner is
given two lists of things and is asked to indicate which
thing in one list belongs with each thing in the other
list, e.g.:

   o Here are the names of seven diseases:

      marasmus, beri-beri, pellagra, rickets,
      heart disease, night-blindness, kwashiorkor

      Which of them do you particularly associate with
      each of the following dietary deficiencies ?
      (Write one disease against each deficiency.)

      1. Vitamin A ....
      2. Vitamin C ....
      3. Vitamin D ....
      4. Protein   ....
      5. Calory   ....

equal
sts

With this kind of question, it is important to have more
things in the first list than in the second. Otherwise,
the learner who knew all but one of the matches would get
that one right automatically. But is we have, say, two or
three more things in one list than in the other, the
learner will still have to choose from three or four
answers for the final match.

nking"
stion

A variation on matching is the "ranking" question.
Here the learners have to decide which thing on the list
ranks first, second, third, etc -- according to some

stated criterion. For example, in the case of the seven diseases mentioned above, learners might be asked to pick out, and arrange in order, the three causing the most fatalities.

Again, the element of guessing may worry some teachers. If you really want to be sure why the learners have chosen the answers they have, you can always ask them to add a note explaining or justifying their answers. This means, of course, that the test will now be a combination of "chosen answer" and "own answer" and must be marked by someone knowledgeable in the subject matter.

Learner's explanation of chosen answer

Nevertheless, such a combination may sometimes be valuable in distance teaching, where the marker may not necessarily meet the learner face to face. The need to explain their answers may reveal those learners who are somehow finding the correct answers in your teaching materials (or in other learners' work) but without really understanding them. Remember:

Useful in distance learning ?

```
***********************************************
*                                             *
*   "OWN ANSWERS" CAN ENABLE YOU TO SEE        *
*   WHAT IS GOING ON IN THE LEARNER'S MIND     *
*   -- "CHOSEN ANSWERS" CANNOT.                *
*                                             *
***********************************************
```

Which to use ? Any one test or assignment can contain both "own answer" and "chosen answer" questions. For which purposes is each best suited ? How do you decide when to use which ?

Mixed tests

Objective questions are most likely to be appropriate when your objectives require that the learner should be able to select from, discriminate between, or decide among a finite range of alternative possibilities. These alternatives might include terms, ideas, quantities, sounds, smells, pictures, actions, objects, and so on.

Appropriate uses for objective questions

*Testing
discrim-
inations*
Thus, if you wanted to test whether your learners could discriminate between the symptoms of pellagra and those of similar diseases, you would need to present them with several "cases" to choose from. **How** to present those cases would be a further problem for you. Would you want the learners to distinguish between written accounts of signs and symptoms, pictures of patients, real patients, or what ? (The fact that learners could recognize a written description might be no indication that they could recognize the real thing.)

*Appropriate
uses for
own-answer
questions*
On the other hand, when our objectives require learners to be able to recall, define, explain, justify, report, invent, sketch out, argue a case, or otherwise come up with their own ideas -- then multiple-choice questions cannot give an appropriate test of their abilities. For such abilities we need "own answer" questions -- even though different assessors may disagree about the quality of a particular answer.

*How long
an answer ?*
As we've already seen, such own-answer exercises may ask for brief responses from the learner, or for extensive ones. In general, we should avoid asking learners for extensive written answers unless we are sure that either:

(a) they already had the necessary compositional skills before beginning the course, or

(b) we are providing tuition in those skills within the course itself.

*Will short
answers
suffice ?*
Even professional adults often turn out to be quite inept -- and certainly unpractised and lacking confidence -- in the writing of essays. This is especially likely to be so in distance courses, where they may have little opportunity to compare their efforts with those of other learners. Short-answer questions (together perhaps with a few multiple-choice items) will often allow for just as thorough a test, and one that is less "contaminated" by

calling on skills that you are not actually aiming to
assess.

Situational Exercises

*Assessing
processes*

Finally in this section, we must mention the kind of
testing in which we assess on-going **processes** -- like the
we assess a learner's ability to carry out an interview
or to prepare a meal following principles of hygiene and
nutrient preservation. To do so, we must be present in
the situation in which the learner is displaying the
ability.

*When products
are
unrevealing*

Such situational assessment is necessary when there is
no assessable product resulting from the learner's
activity. For instance, we might not be able to tell from
the state of the interviewed person or completed meal
(nor from any report the learner might make on either of
these processes) whether the learner had or had not
followed acceptable procedures.

*Must observe
...perhaps
with a
checklist*

If your objectives are concerned with **how** your learners
do or make something, or how they interact with other
people -- then there may be no proper substitute for
watching them, or listening to them do it. For such
assessment, it is useful to produce a checklist of the
points you'll be looking for in their performance. This
will be especially useful if **someone else** has to do the
assessment for you and give you a report. Figure 13.1
opposite is an example of a checklist for use in observing
a learner perform a trouble-shooting task. It tells the
assessor how to describe the task to the learner, what to
look for in the learner's performance, and how to arrive
at a grade.

*Assessing
recorded
performances*

In some cases, it may be possible to assess a learner'.
ability by listening to an audiotape, or viewing a
videotape, of the learner carrying out a practical
activity that you cannot observe "in the flesh". But

Figure 13.1: Checklist for a Situational Test
(Reproduced by permission of the National Coal Board)

     C.198/28

NATIONAL COAL BOARD   COLLIERY APPRENTICE ELECTRICIANS   IT 8

TEST CENTRE.. NAME .... No. ....

DATE ....

Connecting up a three wire signalling system   60 mins.

Connect up the system comprising:

         Two Bells
         Two relays/relay unit
         Two pushes or keys

Check for operation. If you cannot complete the wiring without a circuit diagram you should either draw the diagram yourself or ask the Examiner for one. If the Examiner has to give you a diagram he will deduct some marks from your score but you will not fail the test because of that alone. When checking any safety devices make sure that the Examiner knows you are doing it. Assume you are working below ground in a safety lamp mine. Do not spend more than ten minutes on drawing the diagram.

NB – One of the faults shown below must be prepared on the equipment prior to the test without the candidate's knowledge.

Show by X which of these faults the candidate was required to diagnose and rectify

☐ PUSH/KEY CONTACTS NOT MAKING   ☐ BELL NOT RINGING   ☐ SUPPLY FAILURE

SECTION A. Did the candidate make correct connections to: *(Enter in each box a tick for YES, a cross for NO)*

     ☐ Bells
     ☐ Relays/relay unit
     ☐ Pushes/keys
     ☐ Battery/transformer

SECTION B. Did he check that any intrinsic safety devices:

     ☐ Were in place
     ☐ Were correctly connected

     If the system did not function satisfactorily, did he:

     ☐ Locate the fault
     ☐ Rectify the fault

SECTION C. Did he:

     ☐ Check the operation from both pushes/keys
     ☐ Connect all wires securely
     ☐ Make sure that wiring looked neat and tidy
     ☐ Replace and secure all covers and screws
     ☐ Carry out all connections without the aid of a diagram supplied by the examiner
     ☐ Have a systematic approach to fault location

GRADING. Enter in the box the grade awarded for this test

☐   Candidates should be graded as follows:

     Grade A – Where ALL items in Sections A and B and at least 4 items from Section C are ticked
     Grade B – Where ALL items in Sections A and B and at least 2 items from Section C are ticked
     Grade C – Where ALL items in Sections A and B and less than 2 items from Section C are ticked
     Grade D – Where ALL items in either Section A or Section B are ticked
     Grade E – Where both Sections (A & B) include at least one item marked with a cross

Signed .... *Examiner*

such an alternative might prove inconvenient and costly
and still not enable you to be confident about the
learner's ability.

Setting an Assignment

*Four
main
issues*

So what are the main points to bear in mind when setting
a test or assignment for learners ? Perhaps there are
four main issues to make decisions about:

How big ?

o *How big should the assignment be ?* That is, how
   much time can you reasonably expect your learners
   to put into it -- bearing in mind the amount of
   time they have devoted to learning since the
   previous test or assignment ? (If the assignment
   or test can be seen as contributing to the
   learner's learning -- rather than merely allowing
   its practice or application -- then proportionate
   more time might be allotted to it.)

What testing ?

o *What kinds of exercise might be appropriate ?*
   Follow this guiding principle: Do not set any
   assessment question without asking yourself why y
   are setting it, what underlying knowledge, skill
   attitude it is supposed to be testing, and how it
   relates to important learning objectives.

Feedback ?

o *What feedback might learners be given ?* How can
   learners be provided with feedback that will help
   them learn from their attempt at the assignment ?
   With objective tests, they can, at the very least
   be told what the correct answers were (if not why)
   With "own answer" questions, they need a tutor's
   comments and advice on the work they have produce
   (More about this in the final section of this
   chapter.)

Questions ?

o *How to formulate the questions ?* Many books have
   been written about how to design assessment
   exercises, and I have no space to paraphrase them

here. However, to supplement what I have said on the
subject in the preceding pages, let me add the following:

Writing own-answer questions. With questions (or practical
exercises) that require learners to produce a response
rather than choose among several they are offered, we must
make clear **what kind** of response is required of them.
Suppose, for example, you were asked to answer this
question:

> Is it true that only psychology can provide us
> with valid explanations of criminal behaviour ?

It may occur to you that you could produce some sort of
answer without having a scrap of knowledge about psychology.
After all, you'd need only show that criminal behaviour
can **also** be explained in other terms, e.g. economic,
social, or political.

But would your answer satisfy the markers ? Perhaps
not -- because they might want you to answer it from
particular points of view, or in such a way as to
demonstrate your familiarity with certain approved
authorities on the subject.

And even if you guessed what kind of answer they wanted
from you, you might still be giving them far more of it
than they required. You don't know how big your answer
is supposed to be. You could answer in one word -- No !
(or Yes ! if that's the way you see it) -- or your answer
could fill a very fat volume of case studies and analysis.
Perhaps neither of these is quite what the marker, or the
setter, of the question is looking for.

But why should the learner be left to guess what is
required ? Fortunately, the authors of the assignment
have anticipated our objections. They have provided
detailed notes of guidance for learners. As you'll see
in Figure 13.2 overleaf, they not only say what kind and
how big an answer is required, but also give guidance on

(margin notes:)
Saying
what is
required

...ould you
...atisfy the
...arkers ?

...w big ?

...idance
...eded

how to set about tackling the question. Will your
learners sometimes need such specific guidance ?

Figure 13.2: Assignment Notes for the Learner
(from Open University course D101)

QUESTION AND STUDENT NOTES

This week's assignment consists of a short exercise based on the
four accounts which make up section 3 of Unit 2 (i.e. the pieces
by Sullivan, McIntosh, Worth and Stevens). In not more than 500
words tackle the following topic:

Examine the argument that only psychology can provide us with
valid explanations of criminal behaviour.

1.   Reread through section 3.3.2 'Explanations of behaviour',
     p.84, noting the ways in which explanations of behaviour
     may differ: selection of causal factors, levels of analysis,
     concepts, models.

2.   Write about each of these differences, illustrating them
     from the four accounts in section 3. You might, for example,
     in discussing the second difference, 'that description or
     explanation may be at different "levels of analysis", show
     how McIntosh locates her explanation of the organization of
     thieving in the conflictful nature of society whereas
     Stevens includes genetic and personality factors in his account

3.   When you have completed the analysis above, read the second
     paragraph of section 3.3.2 and try to relate what it says
     (i.e. that different explanations do nto necessarily conflict)
     to what you have so far thought and written. Then go back to
     the original argument about psychology and try to come to a
     conclusion.

4.   Finally, reread what you have written, making sure that your
     ideas are relevant, read clearly, and are expressed precisely.

---

*How much
detail
needed ?*

For some assignment exercises -- especially if your
learners are not in regular contact with tutors or other
learners -- you may wish to give similarly detailed
guidance. For other assignments (and for learners who
can discuss the questions with tutors or other learners),
this will not be necessary.

*A side-
effect of
detailing*

Remember that the more guidance you give as to what
kind of answer is expected, the less chance your learners
have of demonstrating that they do not **need** such guidance

Where you draw the line must depend on your objectives. If you give your learners too many hints and clues, you may be cueing them to demonstrate achievement not of the objectives you initially had in mind but of some lesser, more restricted ones, instead.

Shifting objectives ?

As an illustration, look at the sequence of questions below. They all concern the Swedish political system. But each requires a rather different performance from the learner; each one is testing rather different abilities and insights:

Which question to ask ?

Qu. 1 What aspects of the political system of modern Sweden seem to you most worthy of comment?

Qu. 2 Comment on the political stability of modern Sweden.

Qu. 3 Explain the political stability of modern Sweden.

Qu. 4 Identify and discuss three factors that might help explain the political stability of modern Sweden.

Qu. 5 Identify and discuss three factors that might help explain the emergence of a stable political system in Sweden despite the massive social and economic changes engendered by processes of modernization.

Qu. 6 Which *three* of the factors listed below might best help explain the emergence of a stable political system in Sweden despite the massive social and economic changes engendered by processes of modernization?
(a) Affluence
(b) Gradual economic development
(c) Traditional legitimacy
(d) Civic culture
(e) A homogeneous political culture
(f) Equality
(g) Congruent authority patterns
(h) Elite consensus
(i) The habituation of mechanisms of conflict resolution
(j) Political institutionalization

ducing earner's sponsibility

One by one, the questions become more specific -- leaving the learner less and less responsibility for deciding what is significant about the situation referred to, and in what terms to respond to it. For instance, the learner answering Question 1 may choose not to discuss political **stability**. The learner answering Question 2 may choose to describe political stability without **explaining** it. The learner answering Question 3 may choose to refer to more or to fewer than **three** factors. And so on.

Finally, Question 6 takes multiple-choice form. It tests merely whether the learner can recognize the three crucial factors when they are presented in a list. It could be followed by further multiple-choice questions taking each of the ten suggested factors in turn and asking "If this was one of the three factors you chose, which of the statements below best explains the

Different
abilities
being
tested

contribution made by that factor". But such a sequence of multiple-choice questions would **not** be testing the same abilities as, say, Questions 3 or 4.

Writing multiple-choice items. Here I am concentrating on the "one from several" items that are the staple of objective tests.

Eradicate
irrelevent
difficulties

The essence of writing such a question is to ensure that learners who have the necessary understanding are able to answer it correctly -- while those without it are not. To ensure the first of these, be careful not to introduce **irrelevant** difficulties -- e.g. don't ask "Which of the following is the eponymous hero of a novel by Charles Dickens ?" when it is more appropriate to ask "Which of the following names refers both to the hero and the title of a novel by Charles Dickens ?" (If you wanted to test the learner's understanding of the word "eponymous", this should be done in a separate question.)

Avoid
give-aways

To ensure that learners **without** the knowledge are unable (without guessing) to pick out the correct answers you must be careful to avoid "give-aways". Let me illustrate this, in Figure 13.3 opposite, with a test that breaks every "rule" in the book. Glancing through it, you may feel that its subject-matter is somewhat unfamiliar. Don't let that worry you. The test contains a number of "give-aways" that should enable you to identify the correct answers despite knowing nothing about the (totally fictitious) subject.

Figure 13.3: Spot the Give-aways in this Objective Test

For each of the eight items, underline the <u>one</u> answer
you believe to be correct. Maximum time: 15 minutes

1. The main function of dingle-grabblers is to ruthe

   A. dingles
   B. growks
   C. snitters
   D. beegums

2. Regrallification becomes necessary when

   A. the gudges noogle
   B. the rakob flanes trelsate, and the vosts fail to flonce
   C. the breg fribbles
   D. the hooluphs elgage

3. Nuriles are trassed by yukhorrhoea because

   A. all their obblers are sushed
   B. their fleepers are always tolloidable
   C. the ning-daphle is usually runged
   D. their snarms are never grovid

4. Non-abordal nittering usually involves an

   A. dacklex
   B. grumeld
   C. telloid
   D. ustbile

5. Which of the following are the results of sub-foping ?

   A. grazzed allops and mulced crips
   B. rakols juckested by snallums
   C. a bralious inflaction of plabsts
   D. trass-lomphed vallicles in gled

6. Which of the following is/are essential for breg-slepping ?

   A. stost and rune
   B. rune
   C. phyke and rune
   D. rune and molp

7. The ustbile can be used in

   A. slunthing
   B. freeping
   C. nittering
   D. grunging

8. Which of the following is the correct alternative ?

   A.
   B.
   C. ◄ Don't worry: there's nothing missing here ! DR
   D.

Answers (and comments) overleaf...

*Faults in
questioning*

Here are the answers to the test items shown in
Figure 13.3 -- together with advice on how to avoid the
writing errors illustrated in that test:

1. **A** Don't allow the "correct answer" to contain an
    unintended clue -- e.g. a word (like "dingles")
    that is naturally associated with a word in the
    "stem" (the introductory statement or question).

2. **B** Don't let the correct answer be much longer or
    more detailed than the "distractors".

3. **C** Don't write distractors with qualifying terms that
    are too embracing (e.g. "never", "always") making
    the learner so suspicious as to reject them in
    favour of the more moderate correct answer.

4. **D** Make sure that all answers are consistent with "a"
    or "an" if it is used in the stem.

5. **A** Make all the answers consistent with any single or
    plural verb used in the stem.

6. **B** Don't let one answer be an instance of (or be
    included in) one of the others. (Here, for
    example, if A, C or D were correct, B would have
    to be correct also.)

7. **C** Don't let one item in a test contain a clue as to
    how another item should be answered. (Compare
    item 7 with item 4.)

8. **D** Vary the placing of the correct answer, so as
    to avoid so obvious a pattern as appears here.

*Evaluating
your assessment*

```
******************************************
*                                        *
*  WHETHER OWN-ANSWER OR MULTIPLE-CHOICE, *
*                                        *
*  BE PREPARED TO MODIFY YOUR QUESTIONS  *
*                                        *
*  AFTER TRYING THEM OUT ON LEARNERS.    *
*                                        *
******************************************
```

HOW TO USE ASSESSMENT RESULTS

In response to the questions in our tests and assignments,
learners say and do things. These "things" are the
"results" of assessment. As I mentioned at the beginning
of this chapter, we can use the results in two different

Reporting
and/or
teaching

ways. We can use them to report on the learners' work --
e.g. by grading or marking. Or we can use them as the
basis for teaching -- for helping our learners learn
something new. Or, of course, we can do both.

Reporting on Achievement

As I mentioned earlier, grading (or marking) is not a
necessary part of assessment. That is, we can appraise
our learners' work -- reporting to them or to someone
else about what we find strong, weak or interesting in
it -- without needing to attach a letter grade, percentage

erbal
eports

mark, or the like. That is, we can use words to **describe**
what we see in the work. (Such a verbal report could lead
into teaching the learner, as we discuss in the next
section.)

.as well
grades
d scores

In many situations, however, you will need to report
in terms of letter grades or numerical scores rather than
(or perhaps as well as) words. As an experienced teacher,
you are unlikely to see much of a problem in marking
learners' tests and assignments -- provided you do it
yourself. However, with self-instructional teaching, you
may need to share this task with colleagues.

will be
king ?

At least some of your learners may have their work
assessed by other teachers (call them "tutors") acting on
your instructions. Or perhaps you will have assignments
marked by "proctors" -- advanced learners who have been
through the lessons earlier and are now acting as aides
to you or a tutor. In either of these cases, the question

aring
ks are
ropriate

is: How do you ensure that the mark given to a
particular piece of work is pretty much the same as you
would have given it **if** you had marked it yourself ?

*Three
approaches
to marking*

Impression v analytic marking.   There seem to be three
different approaches to marking an assignment:

1.   impression marking
2.   analytic marking
3.   some sort of compromise between 1 and 2.

With impression marking (much used for essays), one gets
an overall impression of the worth of the work, and gives
an appropriate mark. With analytic marking, one follows
a pre-arranged mark-scheme. The marker is asked to look
for certain features in learners' answers and give so
many marks for this point and so many marks for another.
A clear example would be an arithmetic test where each
expected answer is specified precisely -- and the marker
is instructed to give one mark for each correct answer
and no marks for working that is only partially correct.

*When to
provide a
mark-scheme*

When your assignment consists of a number of short
own-answer questions (or even a practical task), you may
find it quite straightforward to provide assessors with
an analytic mark-scheme. Suppose, for instance, you were
setting items like these:

1.   List the principal components of a balanced diet
     and describe briefly the function of each in the body.

2.   Name five diseases caused by inadequate or
     unbalanced diet.

3.   Calculate the amount of
     (a)   energy
     (b)   protein
     (c)   vitamins A, B, C and D
     (d)   calcium and iron
     in the attached recipe (using food composition tables).

4.   Prepare a meal using the attached recipe, taking all
     necessary steps to minimize loss of nutrients during
     the preparation.

Here it should be possible to tell the marker what to lo
for (and reward) in each case. You could, in fact, give
"model answers". Even with item 4 -- a practical test
where the process rather than the product is to be

assessed -- you could provide the marker with a **check-list**
(like Figure 13.1 on page 313) against which to score
the learner's performance. Furthermore, you could tell

Example of a
mark-scheme
the marker that:

> Item 1 is to be marked out of 12 (1 point for the name
> of each component, 1 point for its function);
>
> Item 2 is to be marked out of 5 (1 point for each
> disease);
>
> Item 3 is to be marked out of 20 (5 points for each
> correct calculation); and
>
> Item 4 is to be marked out of 30 (with so many points
> being deducted for each step not properly
> carried out).

ot so
isy with
issays
However, it is not so easy to devise an analytic mark-
scheme when what you are expecting from learners is an
extended "own answer", e.g. an essay. Look for example
at the "Tutor Notes" in Figure 13.4 overleaf. They were
provided for markers by the author of the essay question
on explaining criminal behaviour that I printed in the
previous section (page 316). (Incidentally, a question
you may like to ask yourself when telling learners what
fferent
formation
· learners
I tutors ?
to include in answers, and markers what to look for in
them, is: How far are you justified in giving **different**
information to each ?)

The notes in Figure 13.4 seem to represent a compromise
approach to marking. They are partly analytic in that
ompromise
roach
tutors are directed to look for certain factors in the
learners' answers. But much is left to each tutor's
impressions as to how much weight to give to one factor
compared with another. Thus, markers might not agree very
closely as to a given learner's grade. (The "teaching"
comments they gave the learner might be quite different
also.)

Figure 13.4:   Tutors' Notes for Assignment Marking
(from Open University course D101)

Assignment 1   TUTOR NOTES

This assignment is intended to get students to think about the nature of explanation in social science by applying some method-ological principles discussed in Section 3.3.2. of Unit 2 to the explanations of crime that are given in Section 3.

Typical answers that follow the suggested framework will consist of a brief paraphrase of each principle (illustrated by examples drawn from the four printed accounts). Direct quotation from Section 3.3.2. is not excluded, though try to check that examples reflect an understanding of the principle that is being quoted. Reward students for clarity and selectivity as against extensive coverage and exemplification which neither reveal understanding nor keep to the 500 words limit.

Students have been asked to come to a conclusion about the explanatory power of psychology in comparison with the other social sciences in question. The conclusion, on one side or the other, or more probably that hinted at in the student notes, is less important than the discussion that has led up to it.

Other frameworks are admissible provided the student has tried to answer the question set. Students may introduce further ways in which explanations differ or want to question what is noted at the beginning of 3.3.2, that social science explanation is based on a deterministic assumption. Reward these provided they contribute to a coherent, relevant answer.

Pros and cons of precise guidance

In general, with open-ended own-answer questions, it is difficult to guide the marker very precisely without exposing learners to the risk that their good (but unpredicted) points will fail to get rewarded. Non-specific guidance, on the other hand, means that a learner's grade will be very dependent on who marks his or her work.

"Agreement exercises"

Where you are relying heavily on impression marking, may be essential to get your markers together for an "agreement exercise" -- letting them all compare the mar[ ] they would give to some sample answers -- before they

start awarding grades in earnest. You may also need to
monitor their marking, from assignment to assignment, by
occasionally marking some of their learners' work yourself.
How much divergence you can tolerate from the grade you
yourself would have awarded may be another issue you need
to resolve.

*Producing
an overall
score/grade*

An overall score. Finally, if you are setting a test or
assignment or examination consisting of several different
items, your markers may need to be told how to reach an
overall score for each learner. Do they simply add up the
marks for each of the separate items and give the "total
achieved" as a fraction of the "total possible" score --
e.g. $5/10 + 8/12 + 11/15 + 9/15 + 16/20 = 49/72$?
Or do they convert it to a percentage ? Or do they arrive
at a letter grade, using some such arbitrary conversion
scale as: 1-14 = E; 15-24 = D; 25-44 = C; 45-59 = B; and
60-72 = A ? If you are a member of a course team, the
procedure will clearly need to be decided in discussion
with your colleagues.

*iscussing
rks with
arners*

Discussing the marking. Will you and/or your markers be
meeting learners face to face ? Or will you merely be
marking work that is sent in to you ? In the former case,
the marking might beneficially be discussed with the
learner -- or even carried out in his or her presence. It
would certainly be possible for markers to question their
learners further about answers that were only partially
correct. They could also ask learners to restate such
answers, or explain them more fully, before deciding a
final mark.

*m marking
tutoring*

The possibility of such discussion -- which could take
place by telephone or even, at a pinch, by letter -- leads
us into the second way of using assessment results.
Regardless of whether or not learners' work is to be
awarded marks and grades, you will still need to consider

how the learners might be helped by the comments and
suggestions of a tutor.

Teaching Through Assessment

*Helping
learners
learn*

Assessment results reveal the learner's strengths and
weaknesses. They therefore suggest where he or she might
be helped by a teacher.

*Teaching
through
discussion*

If the marker is meeting the learner face to face after
the assignment -- and especially if he or she is marking
in the learner's presence -- it is easy to move from
assessing into teaching. A faulty answer will give rise
to discussion; the marker will attempt to elicit the cause
of the lack of understanding and can, there and then, help
the learner to overcome it. The marker becomes **tutor**.

*Teaching
in writing*

If tutors are not meeting learners face to face (or
talking with them on the telephone), they must do rather
as you are doing -- that is, teach the learner in **writing**.
Here they will have an advantage over you, however. They
will be teaching a limited range of points to a particular
learner whose specific difficulties they have already seen
evidence of in his or her completed assignment. Even if
they are also talking with their learners from time to
time, tutors should be encouraged to make the most of
their opportunity to teach through written **comments** and
advice when they return assignments to their learners.

*Deciding on
priorities*

They should be encouraged to direct their comments at
what they believe to be the chief strengths and weaknesse
of each piece of work. They have to decide their teachin
priorities. In order to most benefit the learner, they
may ignore some minor weaknesses in order to help the
learner remedy the major ones. For example, a particular
learner's written report may strike the tutor as poorly
organized, factually inaccurate, full of spelling mistake
and missing the point of the assignment. Yet the tutor
might choose to disregard the first three weaknesses in

order to comment and advise solely on the last one. Here
the tutor might be conscious that there is a limit to the
range of criticism and advice a learner can take at any
one time -- and that even the best organized, most
accurate and immaculately spelled report is wasted if it
is not what the assignment asked for.

Types of tutor-comment. If you want your markers to
provide this tutorial feedback on learners' work, they will
need to consider the variety of types of comment that are
possible. Essentially, you will be asking them to write
down remarks and suggestions that will help their learners
think again about what they have done, and about how they
might do differently another time. The tutor's written
remarks need to convey what he or she would have had to
say if it had been possible to meet the learner face to
face. (With distance learners, it's no good scribbling
"See me !")

Nor will it be sufficient merely to pepper the learner's
work with ticks and crosses and question-marks, underlining
or circling a word here and there. Verbal comments are
essential. But generalized statements of appraisal are
not sufficiemt. Suppose the following remarks were **all**
that a tutor had written on a learner's script:

> *This is quite a fair piece and you
> make a number of points well.
> But some are rather less
> well illustrated than others and
> the argument is sometimes
> weak or not fully expressed.*

These remarks may well be true, but they are unlikely to
help the learner improve. They are too general. The
learner needs to be told precisely **where** and **how** he or she
has illustrated less well, argued weakly, or expressed
less than fully. The learner might also be told what he
or she might have done to avoid these faults.

*Don't
ignore
positive
features*

      However, the above tutor can at least be commended for starting off with some words of encouragement. Some tutors seem to notice only the faults in a learner's work and neglect to mention its positive aspects. Learners won't thank you (or learn much) if all the comments bring them is unrelieved gloom. They need to be told their work has some redeeming features -- or at least some realistic prospect of improving.

      Here are some of the ways in which tutors might teach through their written comments on assignments. You will no doubt be able to identify many more in your discussions with your own tutors or in your own tutoring. Written comments may:

*Some ways of
teaching
through
feedback
comments*

o   Draw the learners' attention to facts they have overlooked or misinterpreted.

o   Suggest alternative explanations or interpretations.

o   Guide learners on the handling of evidence.

o   Show how to use quotations from texts.

o   Draw attention to gaps in the learners' reasoning.

o   Suggest how learners might present their ideas more effectively.

o   Offer new data that will help learners extend their understanding.

o   Ask for further explanation of muddled answers.

o   Demonstrate short-cuts in problem-solving.

o   Draw attention to how a piece of work might have been improved, e.g. in content, balance or logic.

o   Point out relationships between the learners' present work and their earlier work.

o   Commend the learners for any unexpected insights, special efforts or improvement in skills.

The
importance
of tone

Adopting the right tone. The tone of the tutor's remarks is very important. For instance, such comments as those below (all authentic) might be expected to do more harm than good to the tutor-learner relationships:

Examples
of inept
tone

> *This just won't do.*
> *Style !*
> *Disorganized and inchoate.*
> *Your spelling is atrocious.*
> *Clap-trap.*
> *You must get your facts straight.*

Yet the tutor-concern behind such impulsive remarks can be turned into positive guidance -- without sounding
on't sneer
r scold...
either condescending or threatening. Below, for example, are some more comments collected from the margins of learners' assignments. Each has the flavour of **dialogue**
t pursue
nderstanding
in which the tutor is seeking clarification, evidence, or amplification -- or is drawing learners' attention to errors or anomalies -- or is trying to stretch their thinking:

amples of
obing but
n-censorious
mments

o *The meaning is not very clear here. I find what
  it appears to mean very unlikely. Can you
  quote the figures ?*

o *Important point but needs broadening out from the
  specific example. Also did any benefits accrue
  for schools and children ?*

o *If you had given the electronic structures of neon
  and sodium it would have helped show the essential
  difference between them.*

o *Your answer is OK as far as it goes but you do not
  explain why the drop in IE is so large. Look again
  at Figure 7 of the unit and ask yourself what is so
  special about the electronic structure of neon and
  how does it differ from that of sodium.*

o *Yes it is very difficult to assess the effectiveness of the party, either locally or nationally, in this role. I would have welcomed an example on a local issue known to you.*

o *Comment on the results, Chris. Why is there, do you think, such a difference between the least and the greatest ? Should these be taken into the average ?*

Questions rather than answers

Notice that good tutor-commenting may depend more on asking stimulating questions than on providing ready-made answers. As a final example, here is one tutor's response (a kind of mini-tutorial) to a learner's mathematics assignment. The tutor's questions lead the learner in a new approach to the set problem -- which is to decide, given that Set (i) $\{\wedge, \vee, \sim\}$ is an adequate set of connectives, whether Set (ii) $\{\square, \sim\}$ is an adequate set

What does $\{\wedge, \vee, \sim\}$ being an adequate set of connectives mean ? All connectives can be written in terms of $\{\wedge, \vee, \sim\}$.
How do we show that $\{\square, \sim\}$ is an adequate set ? By showing all connections can be written in terms of $\{\square, \sim\}$.
Knowing Set (i) how do we show Set (ii) ? In other words, how can we replace Set (i) by Set (ii) ? How do they differ ?

Guiding your tutors. So, if other people will be marking your learners' tests and assignments, or just offering comments on them, what can you do to help ensure those people give useful advice. Here are five ways of helping

Five ways of helping tutors

1. Discuss with markers the importance of teaching-type comments, and how they might usefully be made. Draw their attention to types of comment, tone, and the need for learners to receive the tutor's response as quickly as possib

2. Show the markers some examples of good and bad commenting on typical learners' work.

3. Ask each marker to examine a few pieces of
    learners' work and record the comments he or she
    would make to each learner to aid improvement.
    (You should do this too.) Then compare notes and
    seek consensus as to how best to help such
    help such learners.

4. Produce general notes of guidance for marking
    tests, assignments or examinations on your course.
    But also produce specific guidance notes about
    each separate piece of work that is to be marked
    and commented on. (See the examples on pages
    323 and 324.)

5. Monitor your markers' marking and commenting,
    from time to time. Find out how the learners
    feel about the kind of feedback (written or
    spoken) they are getting. Have "refresher"
    discussions with any markers whose commenting is
    not as helpful as it could be -- or whose marking
    is too tough, too lenient, or too inconsistent.

*lways
*rovide
eedback

Final reminder. Don't forget that even with objective
test items (multiple-choice questions), learners can still
be given valuable feedback that will help them review
their work and improve it. At the very least, they can be
told which are the preferred answers. Better still, they
can also be told why. Furthermore, for every question
they may have gone astray on, they can be directed to
specific teaching material in order to brush up their
understanding. Similarly, even with an end-of-course
examination, it is worth considering how learners might
be given feedback that might help consolidate their
learning or aid their approach to future courses.

SUMMARY

Here, to sum up, are the main questions you will need to
answer when planning your assessment strategy:

*The main
concerns
for an
assessment
strategy*

1. Is there any necessity for occasional tests or assignments ? Or will the self-assessment encouraged by "activities" be sufficient ?

2. If you do need tests or assignments, how frequent should they be ? And how time-consuming ?

3. Which of them can be self-assessed, and which should be sent to a tutor for marking and/or comments ?

4. Which lesson or course objectives will each test or assignment be aimed at ?

5. What kinds of question -- e.g. objective or own-answer (short or long) -- are appropriate ?

6. How can questions best be posed so as to reveal the learners' true knowledge, skills and attitudes ?

7. If some objectives need "situational" assessment (in the presence of an assessor), how can this be arranged ?

8. Must some assessment be carried out under controlled conditions -- e.g. to a time-limit, in the presence of an invigilator, and without access to reference books or consultation with colleagues ? (In other words, is a formal examination needed ?)

9. How can learners be provided with appropriate feedback that will aid their learning ?

*Compare these
with the
questions on
pages 76/77*

10. How can the marking and/or commenting of tutors be made as effective as possible ?

```
*************************************************
*                                               *
*   DO ALL YOU CAN TO MAKE EACH ASSESSMENT      *
*   A LEARNING EXPERIENCE -- AND NOT JUST A      *
*   FORMAL CHECK-UP ON WHAT HAS BEEN             *
*   LEARNED ALREADY.                             *
*                                               *
*************************************************
```

14. EVALUATING YOUR LESSONS

*Why
evaluate ?*

However carefully you design a lesson, you can't expect to produce perfection in your first draft. It will be capable of improvement -- either in its subject-matter content or in the effectiveness of its teaching (or both). Hence the need for evaluation.

WHAT IS EVALUATION ?

*answering
questions*

Evaluation is the process of getting various people's reactions to your course or lesson -- with a view to improving it. What do people think of your lesson ? What is it like to work with ? How effectively does it teach ? What unexpected problems arise ? What needs changing ? These are the kinds of question that evaluation might answer.

Why Bother ?

*convincing
others*

There are many reasons why you should care about evaluation. One reason is that many people may need **convincing** that your new approach to teaching is worthwhile -- especially if self-instruction is not yet well-established in your institution. You may need to prove to sceptical administrators, employers and other teachers that the results can be as good as, if not better than, those obtained by the traditional lecture-plus-textbook approach.

*convincing
yourself*

*improve
learning*

Also, you may need convincing yourself that all your planning and preparation time has been well spent. The chief and educational reason for caring about evaluation, however, is that it can lead to noticeable **improvements** in your teaching -- and therefore in your learners' learning.

Types of Evaluation

In this chapter, I discuss three types of evaluation, the second of which has two forms. I list them below in the order in which you would normally carry them out:

Three types of evaluation

o Critical commenting.

o Developmental testing -- including face-to-face tryout and field trials.

o Continuous monitoring.

CRITICAL COMMENTING

In this form of evaluation, you get people to read your draft lesson carefully and offer you their critical but, let's hope, constructive comments. Who might usefully read it and offer such comment ? You might ask:

Who might comment ?

- fellow course team members (if you have any);

- other subject-matter experts;

- tutors who are familiar with learners like yours; and

- learners who have recently been studying in the same subject area.

Kinds of comment

Such "critical friends" may take issue with you over fundamental matters of content, style, and teaching strategy. Or they may find nothing to suggest but minor enhancements. Either way, their response may well be sufficient to renew your own incentive to take a fresh hard look at the material -- and do more critical commenting of your own -- before trying it out on some learners new to the subject.

Course Team Discussions

If you are working in a course team, it is essential that **at least one** of your colleagues should be persuaded to offer you considered comments on your lesson. These can either be put in writing or be spoken face-to-face, privately or in a course team meeting. Course team

The pros

discussion of each draft lesson can be valuable. Matter general principle often emerge and lesson authors can le from discussion of one another's drafts. However, such

and
the cons

group analysis can be threatening to the individual author unless the working relationship is a sympathetic and mutually supportive one.

Figure 14.1: Extracts from a Subject-matter Expert's Comments on a Lesson about Educational Administration

Page 30

I was very impressed by the organization chart. But do make clear that this is just an example (and not very typical).

Page 31

Para 7.3 will get you shot ! If you go to press suggesting that the Chairman is the political adviser to the Chief Education Officer you will be slaughtered -- quite rightly. The CEO is the professional adviser to the Education Committee. You have it exactly back-to-front.

Page 33

There are LEAs which are not Counties. Please try not to make students think their County Council representative is automatically an LEA representative, or that all Counties are LEAs and Districts are not. I know it is complicated, but it is important.

Page 35

What a nice Authority your Mr Edwards works for. In most authorities I have known, a letter like that from an AEO would produce apoplexy all round. Formality is still the order of the day. You may not like it, but it is so, and the course should reflect it.

Page 41

The management of the Council as a body (rather than as a collection of separate enterprises) is a fairly simple concept which you seem to have hidden behind jargon ("corporate management") that the student will not understand.

Areas of Commenting

There are two main aspects upon which you might invite
critical comments:

- subject-matter content; and

Two aspects

- likely teaching effectiveness.

You may ask all your commenters to consider both; or you
may ask some to concentrate on one aspect and some on
another. For instance, you might send your lessons to
subject-experts (inside and outside your institution) to
comment on content; while you get tutors and experienced
learners to speculate about the likely teaching

*Specialized
commenting ?*

effectiveness of your materials. Figure 14.1 shows the
kind of useful comments that may come in from a subject
expert -- in this case, an expert on educational
administration.

You may wish to offer your commenters a **checklist** to
guide them as to the kinds of issue you'd like them to
address. Here are two checklists, one for subject-matter
content and one for likely teaching effectiveness. They
are simply examples; you may well have more apt questions
of your own that you'd want to ask.

Subject-matter Content -- Checklist

*Questions
about
content*

o Are the aims and objectives sufficiently explicit ?

o Do the aims seem worthwhile and relevant to what
learners perceive as their needs ?

o Do the objectives support the aims ?

o Are there any additional aims and objectives that
should be included ?

o Is the content appropriate to the objectives ?

o Is it factually correct ?

o Is it up-to-date ?

o Are there any important omissions ?

o Is there any redundant material ?

o Does the material hang together logically ?

o Does it avoid over-simplification and
   over-generalization ?

o Is it balanced, and careful to recognize
   opposing viewpoints where appropriate ?

o Does it use evidence responsibly ?

o Does it contain any unsatisfactory examples,
   analogies or case studies ?

Likely Teaching Effectiveness -- Checklist

*Questions
about likely
effectiveness*

o Will learners understand what is expected of them ?
   (Is there enough study guidance ?)

o Do you think learners will have difficulty achieving
   any of the listed objectives ?

o How long would you expect learners to take over
   each section ?

o Does the material seem pitched at the right level
   of difficulty and interest for the intended learners ?

o Do the examples, analogies and case studies seem
   relevant to learners' interests and are they
   sufficiently illuminating ?

o Can you suggest any additional examples, analogies
   and case studies ?

o Can you identify any sections that are likely to
   cause **problems** for learners ? Why ?

o Are all new terms adequately explained ?

o Is the number and distribution of activities and/or
   self-tests about right ?

o   Are all the activities worthwhile and practicable ?

o   Does the assignment or suggested follow-up activity (if any) seem appropriate ?

o   Can you suggest any further ideas for activities, tests or assignments ?

Summary

So, here is a rough order of events concerning the type of evaluation we've discussed so far:

Order of events

1.   Decide who might offer useful comments.
2.   Finish your first "public" draft.
3.   Send it to the "critical friends" named in 1.
4.   Revise your lesson in the light of comments.
5.   Proceed to next stage of evaluation --
        developmental testing.

DEVELOPMENTAL TESTING

From speculation

So far you will have collected opinions about the content of your lesson and **speculations** about its likely teaching effectiveness. These latter speculations do remain guesswork -- even when you have "critical friends" who are brilliantly intuitive and frequently correct. You won't know definitely whether, what and how well your material teaches until your lesson is studied by learners who are new to the subject.

It will then be no good saying "Well, I taught them; b they just didn't learn". If they don't learn, or otherwi find the experience uncongenial, then your lesson is at fault. It needs revising. That is the purpose of developmental testing.

...to trying it out

Developmental testing involves us in trying out our lesson on "sample" learners and revising it before we publish the final version. Clearly, these sample learner

*Choosing
sample
learners*

should be as like our intended learners as possible in background, motivation, etc. But they will not necessarily be studying the lesson under exactly the same conditions. For example, an individual sample learner may not even be asked to read all the lessons in your course. Nevertheless, such sample learners can give us invaluable help in improving the lesson for the benefit of future learners.

There are two main forms of developmental testing:

*Two forms
of testing*

o Face-to-face tryouts

o Field trials.

Face-to-face Tryouts

*One lea-ner
at a time*

For this kind of developmental testing you will need two or three sample learners with whom you will work, **one at a time**, through the second draft of your lesson.

*Test your
learner ?*

How to begin ? Sit down with your learner in a quiet place where you can avoid being disturbed for an hour or two. Check -- with a test if necessary -- that he or she is competent to begin on the lesson. That is, has your learner already acquired whatever prerequisite abilities you are expecting of learners ? (These may have been acquired by reading previous lessons in your course.)

*What do
they know
already ?*

It may also be worth testing your learner on the concepts you are covering in the present lesson. It is just possible that he or she is (somehow) already familiar with them. If so, this learner's responses will not imply much about those of the learners it is eventually intended for. (In short, the learner who knows it all already -- like the learner who doesn't know enough to begin -- will not be typical of your "target audience".) There is another reason why it is worth your finding out about the learner's **prior** perceptions of the concepts in your lesson: it may help you understand how he or she reacts to your handling of them.

Make sure your learner understands the purpose of your collaboration -- that the lesson is on trial, not the

*Explain
purpose*

learner. Admit that you expect there to be weaknesses in
the teaching and that you hope, with the learner's help,
to eradicate them before it goes into wider circulation.
Obviously, the more lessons a particular learner tries out
with you, the more relaxed he or she will be -- and the
less likely to influence his or her approach to the
material.

*Observe and
make notes*

So, get your learner started. Observe how he or she
works through the lesson. What sequence does your learner
follow -- and from what starting point ? How does he or
she respond to your activities ? And are there passages
that seem to bore or annoy or cause your learner undue
difficulty ? If you have to explain anything orally, make
a note of what you say, because you may decide you need to
write it into the next version of the lesson. You may also
want to make a note of any comments your learner offers
about the difficulty, relevance, interest or effectiveness
of various parts of the lesson. And how long is your
learner taking to work through the various sections ?

*What has
learner
learned ?*

When your learner has finished, test again to find out
what he or she has learned. This should lead you into a
critical discussion of your lesson. Which parts has your
learner learned most from ? And from which parts has
little been learned ? Can your learner suggest why this
might be ? How does the learner's present understanding
compare with what he or she already knew about the topic ?
What changes would he or she like to see in the lesson ?

*Discuss
possible
improvements*

How such a discussion might go, and the kinds of
improvement that might be suggested, will vary according
to you, your learner, and the sort of learning materials
being tested. Much depends on your rapport with the
learner and on your ability to get him or her to level with
you -- rather than holding back for fear either of being
thought "thick" or, alternatively, of hurting **your** feeling
about your precious lesson. (Some authors prefer not to

mention that they wrote the lesson being tested.)

Try with more learners

Once you have corrected any glaring errors or weaknesses revealed by your first learner, you can try the lesson out with one or two more. Take particular note of any reactions they have **in common**. They may all make similar mistakes on a certain activity, for instance; or all may suggest that a certain passage is patronizing or obscure.

Weighing your learners' comments

Weigh the words of your try-out learners carefully. Some comments will seem trivial; others richly insightful. Remember, they are most unlikely to have revealed all the weaknesses in your lesson. But at least the responses should help you seek out further weaknesses yourself. Consider whether or not your learners' comments are likely to be typical of future learners. Are some of them personal and unlikely to be repeated ? Do some of them suggest areas of weakness that would crumble under general scrutiny ?

Ways of revising your lesson

When you have digested all your learners' comments, do what seems necessary to amend your lesson:

o   Cut out irrelevant material.
o   Expand any explanations that are too terse.
o   Insert more practice exercises where called for.
o   Allow for additional summaries or reviews.
o   Shorten your elephantine sentences.
o   Sharpen your analogies.
o   Insert more homely examples.
o   Tie your pictures more closely to the text.
o   Make better use of additional media.

In short, improve your lesson.

try this proach

You may feel, of course, that face-to-face tryout is too time-consuming or difficult to arrange for every lesson. Nevertheless, I would strongly urge you to evaluate at

least your **first few** self-instructional lessons in this way
Also, you may want to return to face-to-face testing for
any subsequent lessons in which you are trying out novel
approaches or are presenting learners with unusual learning
problems.

Can help
your future
teaching

The fact is, face-to-face tryouts -- in which you can
observe the learner at work on your material -- can
contribute a great deal, not just to the development of
a particular lesson but to **your** development as a "teacher
in print". Many competent practitioners of
self-instruction will admit that much of their expertise
derives from the insights and awareness developed in their
early experiences of trying out materials face-to-face. I
can be a disturbing experience -- "How can they possibly
be having trouble with such carefully written material ?"
but one with a lot to teach the teacher.

However, such a tryout will not give you all the
information you need. After all, the situation is rather
artificial. Your eventual learners will not have you
sitting alongside them as they work through your lessons.

Also need
field trial

So, having revised your material in the light of a face-
to-face tryout, you may then evaluate it more "naturally"
in what I have called a **field trial**.

Field Trials

For this you will need a large group of sample learners,
say 20 or 30. You will have them use the lesson in much
the same circumstances as the learners for whom it is
eventually intended. For example, this may mean their
reading it in their own homes at whatever time best suits
them. Or it may mean their taking it off to the library
or all coming together to read it in one room, with or

Normal
working
conditions

without a tutor or proctor to call on in emergencies. A
to create whatever would be the normal working condition

How are you to find out how learners use your lesson
and what they have got out of it ? Can you find out
without being with them while they are learning ? Yes,
to some extent. You can, for example:

*Ways of
collecting
information*

o Require them to tackle a test on the lesson, before
   and after working through it, and to hand in their
   results.

o Ask them to fill in a "log sheet" and/or
   questionnaire (see Figures 14.2, 3 and 4 for
   examples) -- in which they might comment, for
   instance, on:

   (a) How long they took over the lesson.
   (b) How easy/interesting/useful it was.
   (c) What they liked and disliked about it.

   The answers to (a), (b) and (c) may be illuminating
   in their own right. But they are likely to be even
   more so when compared with learners' responses to
   other lessons in the series.

o Interview some of the learners afterwards to discover
   their general impressions of the lesson and how they
   think it might be improved.

None of the procedures mentioned above makes the situation
of the field trial learners very much different from what
might be the "normal" working conditions. However, they
do fail to collect one kind of useful information that is
richly available in face-to-face tutorial tryouts. That
is, field trials may give us little information about **how**
the learner tackles the material. Even if it were realistic
to have all learners working together in one room -- and
that seems unlikely -- we could not follow the minute-by-
minute progress of each one.

*But how did
learners
work ?*

The nearest we can get is to ask the learners themselves
to record their reactions as they work. This does, of
course, make their situation different from that of the

*eeping
ecords*

learners for whom the material is intended. Nevertheless, you may feel that the "artificiality" of writing down reactions is worth enduring for the sake of the insights that may be forthcoming.

Spontaneous comments

Free comments. The simplest way of getting moment-by-moment reactions is to invite learners to write their comments in the margin of the text as they read -- or in a separate notebook with non-book materials. Below are some comments of this kind I have had from learners. (Some are quite similar to the comments one may get from experts. As you will notice, such remarks are likely to persuade one to take another (evaluative) look at one's lesson:

Examples

> I've lost the drift of the argument.
>
> Too many technical terms all at once.
>
> Sexist !
>
> This paragraph is contradicting itself.
>
> I am getting quite intrigued now.
>
> So dull, I don't want to go on.
>
> Too long-winded.
>
> We need photographs to appreciate this distinction.
>
> What is this supposed to be an example of ?
>
> Beautifully clear and logical.
>
> Can't you give another worked example before this exercise ?
>
> What has this paragraph got to do with the topic ?
>
> Superficial -- nothing to think about here.
>
> How is this different from the word's everyday meaning ?
>
> I could do with a summing-up about here.
>
> I'd need to try this out in the workshop to be convinced.
>
> What am I supposed to do with this information ?

Figure 14.2: A Tester's Log Sheet

TESTER'S LOG SHEET

1. YOUR NAME C.B. Russell

2. TITLE OF COURSE UNIT KANT, Units 17, 18

SECTION	STARTED AT	FINISHED AT	TOTAL TIME	YOUR COMMENT ON THE SECTION AS A WHOLE
1.1 – 2.8 (pp. 1–20)	4.20	5.0	.40	Clear & well presented
	6.40	7.30	.50	Since I have no experience of philosophy, I am glad that you are introducing it gradually
3.1 – 3.6 (pp. 21–57)	7.30	9.30	2.	The difficulties started when you asked me to read long passages from Kant. I did not feel properly prepared for this.
	11.15	1.00	1.45	
	2.30	3.45	1.15	
	6.30	8.00	1.30	
4.1 – 6.2 (pp. 57–97)	2.	3.20	1.20	I became saturated, and lost the thread of your commentary. I was not sure what the Exercises required me to do.
	4.50	6.30	1.40	
	9.	9.45	.45	
Assessment Exercise (p. 98)	9.30	11.15	1.45	My problem was whether to confine myself to the Autonomy of the Will, or to try a broader approach. The latter seemed to give me a better chance of showing what I know.
	1.30	3.40	2.10	
	7.00	9.00	2.	
	10.00	1.20	3.20	
TOTAL TIME (INCL. ASSESSMENT)			21.40	

Figure 14.3:   End-of-Unit Questionnaire (Part One)

END OF UNIT QUESTIONNAIRE (Part One)

1. Name: 2. Unit title/No.

 J. Brodie   *No. 19*

3. What did you particularly like about this unit?

 The examples discussed are basically interesting but

4. What did you particularly dislike? *Most of my time and effort was spent struggling with the sociological terms & the writing style of sociologists. The overall themes & concepts are difficult to master because of the language barrier.*

5. Were there any sections, concepts or words that you found particularly difficult, or not well explained? If there were, please give details.

 The terms were copiously explained but with definitions that were hard to recall during later reading. Repeated re-reading & refreshing of memory was necessary during difficult & complex passages, e.g. first paragraph of section 3.1

6. Can you suggest what might have helped you in these cases?

 Use the same definitions in self-assessment questions as are printed in text: 'action', 'role', 'norms', etc.

7. Do you have any other comments about this unit?

 As with other sociologically-based units, my difficulties stem from the terminology. Other disciplines' approaches to the same topics (crime, unemployment, immigration, etc.) seem to overcome this difficulty & get their message across using more familiar, or at least more clearly defined terms.

Figure 14.4: End-of-Unit Questionnaire (Part Two)

END OF UNIT QUESTIONNAIRE (Part Two)

1. NAME .... *K. Mitchell* .... 2. Course Unit. *Unit 12* .....

Put a tick in the appropriate box for each of the questions below:

3 How much of the subject matter of the unit was already familiar to you?
- All of it
- Most of it
- About half
- A small amount
- [✓] None at all

4 To what extent did you enjoy working through the unit?
- I liked it very much
- [✓] I quite liked it
- I felt indifferent to it
- I rather disliked it
- I disliked it very much

5 How difficult did you find the course unit?
- [✓] Very difficult
- Fairly difficult
- Neither too difficult nor
- Fairly easy   too easy
- Very easy

6 How difficult did you find the assignment exercise which followed the unit?
- Very difficult
- [✓] Fairly difficult
- Neither too difficult nor
- Fairly easy   too easy
- Very easy

7 Do you think the unit gave you enough practice in using the ideas it contained?
- Too much practice
- [✓] Neither too much nor too little practice
- Too little practice

8 In view of the amount of time the unit required of you, do you feel you learned as much as you might have expected from it?
- I learned a great deal
- [✓] I learned a reasonable amount
- I learned too little

9 If this course unit were considered typical material from the course for which you have applied, how would your experience of it affect your desire to take this course?

My desire to take the course would be:
- Very much increased
- [✓] Somewhat increased
- Unaffected
- Somewhat decreased
- Very much decreased

10 Are you willing to test further units?
- [✓] Yes
- No

11 Please give overleaf any other general comments that you would like the author (or illustrator) to take into account when revising this course unit for publication.

Field trial questions. As well as, or instead of, inviting free commenting, you can include special "field trial questions" in your lesson. That is, in addition to whatever activities and exercises your eventual learners will be asked to tackle, you can ask questions that invite your test learners to give information about their use of your materials.

Specific questions

For example, at the beginning of the lesson, right after your statement of aims and objectives, you might print the following:

Example

```
In the space below, say what is your reaction
to the author's aims and objectives.
(e.g. Are they clear to you?  Do they seem
relevant? etc.).



```

How long did it take ?

At the beginning of each section within a lesson, you may have a box as follows:

Time started	

-- and a "Time finished" box at the end.

After each major activity, question or exercise -- especially one that relates to a major objective -- you may ask a set of questions such as the following:

*Questions
about
activities
(exercises)*

1. Write down your answer to Exercise X in the space below.
2. How long did the exercise take you?
3. Was it clear what you were supposed to do?
4. How easy was it?
5. Did you consider it a worthwhile exercise?
6. How similar did you think your answer was to the author's?
7. What was your reaction to the author's discussion of answers?
8. If you were not satisfied with your answer, a) what did you do about it? And b) how do you account for your getting it wrong?
9. If you didn't tackle Exercise X, please say why not.

Thus, when you get back the printed lesson at the end of the field trial, you will get not only the learners' written answers to the key activities but also their comments on those activities.

After each section of the lesson you may include such questions as:

*erall
view
estions*

1. How long did this section take you?
2. Without referring back, summarise the author's main points in not more than 100 words.
3. How difficult was the section?
4. How interesting was it?
5. Did it seem clearly related to the aims and objectives of the lesson?
6. How useful or relevant were the diagrams, cartoons, tables, etc?
7. Can you suggest any ways of improving the section?
8. Do you have any other comments about the section?

NB With all such "field trial questions", make sure you **leave sufficient space** on the page for learners to write in their answers.

Analyzing reactions

Group discussion. When learners have completed their work on the lesson and returned their annotated copies to you, then you will be able to analyse their reactions along with their test results, forming an overall picture of how they responded to the lesson, how long they took over it, and what they learned from it. You may then be able to meet with a group of them to discuss common reactions and suggestions for improvements. Key questions to ask in such a discussion (or in a questionnaire if you cannot get together with your field trial learners) are:

Key questions to discuss

o   What did you like most about the lesson ?
o   What did you dislike most ?
o   What changes would you recommend ?

You can then put the finishing touches to your lesson and have it printed up for regular use by the learners it was always intended for. However, those learners may still respond differently from your developmental testers. So you can't assume that your concern with evaluation will now be at an end.

Evaluation must continue

CONTINUOUS MONITORING

Once your lessons are in regular use with your intended learners, presumably as part of a course, you will need to keep them under review. After all the developmental testing you may be pretty sure that you've got some reasonable lessons. But surprises do happen. These learners are studying "for real" and may reveal new weaknesses or peculiarities in your materials. This is especially likely if you use the same set of lessons again and again over several years, perhaps with the learners gradually coming to differ from those you originally wrote for. So, continue to monitor your lessons and be prepared to amend them where problems or opportunities dictate.

The need for monitoring

Continuous monitoring takes two forms:

o Casual evaluation.

o Deliberate evaluation.

These may lead to changes not just in the lesson materials but also in many other aspects of the course.

Casual Evaluation

This kind of evaluation arises from things we "just happen to notice" during the life of the course. Here are some examples of things we might happen to notice, or have brought to our attention:

o Learners are dropping out of the course.

o One of our set books has gone out of print.

o Learners are getting increasingly late with their assignments.

o Other teachers are complaining about our learners.

o Some of our lessons are unpopular.

o Learners are not turning up for practical sessions.

o Some of our tutors feel constrained by the assessment system.

o Bad weather ruins an important field trip.

o Work done by previous learners is being plagiarized by the present group.

o Many employers are not providing the promised support facilities.

o Learners are spending far too long on the audiotapes.

o A major advance is reported in the knowledge underlying one of the main topics in our course.

o Assessment results indicate ineffective teaching in certain sections of the course.

*Who
notices ?*

Such items may arise from our own observations -- e.g. assessment results. Or they may be reported by learner tutors, or anyone else (e.g. employers) with whom our learners and tutors have contact. We may or may not be able to do anything about the problem (or opportunity) indicated, but we should aim to be aware of it.

Deliberate Evaluation

*Answering
specific
questions*

Deliberate evaluation differs from casual evaluation in that we are actively seeking answers to specific questi about our lessons and the course. For example: Can the written guide to the course be improved in any way ? A learners without previous practical experience coping reasonably well ? Is the home experiment kit being use Do tutors feel that the on-site sessions are serving th purpose ?

*Gathering
reports*

If you are not teaching all the learners who study yc lessons yourself, it is essential to obtain regular reports from the other teachers. In the Open Universit the central course team thus keeps in touch with the regional tutors who assess learners' assignment work; and obtains from them evaluative reports on the course and how learners are coping with it. (See Figure 14.5 tutors' comments on one block of a course.) Even with on-site Keller Plan courses, student proctors may see more of the learners' work than do the staff-members whc devised the course. They should be encouraged to report regularly, either in writing or in discussion.

*Face-to-face
discussions*

Discussions and interviews. Deliberate evaluation can o be conducted in group discussion with tutors and/ or learners -- provided you can get them together for the purpose. With an on-site course, teachers might usefull get together weekly to discuss progress. With a Keller Plan course, any advanced students acting as "proctors"

Figure 14.5: Tutors' Comments on One Block of a Course

Tutor Number	Comments
86	Unit 10 reading, Deutsch in particular, seemed to cause students some difficulty, in spite of the summary in Unit 10. The article is good, however, and I found that a tutorial session cleared most of the problems. New tutors might be alerted in advance next year.
58	My own criticism is directed at Unit 10 which I consider to be far too vague and pitched at far too high a level of generalization. It appears to be out of keeping with the course so far. Perhaps a more interesting exercise would be to look at some situation in more detail. This would enable the incorporation of section 4, the controls of politics on communication, to be brought out in an integrated way rather than as a postscript.
26	Some of my students are critical of what they describe as the 'jumping about' nature of the course, i.e., a tendency to spend too little time on one topic area before switching to a distantly related theme. I think they would prefer more discrete blocks of emphasis on a particular social science.
28	This is the best block to date.
11	Unit 07 seems excessively technical containing matter not of obvious interest to social science students. This is my reaction with which students appeared to agree (out of politeness?). Unit 09 again seems too technical and more appropriate to a course in physical transport rather than social science aspects. Also appears totally to fail to integrate with earlier Units concerned with natural resources—so that there is no discussion of relative efficiency of fuel usage of different transport modes nor of fossil fuel constraints on transport technology and usage. These are topics most likely to interest D101 students I feel. Also are D101 students likely to be so interested in location of Turkish Railways?
44	07: written work by students showed that they had not grasped the significance of the concept of 'deep structure', despite the SAQ and CMA questions. Suggest that SAQ4 (p. 39) be broken down so as to draw out separately the elements of the definition given on p. 72. Unit 10 looks deceptively short and coming at the end tended to be rushed. I think that the Unit would come better after 08. The spatial factor is less demanding in comprehension because more concrete.

Relieving anxieties

will have much to contribute to these meetings. They may also be feeling certain anxieties about their role, and these may be surfaced in the discussion. If participants cannot be brought together, perhaps you can interview them instead (on the telephone if necessary).

And/or a questionnaire

Using questionnaires. However, both discussions and interviews may be difficult to arrange, especially with distance courses. As an alternative (or as a supplement) you might collect information from course participants by means of a questionnaire.

Getting advice

The design of questionnaires is an art in itself, and have no space to go into details. If you do need advice, it may be worth considering whether there is a colleague within your institution (e.g. in social sciences) who has experience in questionnaire design and survey techniques.

Three types of question

To get you started, it is worth noting that the questions used in questionnaires normally fall into three basic categories:

The rating question

1. A question, together with several alternative answers expressing different ways of rating some aspect of the course. The learner is asked to choose whichever one he or she agrees with. For example:

Example

> How clear do you feel about what the project
> will be demanding of you ?
>
> (a) Very clear
>
> (b) Fairly clear
>
> (c) Rather unclear
>
> (d) Very unclear
>
> (e) I've not thought much about it yet

Alternative rating

An alternative form is to pose the question as a statement with which learners are asked to indicate the extent of their agreement or disagreement. For example:

Example

> Would you agree that the demands likely to
> be made on you by the project are now
> clear to you ?
>
> (a) Very much yes
>
> (b) Yes
>
> (c) Haven't thought about it yet
>
> (d) No
>
> (e) Very much no

*Which applies
to learner ?*

2. A question inviting the learner to look at several answers and choose whichever ones apply to him or her. For example:

Example

> For Lesson 12, which of the following aspects
> do you believe might have been improved in
> some way ?
>
> (i)   Aims and objectives
>
> (ii)   Study guide
>
> (iii) The case study
>
> (iv)   Activities
>
> (v)   Feedback on activities
>
> (vi)   The set book readings
>
> (vii) End-of-lesson test

*nviting
ree comments*

3. Open-ended questions inviting learners to make a free response, writing down their comments. For example, as a follow-up to the last question mentioned above, one might ask:

:ample

> What do you believe should be done to improve
> those aspects you have picked out ?

*at do
u need
know ?*

Clearly, what you ask questions **about** will vary from one course to another. It will also vary according to the point within the course at which your questionnaire is to be completed, and according to the kinds of decision you hope to be able to make in the light of the answers.

*y out
draft*

The best way of ensuring that your questions are as clear and unambiguous as possible is to try them out on a few people in draft form. That is, developmentally

test your questionnaire through tutorial tryout. If you
cannot find appropriate learners to vet your draft
questionnaire, then friends, spouses or colleagues may
be able to oblige by pointing out weaknesses and
obscurities that have escaped your notice.

Meaning of
responses ?

Even the best of questionnaires, however, may produce
answers that are hard to interpret. What do learners **mean**
when they identify a particular lesson as "difficult",
"too long" and "very interesting" ? Do they all mean the
same thing ? Ought we to be doing anything about it ?

```
********************************************************
*  IT CAN BE VERY ILLUMINATING TO INTERVIEW           *
*  SOME OF THE LEARNERS WHO HAVE COMPLETED             *
*  YOUR QUESTIONNAIRE.                                 *
********************************************************
```

USING EVALUATION DATA

How to
use data ?

The ultimate and over-riding question in evaluation is
"So what ?" That is, what are we to **make** of the
information we collect ? How are we to use it ?

Improvement

The aim of evaluation is to understand our course and
how learners interact with it -- with a view to sustainir
it, developing it and, where possible, **improving** it.
(Check the four aspects of course planning depicted in
Figure 3.1 on page 36.) The improvements you make to
your lessons, and other aspects of your course, will
ideally benefit learners who are **currently** working with

Who will
benefit ?

Some changes cannot be made fast enough, however, so som
improvements will benefit **future** learners only.

Examples of Course Improvement

Kinds of
improvement

Let us look briefly at the kinds of improvement that mig
be made in the light of evaluation findings:

A distance course. This first example is a set of recommendations compiled for a distance learning course by my colleague, David Hawkridge:

Improvements to a distance course

Evaluation findings	Recommendations for course changes
1. 40% of students consider workload on Lessons 3 and 4 to be at least 50% greater than for other lessons.	Remove the exercise on p. 64. Eliminate items (c) and (f) from the reading list.
2. 30% of students report that local resources are not available for carrying out the mini-project in Lesson 7.	Replace the mini-project with an essay so that no students are placed at this kind of disadvantage.
3. 52% of students do not find the tapes for Lesson 3 to be useful.	Change the third assignment so that it is based on both the printed material and tapes, or eliminate tapes, or revise tapes so that they are more useful.
4. Students (12%) want additional material on the mathematical aspects of Lesson 9.	Recommend appropriate remedial text if available, *or* prepare suitable material.
5. Academic colleagues (5) want inclusion of alternative material to counter allegations of bias in Lesson 9.	Do not alter materials. Include a summary of their allegations. Add an alternative text to list of recommended books.
6. 70% of students want fewer assignments.	Replace the project with an essay (see 2 above) and replace essay C with a quiz-type test, self-marked.
7. Less than 30% of students tackled either of the two integrative, 'course-as-a-whole' questions in the examination; and marks on those two questions averaged 20% below those gained on the questions of more limited scope.	Make the tackling of one integrative question compulsory in the examination; re-write final section of last lesson so as to give students practice in reviewing course to establish overarching principles and general insights.

An on-site course. The second example is an extract from a lengthy report by Will Bridge on the evaluation of a Keller Plan course in particle mechanics. It is particularly interesting here in reminding us that evaluation can suggest changes in many aspects of the course in addition to the teaching quality of the learning materials:

Improvements to an on-site course

The outstanding problems in the initial trial in 1972/3 had been the hurried and crowded nature of the test sessions, the students' slow overall progress which resulted from this, and the lack of a steady routine for them to keep to. To tackle the first problem, it was decided to use a larger classroom (seating approximately 50 students), and to try using fast students on the course to test their colleagues on those units the fast students had passed. The problem of slow progress was tackled by fixing deadlines for passing each of a minimum number of eight units throughout the course. A course-work mark scheme was arranged so that students were given one mark (equivalent to just less than one percent in the final grading) for being a 'tester', and one mark for each test passed before a deadline.

Another changes was made to the course for 1974. The units were re-arranged in a branching pattern, so that after a student had covered two introductory units, he was given some freedom as to which units he studied. This change was partly because the needs of the electrical engineers differed somewhat from those of the physical scientists, and partly because it was thought that different students might choose different sequences through the course.

With these changes the course was re-run in 1974. The staffing continued at the same level, but was supplemented by between two and four student testers employed at any one period. There were a number of improvements. A majority of the students completed at least the core of eight units, and there was no drop-off in attendance attendance over the two terms. This time I was the evaluator. I interviewed one third of the students, and looked for the reasons for these improvements. Overall, it seemed that the guidance the deadline provided did help students, particularly the weaker ones, to work steadily. They were also influenced by the (small) credit given for this.

It emerged from two questionnaires that, although throughout the year the student testers were found to be approachable and adequately knowledgeable, early on in the year they had not been sure about exactly what to do. For example, they did not know whether or not to accept correct answers which were not got by the same means as the answers provided by the model solutions, and they were not sure whether or not verbal explanations of written answers could be accepted. Some of the testers learnt by experience what to do, and in consequence became more acceptable.

The branching pattern was popular, although many chose the same sequence as the previous linear one.

However, there were still problems. Complaints about the workload continued, now coming also from weaker students who had previously dropped out. Also, students were still not convinced that they thoroughly understood units they had passed, some thinking the test questions not deep enough, and others thinking that tests did not cover all of each unit ...

from:

Bridge, W. (1977) 'Changes in a self-paced course' in *Individual Study in Undergraduate Science*, W. Bridge and L. Elton (eds), Heinemann, London.

*Never stop
monitoring*

The evaluation and improvement of that Keller Plan course continued year by year. Some intended improvements turned out to have the opposite effect -- e.g. giving students extra credit for passing units regularly may have been responsible for the cheating that was detected in some tests. Continuous monitoring is a continuing necessity.

Towards Re-making Your Course

*The eternal
questions*

Each time your course runs, ask yourself questions like these:

- o Did the course attract enough learners ?
- o Were they sufficiently qualified ?
- o Did enough of them finish the course ?
- o Was the standard high enough ?
- o Was the course cost-effective ?
- o Were the learners satisfied ?
- o Were the teachers/administrators satisfied ?
- o Were others (e.g. employers) satisfied ?
- o What needs to be changed ?

*'rom
'olling
'emake...*

Some changes you will be able to make from one year to the next -- supplementing this text, replacing that audio-cassette, re-scheduling the weekend practical sessions -- in a kind of "rolling re-make" of the course. But, eventually, the answer to that final question above may well be PRACTICALLY EVERYTHING. Sooner or later, evaluation may suggest you need to start on designing a new course entirely. Back to Chapter 3 !

*o total
ewrite*

FINAL CHECKLIST FOR LESSON EVALUATION

In case you think I've wandered too far away from the evaluation of individual lessons, the checklist below should remind you of what might be done. Go through as many of the following steps as possible:

*Checklist
for lesson
evaluation*

1. Criticize your first draft yourself, using a checklist like those shown on pages 336-338.

2. Offer your second draft for critical commenting by friends, colleagues and other experts, using similar checklists.

3. Repeat your own critical reading in the light of their comments and suggestions.

4. Carry out any improvements indicated by critical commenting.

5. Tutorially tryout your lesson on a few learners individually.

6. Carry out any improvements suggested by the tutorial tryout.

7. Write in "field trial questions" after major activitie and at the end of sections, and compile any necessary questionnaire ready for field trial.

8. Run field trial with twenty or thirty learners.

9. Discuss possible improvements to lesson with field trial learners after analysing their responses.

10. Carry out "final" revisions to the lesson.

11. Print it -- but be prepared to revise it yet again, and eventually perhaps replace it, in the light of continuous monitoring of the course as a whole.

```
************************************************
*                                              *
*  DON'T JUDGE A SELF-INSTRUCTIONAL COURSE     *
*  BY THE ELOQUENCE OF ITS DEVELOPERS OR       *
*  THE GLOSSINESS OF ITS PACKAGING -- THE      *
*  PROOF OF THE PUDDING IS IN THE EATING       *
*  (AND IN HOW WELL IT STAYS DOWN).            *
*                                              *
************************************************
```

15.   STARTING, KEEPING GOING, AND FINISHING OFF

Tips,
guidance,
reminders

This brief final chapter consists chiefly of a few tips
to get you started on your lesson-writing; some guidance
about certain editorial chores you'll need to carry out
while the work is in progress; and some final reminders
about how to bring it all to a satisfactory conclusion.

STARTING TO WRITE

Here are some practical tips, most of which have helped
me at some time or other. Perhaps some of them will be
useful to you also:

When start
writing ?

o Allow yourself just so much time for preliminary
   reading and research (hours or days, according to the
   number of lessons and the newness of the topic) and
   be strict about deciding the day on which you will
   actually start writing your first draft of the lesson.

Deadline

o If you do not already have an official deadline for
   completion, set yourself one. Preferably arrange it
   in such a way that you will suffer some inconvenience
   or embarassment if you fail to meet it. For example,
   you might agree with some "critical friends" that you
   will have the first draft of your lesson available for
   them to read by a certain date.

any sequence

o Don't feel constrained to write the lesson in the
   sequence it will be read by learners, if this doesn't
   suit you. If you find the beginning difficult, start
   somewhere else. Begin, perhaps, by writing an exercise
   or case study, or any part of the lesson that seems
   particularly interesting or "of the essence". The rest
   can then be written around it.

irst draft
ot to be
erfect

o Don't aspire to perfection in your first rough draft.
   Aim to cover the ground as fast as possible, getting
   the broad flow of ideas and activities established.
   Only then should you let yourself go back to your

source materials and references to check on any
dubious details.

*Arrange for
concentration*

o Try to arrange a period of writing time -- several
   hours or, better still, a couple of days -- when
   producing your lesson will be your only task. If
   possible, find a place where no-one can burst in for
   an impromptu meeting and where no phones ring.

*Carry a
notebook*

o If your lesson-planning and writing spreads over
   several days or longer, you may find you do a lot
   of "writing" in your mind while walking the dog or
   in the intervals of attending to other business.
   Always keep a notebook on you, so as to record the
   sudden "brain-waves" that might otherwise be forgotten.

*Think of
named
learners*

o As you write, keep in mind one or two individuals you
   know who might be typical of those for whom your
   tutorial-in-print is intended. Ask yourself, page by
   page, how Sid or Sue (or whatever their names are) might
   respond to your words (and pictures) of wisdom.

*Why are you
telling them ?*

o Never assume that just because you've spelled out the
   information on the page it will necessarily mean
   anything to your learners. Unless you constantly ask
   yourself "Why am I telling them this ?" and "What do I
   want them to do with it ?" -- and reach satisfactory
   answers -- the information may remain inert.

Don't skimp

o Resist the temptation to do the job less well than you
   know you could -- e.g. when you realize that a vivid
   example or a pictorial representation would be far mor
   telling than a straightforward verbal explanation
   (however clear) but would involve you in extra
   thinking time.

*If you
get stuck*

o If you get stuck on one section of your lesson, don't
   give it all up and go off to attend to whatever other
   duties you might be neglecting. Instead, try turning
   your attention to some other aspect of the lesson (or

another lesson) and come back to the troublesome
section later on.

*Break off in
full spate*

o When you break off writing for the day, try to do so in
   the middle of a "good patch" -- so you'll find it easy
   to get started again next time.

o And, in general:

```
****************************************************
*                                                  *
*   AIM TO ENJOY WRITING YOUR LESSON: IF YOU        *
*                                                  *
*   DO, YOUR LEARNERS MAY ENJOY READING IT.         *
*                                                  *
****************************************************
```

EDITING YOUR FIRST ROUGH DRAFT

Your first draft will probably be handwritten and
full of corrections, additions and crossings-out. But

*Criticize
yourself*

don't hand it over to your typist as soon as (let alone
before) you have written the last word. Before you do,
criticize it.

To give direction to your criticisms, consider your
lesson in the light of each of the following questions
(or work out a checklist of your own):

*Checklist
for self-
criticism*

o Does the structure of the lesson seem sensible and
   coherent -- with introductions or previews, and
   summaries or reviews used where appropriate , and
   will learners be able to appraise it as a whole before
   tackling it in a detailed way ?

o Have I taken adequate steps to motivate the learners
   and make clear to them how they might tackle the material
   and what they might expect to get from it ?

o Have I pitched the lesson at the right level of
   difficulty -- challenging without being inaccessible --
   and consistent with the prerequisite abilities I say
   I am assuming of learners ?

Checklist for self-criticism

o   Is the tone that of a friendly but rigorous tutor,
    lively and interesting, light of touch, and with
    humour (and humanity) admitted where appropriate ?

o   Is my language plain and straightforward (e.g. calculate
    Fog Index) -- with words and sentences reasonably
    short, and technical terms used only when essential
    (but properly defined and explained) and gobbledegook
    excluded altogether ?

o   Have I avoided sexist language -- language that seems to
    refer to people of one sex only when, in fact, either
    might be involved ? For example, writing "he/him/his"
    when I might more accurately have written "he or she",
    etc (or recast the sentence so as to avoid the pronouns
    altogether).

o   Have I used analogies, examples (and non-examples),
    case studies, and pictorial illustrations wherever
    they might make a worthwhile contribution to the
    learner's understanding ?

o   Does my argument contain any unexplained gaps or
    redundancies or illogical jumps that might irritate
    or confuse learners ?

o   Have I built in sufficient questions, exercises and
    activities to encourage learners in self-assessment
    and enable them to develop their understanding towards
    the objectives of the lesson ?

o   Does the lesson incorporate non-print media -- e.g.
    practical work, listening to audiotape, discussion
    with other learners -- where these might be more
    appropriate than print ?

o   Are any assignment items related to the aims and
    objectives of the lesson, clear in what they demand of
    the learner, and can I ensure that any given learner's
    work would be assessed in much the same way, whoever
    marks it ?

o Is the learner's likely workload (in terms of study
   time) reasonable for the topic of the lesson ?

*Reading
aloud*

When you have made any amendements to your lesson suggested
by these questions, **read it aloud** -- and tidy up any
passages that still sound pompous, long-winded or unduly
complex. Watch out also for jarring repetitions of a word
or phrase -- e.g. you may find you have begun two or three
sentences in the same paragraph with "However".

*Safeguarding
your drafts*

One final point: Never let your one and only copy of
the first draft (or any other draft) out of your possession.
Much good material has been lost that way. As your
handwritten draft swells and changes, and especially
before you hand it over to your typist:

```
****************************************
*                                      *
*    PHOTOCOPY IT -- AND STORE THE COPY *
*    SEPARATELY FROM THE ORIGINAL.      *
*                                      *
****************************************
```

*With a
word
processor*

And if you're using a word processor -- make frequent
paper copies of the material you hope is still stored
safely on disc.

TYPING YOUR DRAFT

*Briefing
your
typist...*

Unless your lesson is one of a series and your typist
already knows how to lay it out on the page, don't just
hand over your manuscript and hope for the best. Give
your typist **written** instructions and/or some sample pages
typed as you would like your lesson to be typed.

and printer ?

Below is one possible set of guidelines for a typist.
Your requirements may be different. If your material will
eventually be printed, you may need to develop a similar
set of guidelines for your printer.

Guidelines for typist/printer

Please:

o Type on A4 paper.

o Lay out the body of the text within the boundaries indicated on the attached specimen (i.e. 5 cm margin on left; 2 cm on right; 3 cm at top; 3+ cm at bottom

o Leave right-hand margins unjustified.

o Type in 1½ spacing Elite, except where indicated otherwise in the manuscript.

o Distinguish between the three grades of heading as shown in the manuscript.

o Start each section with an A-heading at the top of a new page, left or right as the case may be.

o Between foregoing text and a B-heading, leave 3 lines of space; before a C-heading, 2 lines.

o Below A- **and B-headings**, leave 2 lines of space before ensuing text. With C-headings, text to continue on same line.

o Leave **3 lines** of space above and below boxed items.

o Leave 2 lines of space between paragraphs except when preceded by a heading.

o Leave 3 lines of space between preceding paragraph, and 4½ lines of space between stopper and following paragraph.

o Indent each new paragraph to fifth character unless preceded by a "stopper"-rule or a heading, in which case pull out to margin with A- and B-heading (and run on with C-headings).

o Do not hyphenate words at the end of a line.

o Do not end a line with the first word of a new sentence.

o   Avoid having one word on its own at the beginning of
    a line, as happens in the sentence you are reading
    now.

o   Do not strive to finish each page on the same line.
    If necessary, a page can over-run by up to two lines
    of type (e.g. to complete a section) or can stop
    short after three lines.

o   Do not start a new paragraph or have a heading on
    the last one or two lines of a page.

o   Do not end a paragraph on the first line of
    a new page.

o   Insert attached illustrations exactly where shown
    in the sequence of text. Where the illustration is
    not attached, leave the amount of space indicated
    in the manuscript. Do not fill space near the bottom
    of a page by typing text that is meant to be read
    after a subsequent illustration. If the space is
    not big enough for the illustration, leave it blank.

o   Treat boxed items as illustrations. That is, do not
    split one between two pages unless it is too big to
    fit on one page.

o   Leave me to write in the side-headings by hand and
    to insert Letraset heading on title-page.

Are your
guidelines
being
followed ?

While your typist is typing your lessons, keep in touch.
Your guidelines may not be as clear or as comprehensive
as you may think. Check whether your typist is having
trouble interpreting them. Amend them and add to them
where necessary. (Even if you are typing your own
lessons, it is sensible to think out your own guidelines
in advance, rather than trying to make them up as you
go along.)

GETTING COPYRIGHT PERMISSIONS

*Other
people's
copyright*

Will your lesson reproduce any materials -- e.g. words,
pictures, recorded sound -- for which someone else holds
the copyright ? If so, you will need to obtain written
permission from the holder of the copyright. You can
send off for this while your typist is at work on your
lesson, if you have not already done so.

*Seek
permission
early*

Actually, it is best to start requesting permission
as soon as you are reasonably sure you want to use any
particular material. You will sometimes have difficulty
tracking down the copyright holder (who may be the author,
or the author's employer, agent or "estate"). A reply may
be slow in forthcoming; and you may, in any case, be
refused permission to quote or else be asked so high a fee
that you need to consider whether the material really is
all that essential.

What is Copyright Material ?

*All writing
copyrighted*

It is wise to act on the assumption that any piece of
writing (even a letter or a shopping list) is protected
by the laws of copyright. That is, during the period of
copyright -- 50 years from first publication or from the
death of the author (whichever is the later) -- permission
to reproduce it or any "substantial part" of it, can be
given only by the holder of that copyright.

*...and
pictures*

*...and
sound*

The same is true for pictures (e.g. drawings and
paintings, photographs and diagrams, etc) and for recorded
speech or music and moving pictures. Use any such material
without permission and you could be involved in an
expensive court action for infringement of copyright.

What is Infringement ?

*Substantial
part ?*

The Copyright Act of 1956 indicates that infringement
occurs when more than a "substantial part" of a work is
reproduced without permission. Unfortunately, "substant

part" is not defined. However, some general rules of thumb are widely followed by publishers. If, for example, you are quoting an author's **prose** merely because it expresses something more elegantly or more forcefully than you think you could do yourself, then 50 words is about the most you should use without seeking permission. (Though, of course, you must still place those words within inverted commas and name their author -- and somewhere mention the work from which the quotation came, together with its publisher and date.)

How much to quote ?

50 words ?

With **poetry**, even 50 words may be too many to quote without permission, since they would form a "substantial part" of a short poem. Once court case held that four lines were a "substantial part" of a 32-line poem. Better not to quote more than three or four lines or one-tenth of the whole poem, whichever is the smaller.

Less if poetry ?

If, on the other hand, you quote other authors' words not as a decoration to your text but in order to comment on or criticize their ideas (as in a scholarly article or review), then you are safe in quoting much more. In such cases, it is widely regarded as "fair dealing" to quote, without permission, a single prose extract of up to 400 words, or a series of shorter extracts (none more than 300 words) totalling a maximum of 800 words -- provided this does not amount to more than 10% of the total (as it might, for instance, in a newspaper or journal article). In reviewing or criticizing poetry, quoting up to 40 lines -- or 25% of the total, which is less -- is generally considered "fair dealing". Nevertheless, as mentioned above, you should give a full reference to the source of your quotation.

ore if riticizing

ir dealing

So, unless you are confident that your use of the quotation would be seen as criticism or review:

```
*****************************************
*                                       *
*    SEEK PERMISSION FOR ANY QUOTATION   *
*    OF MORE THAN 50 WORDS.              *
*                                       *
*****************************************
```

Pictures and sound

With copyright illustrations, recorded sound, and video or film material, the idea of "fair dealing" is not recognized. So you should seek permission for even a fragment of a picture or a split second of an audio or visual recording.

Ideas are not copyright

Nevertheless, it is worth remembering that there is **no copyright protection for ideas or facts**. Copyright applies only to the actual words or pictures through which these ideas **or facts** are expressed. On the one hand, this means that you would risk infringing copyright if you were to use the same words or pictures, without permission, in another medium, e.g. making an audio-tape of a written text. But, on the other hand, you may avoid infringing copyright by re-expressing an author's ideas in your own words, or re-drawing an illustrator's pictures in a different style. If you followed them too closely -- without mentioning the source of your inspiration -- you might be accused of plagiarism instead.

...but beware plagiarism

Who Holds the Copyright ?

Identifying copyright holder

To obtain permission, you will need to identify the copyright holder. If you are wanting to quote from a book, you will probably find the name of the copyright holder among the small print on the <u>reverse</u> of the title page. Usually it will appear in a "copyright notice", naming either the author(s) or the publisher, e.g.

Copyright © 1984 Winifred Smith

Write to the author at the publisher's address. If you want to use illustrations and the illustrator is not given a separate copyright notice, assume that the publisher is the copyright holder. With articles from newspapers or journals it is safest to assume that the publisher if the copyright holder, unless the article carries a separate copyright notice.

*Picture
copyrights*

The copyright in photographs, engravings, etchings and prints (as in painted or drawn portraits) belongs to the person who commissioned them. (If no-one paid for them to be produced, then the artists are regarded as having commissioned themselves.) With other paintings and drawings, copyright belongs to the artists, unless they have specifically assigned it to someone else. In none of these cases can you assume that the present owner of the work is also the copyright holder -- even though they may think they are. If you are wanting to use a photograph of a painting, you may need to obtain permission not only from the person who commissioned the photograph but also the person who holds the copyright for the painting.

*Your own
photographs*

Incidentally, if you plan to print photographs you have taken yourself, and they include recognizable images of any living persons, you will need to seek their permission first.

*Broadcast
material*

The copyright of all radio and television material will belong to the broadcasting company. Films, audio-recordings and video-recordings should identify the copyright holder by means of some kind of copyright notice on the packaging and/or on the material itself. Needless to say, as with illustrations, the fact that you may own a copy of the material does not give you the right to reproduce it.

Writing for Permission

Write to the copyright holder, keeping a copy for your files. Give the following information:

*hat to
ll holder*

o Full details of the work from which you wish to copy.

o A photocopy of the extracts or illustrations you wish to reproduce (or a tape of audio/video extracts).

What to tell
copyright
holder

o Any deletions or amendments you might want to make.

o The author(s), title, publisher (e.g. a college or a commercial organisation), expected date of publication of the work in which wish to quote the material.

o If you will be publishing to a small number of learners especially if you will not be charging for the material this might be worth mentioning to deter any copyright holder who might be tempted to ask a huge fee.

o An assurance that you will acknowledge the source of your quotations (on the relevant pages and/or on an introductory page, whichever you intend). Incidentally illustrations are usually acknowledged in the caption by saying "from" (whatever the source) if the illustration is reproduced in its original form, or "after" or "based upon" if it has been re-drawn.

Protecting Your Own Copyright

Your own
copyright

In the UK, copyright is automatically established the moment a work is written (whether published or not). It may be vested in your institution if you are writing as part of your job; in you, if you are writing as an extra, spare time activity. (The accepted test of whether you or your institution is the copyright holder is to ask whether you could reasonably be dismissed for refusing to produce such material). Despite the automatic protection, it is sensible to print the copyright notice on your work, i.e.

Copyright © 19XX Name of holder

Further Guidance

Copyright is undoubtedly a complicated business. Yet t
development of self-instructional courses can be much e
by incorporating already published material. If you

If you need
more help

believe you need further guidance on how to do so witho
breaking the law, and if there is nobody in your instit

who can offer specialist help, you should be able to obtain
advice from the Council for Educational Technology in London

CORRECTING YOUR PROOFS

*What are
proofs ?*

The word "proofs" normally refers to a sample copy of your
finished text, provided by the printer so that you can
check its accuracy before multiple copies are run off.
However, we can use the same term also for a photocopy of
the draft your typist has just finished typing.

*Who should
check ?*

If you can, try to ensure that at least one other
person besides you and the typist reads the proof copy.
You are the best person to ensure that your typist has
followed the layout you intended. However, authors have a
tendency to "see" the word they intended, regardless of
what has actually been typed. So, mis-spellings,
incorrect numbers, and the like, may be spotted more
readily by someone else who can compare your typist's
draft, word by word, with your original.

*hat to
heck*

The main points to check are these:

o Have your instructions about layout been followed ?

o Are pages numbered correctly ?

o Does the text contain any errors (e.g. spelling
   mistakes or missing words) that need to be corrected ?
   If so, make your corrections on the photocopy, not
   on the original.

o Has the cold clarity of type revealed anything in the
   text that learners would find hideously offensive,
   confusing or incomprehensible ? If so, change it;
   but resist the temptation to fiddle about with **minor**
   "improvements". Any extensive alterations now will
   waste the typist's time and may cause layout problems.
   (Better to save them for the perhaps extensive
   re-typings that may result from developmental testing.)

o Do you need to paste in any illustrations, draw any
   boxes or arrows by hand, or add any Letraset headings ?
   (Don't do this until your typist has completed any
   necessary corrections.)

Symbols for Correcting Proofs

Your aim in correcting proofs must be to communicate
clearly with your typist and/or printer. You need to draw
their attention to points in the type-written (or printed

Use agreed
symbols

text where they are to make a change -- and tell them
exactly what that change is to be. This you will do by
marking the proofs with symbols **agreed** between you. Any
agreed symbols would do; but those I give in Figure 15.1
are very widely used.

Notice that the nature of your corrections should be

Use the
margins

indicated in the left-hand **margin** of the page. Within
the text itself, it is preferable to indicate only the
place where the correction is to be made. (Your typist
may or may not be able to decipher corrections made
between the lines; printers generally discourage them.)

If you have several corrections to make on one line,

Separating
corrections

they should be indicated in order from left to right
in the margin, each being separated from its neighbours
by the oblique mark (/). If, heaven forbid, you have
so many corrections that you can't indicate them all
in the margin (or even both margins), write them on
a separate sheet and staple it securely to the page.

When your instruction to the typist/printer is given

Ring
instructions

by a word or phrase, e.g. "stet" or "take back", put a
around it so as to decrease the possibility of its
getting incorporated into the text by mistake.

```
*************************************************
*                                               *
*  MAKE ALL YOUR CORRECTIONS ON A PHOTOCOPY     *
*  -- NOT ON THE ORIGINAL TYPESCRIPT.           *
*                                               *
*************************************************
```

Figure 12.1: Proof-reading Symbols

	① If you want to make this kind of CORRECTION	② Make this mark in the MARGIN	③ And make this mark in the TEXT
INSERTIONS	To delete unwanted material	⌐	(line through unwanted material: / or —)
	To change your mind about a correction, saying "leave it as it was"	*stet* (and cross out marginal mark for the previous correction)	‑ ‑ ‑ ‑ ‑ ‑ ‑ ‑ ‑ ‑ (under the material that is to be left as it was)
	To insert material that has been omitted	*copy missing* (attach original page with omitted material clearly indicated)	⋏ (at point where the omitted material is to be inserted)
	To insert new material	(Write out the new material, followed by ⋏)	⋏ (at point where the new material is to be inserted)
	To underline a word or phrase	*underline*	(under relevant words)
	To have an abbreviated expression spelled out in full	*spell out* (and indicate how)	(King the expression)
PUNCTUATION	To <u>insert</u> a		
	full-stop (period)	⊙	⋏
	colon	⊙	⋏
	semi-colon	;	⋏
	comma	,⋏	⋏
	question mark	?⋏	⋏
	exclamation mark	!⋏	⋏
	apostrophe	⋎	⋏
	hyphen	/-/	⋏
	dash	/--/	⋏
	oblique	/|/	⋏
	parentheses	(/)	⋏⋏
	single quotation marks	⋎/⋎	⋏⋏
	double quotation marks	⋎⋎/⋎⋎	⋏⋏
			} (at point(s) where the mark is to be inserted)
	To <u>substitute</u> one of the above punctuation marks for an existing character	(As above)	/ (through character to be replaced)

Continued overleaf...

Figure 12.1: Proof-reading Symbols (CONTINUED)

	CORRECTION	MARGIN	TEXT
TYPESTYLES	To change one typestyle for another:		Make this mark under letter/words to be altered / Ring the letter/words to be altered
	Change to:		
	italics	*ital*	_____ / ⬭
	upright (Roman), not italics	*rom*	_____
	capital letters	*cap(s)*	≡≡≡
	lower case (small) letters	*l.c.*	_____ / ⬭
	bold type	*bold*	∿∿∿
	another named typeface (e.g. san serif)	*san serif*	⬭
SPACING & LAYOUT	To start a new paragraph	*np*	⌐ (before the word that is to begin the new paragraph)
	To run two paragraphs together as one	*run on*	⌐ (linking the last word of the first paragraph to the first word of the second)
	To move a line of type:		⊢ left-hand edge of type)
	to right	⌐	(enclosing material to be moved and showing how far)
	to left	⌐	(up to beginning of material to be moved)
	To centre material on page (or column):	*centre*	(around material to be centred)
	To move a letter or word from:		
	end of one line (or column or page) to beginning of next	*take over*	(around letter/word)
	beginning of one line, etc., to end of previous	*take back*	(around letter/word)
	To transpose (change places of letters/words	*trs*	⌐⌐ (between letters/words to be transposed -- number to show order if necessary)
	To transpose lines:	*trs*	(around lines)
	To insert space:		
	between letters or words	#	⋀ (between letters or words)
	between lines	# (Can also say how much, if not obvious)	⊱(between lines to be spaced)
	To close up space:		
	between letters or words	*less #*	(between characters to be joined)
	between lines	*less #*	⊂ (linking the lines that are to be closed up)

For complex
corrections
If some of your corrections seem too complicated for
these symbols, use a separate sheet of paper to write or
type out exactly how you want the relevant piece of text
to look -- and attach it to the proofs with a marginal note
to your typist or printer.

Example
Figure 12.2 illustrates the use of the symbols in
correcting the text that now makes up most of page 374
in this book.

Figure 12.2: Proof-reading Symbols in Action

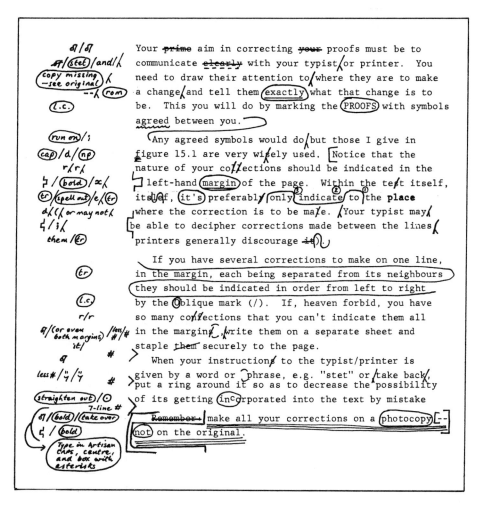

TOWARDS A FINAL DRAFT

So you have finished proof-reading what will be the first
"public" draft of your lesson. This you will take to
perhaps two further drafts, improving your material in
the light of evaluative comments -- first from colleagues
and then from "guinea-pig" learners. I can sum up these
final stages of producing your lesson by referring you
to the advice and checklists given in Chapter 14. That
is, once you are in a position to turn out multiple copie
of Draft 1:

*The final
stages*

o Get critical comments on Draft 1.

o Correct and re-type where necessary to produce Draf

o Developmentally test Draft 2.

o Correct and re-type where necessary to produce the
    final draft.

A dilemma

Of course, one could go on titivating a draft lesson for
ever. But, in these final stages, one has to struggle
with what may seem like a dilemma -- viz, to get it **righ**
or to get it **finished**.

You are no doubt working to a deadline, and you **must**
your lesson finished. But will it ever be "right" ? Ye
but only so long as you accept that "right" does not hav
to mean "perfect". In this imperfect world, right may
often be less than perfect -- but will still be good
enough. (And still sufficiently hard to attain !)

*Don't wait
for
perfection*

Better to settle for producing a succession of
90%-perfect lessons than to refrain indefinitely from
publication in the hope that one day you'll turn out a
hundred-percenter. If you ever do, you'll be the first

INDEX

Abstract v concrete: 142-143,215,221
Access devices: 163-179,293
Active v passive verbs: 218-220
Activities: 36,80,83,84,95,97,99,101,103,104,107,111,114,115,
       119-135,137,138,147,148,152,155,161,173,175,176,198,199,
       206,240,247,248,251,258,293,298,302,348,349,337,364
Adapting existing materials: 30-31,87-91,92,108,127-128,159,205,
       265,368-370,372
Aims: 15,39,43-44,80,257,336
Algorithms: 55-56,186
Alice (in Wonderland): 181
Analogies: 143-144,148,193,195,337,364
Analytic v impression marking: 322-325
Answers:
     Author's, 93,95,97,99,101,103,105,107,111,133,248
     Learner's, 93,95,97,99,101,111,126,132,248,315-320,322-325
Ascham, Roger: 211
Assessment: 19,32,39,47,76-77,80,265,301-332,364
     formative, 302-303
     methods of, 305-320
     purposes of, 302-305
     summative, 303
     timing of, 303-304
     using the results, 321-331
Assignments: 26,84,148,303,304,314-320,321,332,337,364
Attitudes: 46,75,76,80,99,111,191,314
Audio-cassettes, use of: 243-250,251,257,258,266
Audio material: 72,84,101,103,107,128,159,221,236,238,240,
       242-250,371
Audiovision: 247-250,252,257,273

Backward chaining: 65-66
BBC: 242,253
Blobs: 154,229
Bold type: 101,103,111,164,179,221,229,291
Borders: 188,297-298
Boxes:
     for answers: 95,97,122,132,248,348
     for display: 154,188,228,294,298,367
Bridge, W.: 357,358
Broadcasting: 242-243,253,371

CAL (See Computer Assisted Learning)
Camera ready copy: 280
Capitals: 179,221,229,291
Captions: 152,154,182,194,197,199,286
Cartoons: 94,112-113,188,190,191
Case studies: 111,129,146,156,158,217,337,364
Casual evaluation: 351-352
Causal sequence: 63

CBT (See Computer Based Training)
Charts: 188,196,202
Checklists: 31,32,36,39,40,48-49,75,76-77,79-80,82-83,88-89,
        129-135,221-222,229,231-232,233-234,247,255-256,257-258
        265-266,272,273,328,330-331,332,336-338,341,359,360,
        363-365,366-367,373-374,378
    Using, 114,135,167,313,316,317,323,336
Chronological sequence: 62
Colleagues' comments: 78,79,159,160
Columns: 97,111,114,152,284,287
Colour, use of: 97,101,111,133,175,200,288-289
Commenting:
    on teaching materials, 78,79,159,334-338,344,345,346-350,
        352,353
    on learners' work, 268,314,323,326,326-330
Communication: 24-25,47,269
Computer assisted learning: 261-266
Computer based training: 261,263
Computers: 211,251,257,258,261-266,307
Computer teaching: 261-266
Concentric circles (sequence): 63
Concepts: 48-49,54,124,125,129,138-148,221
Concept analysis: 48-49,139,141
Concept maps: 51-53,165,168
Concrete v abstract: 142-143
Constraints: 26
Content of courses: 38,39,47,48-60,61,78,80,268,336-337,336
Contents lists: 164-165,171
Continuous monitoring: 78,350-356,359
Contractions: 208-209
Conversational style: 207-211,229,231,248
Conversation: 156,157,159,207,223,244
Copyright: 159,189,205,206,250,368-373
Council for Educational Technology: 373
Course authors: 19-20,21,79,127,248
Course teams: 20-30,325,334
Critical friends: 21,334,338,361

Decisions: 23-24,55,135,355
Definitions: 48,148,149,176,221
Deliberate evaluation: 352-256
Demonstration: 240,268,271
Description: 193,194
Designers (graphic): 20,22,275,295,299
Developmental testing: 78,79,84,133,135,159,205-206,338-350,35
    Face-to-face tryouts: 339-342,343
    Field trials: 342-250
Diagnostic testing: 140
Diagramming: 49-58
Diagrams: 49-58,101,105,123,133,262
Discovery learning: 125,146,147,151
Discussion: 43,119-120,122,207,244,251,252,266,271,334-335,
        340,350,352
Distance education/learning: 9,10,86,161,237,245,253,266,269,
        270,311,327,354,359

Distractors: 308,320
Double page spreads: 114,145,152,153,199,287
Dramatizing: 156

Editors and editing: 20,21,275,363-365,373-377
Educational technology: 15,21,51,373
Effectiveness (of teaching): 47,78,336-337,338
EG-RUL: 125,149-151
Entry tests: 80
Essays: 307,311,322,323,
Evaluation: 36,47,77-78,80,266,320,333-360,378
    Using evaluation results, 356-359
Examinations: 26,32,302,303,331,332
Examples: 99,114,124,138,141-143,144,146,148-151,217,248,262,
        337,364
Exercises, testing: 306-320
    paper-and-pencil, 306-312
    situational, 306, 312-314
Existing materials:
    Adapting: 30-31,87-91,127-128,205,265,368-370,372
    Analysis of samples: 93-115
    Ways of using: 92,108
Experiments: 238,240-241,246,247,263
Explanation: 193,194,262,337

Face-to-face teaching/learning: 10,11-13,32,120,129,161,237,266,
        268,301,339-342
Face-to-face tryouts (of material): 339-342,343
Feedback, 77,93.95,97,99,105,107,109,111,114,115,119,129,130,
        132,133,134,135,137,138,147,176,199,247,248,258,262,268
        293,314,326-331,332
Feurzig, W.: 264
Field trials (of material): 342-350
Film: 72,240,288,370,371
Flow diagrams: 68,165,166,228
Fog Index: 230-231,364
Footnotes: 103,105,159,284
Formative assessment: 302-303
Fritts, H.C.: 54

Generalizing: 142,337
Glossaries: 176,244
Gobbledygook: 212,213,214,215,364
Grading: 76,268,271,301,321-325,364
Gramophone records (discs): 103,244
Graphic conventions: 198-199
Graphic devices: 99,103,105,132,154,174-175,187,200,295,297
Graphs: 188,196
Group work: 129,252,266
Gunning, R.: 230

Handwriting: 172,291,292
Harrison, R.: 43
Hawkridge, D.: 51,357
Headings: 164,170-172,210,293,294-295,373,366,367
Hierarchies: 67,148,170

Home experiment kits: 107,236,237-238
Human contact: 266-272
Human interest: 156,210,231
Humour: 94,155-156,211,364

Illustrations, 114,129,152,189,193,364,370,371,372,373,367
Impression v analytic marking: 322-325
Improvement of courses/materials: 33,36,39,77,78,206,266,333,
        340,341,350,356-359,373
Indenting: 133,154,164,294
Indexes: 178-179
Instructions (to readers): 172-173,286
Interactive video: 86,251,252,261
Interviews: 84,122,234,244,343,352,354,356
In-text questions: 121,128,129
Introductions: 168,169,170,173,363
Italics: 111,133,222
ITQs: 121,128,129,248,302

Jargon: 103,220-223,364

Keller Plan: 9,271,352,357,359
Kits: 72,107,237-238
Knowledge: 46,76,80,167,234,314

Landscape format: 111,283,284
Layout: 97,101,107,111,114,115,152,199-200,281-289,298,366-367,
Learners, learning about: 39-43,338-350
Lectures: 81,82,207,245,333
Letterpress printing: 280-281,289,297
Lewis, B.N.: 56
Lewis, R.: 134
Lightness of touch: 155-156, 210-211,364
Line width/spacing: 284,285,293
Linking lessons: 103,168,221
Lists: 154,228,294
Logical v psychological order: 66,142
Low-cost production: 33,93,101,299

Main ideas: 138,176,227,228,272
Maintenance of courses: 32-33,78
Marking (grading): 76,268,271,301,321-325,364
Mark schemes: 322,323
Manpower Services Commission: 87
Margins: 97,101,105,107,115,152,159,172,221,284,286,287,374
MARIS: 87
Matrix: 57
McGuiness, M.: 153
Media (choice/use): 39,47,72-75,80,161,233-273,277,364
        essential questions, 75
        functions of, 72,74
        learning stimuli in, 74-75
        notes, 257-260,(egs on pp 235,236,239,245,249,259,260),26
        types of, 73
Media specialists: 21,250,251-252
Misconceptions: 129,206

Model answers: 322
Models: 238-240
Monitoring, continuous: 78,350-356,359
Montage: 191,192
Multiple-choice questions: 97,122,308,311,318,331

National Extension College: 87
Non-examples: 124,141-142,144,148,149,364
Numbering of paragraphs: 172,284

On-site self-instruction: 10-12,237,245,252-253,266,269,271
        357-359
Objectives: 11,15-16,39,43-47,52,74,75,80,93,115,128,129,139,
        166-167,168,178,211,220,234238,257,305,311,317,332,348,
        336,337,364
    course v lesson, 47,304,314
    types of, 46,
    value of, 46-47,
    writing, 45,
Objective tests: 306,307-310,311,314,331
Offset litho printing: 280,281
Olivetti: 201
Open learning: 9,10,86
Open University: 9,15,20,87,91,92-118,145,158,160,166,169,177,
        190,192,194,204,235,236,237,238,239,242,246,248,249,253,
        254,259,260,261,262,352
Open Tech Unit: 87
Overloading: 58-59,202,203,227
Overviews: 168

Packaging of lessons: 275-278
Page format: 283,366-367
Page size: 282-283
Paper-and-pencil exercises: 306-312
    objective tests, 306,307-310,311
    own answer tests, 306-307,311
Paragraph length: 227-228
Patterned prose: 182
Personal interaction: 72,120,270-272,312
Personal pronouns: 207-208
Photocopying: 279,291,365,374
Photographs: 11,110,189,194,246,280,288,371
Pictorial approach: 181
Pictures: 74,81,111,114,115,129,143,152,181-206,286,368,370
    functions of, 190-197
    using, 198-206,240,247,247,251,287,288,364
    still v moving, 101,240,253-255
Place-to-place sequence: 62
Plain writing: 211-229,231-232,364
Pope, A.: 213
Portrait format: 111,283,284
Post-tests: 176,177,178
Practical work: 72,84,107,122,234-241,246,258,259,266,268,271,
        312,313,322
Practice: 138,147-148,151
Pre-requisites: 36,80,140,141,363

Pre-tests: 167,178
Principles: 54,124,125,129,138-148
Print: 72,80,233,247,248,257,262,284,288
Proctors: 12,271,321,352
Problems (faced by learners): 12,59,85,114,120,137,144,152,172,
        228,237,248,253,267,277,278,284,301,311,337,364
Problem-centred sequences: 64
Process (v product): 58,306,312,322
Production costs: 33,86,93,101,299
Production schedules: 26-30,79,361
Product (v process): 58,306,312,322
Profiles: 33
Projects: 59-60,70,241,268
Pronunciation: 221,244
Programmed learning: 14,15,86,130
Proofreading symbols: 374-377
Proofs, correcting: 373-378
Psychological v logical order: 66,142
Punctuation: 228-229

Quantification: 195-197
Questionnaires: 42,43,123,343,346-347,354-356
Questions: 95,97,103,107,121,122,124,125,127,128,130,132,133,
        148,161,169,174,197,200,201,247,251,258,271,308-312,
        314-320,332,348,349,352,354-356,364
Quoting: 156,159,369,372

Racism: 203-204
Radio: 242-243,257,258,371
Readability: 207-232
    measuring, 229-231
Reader-stoppers: 93,95,97,99,101,103,105,109,132,133,135,188,
        293,298
Reading speeds: 83-84
Recorded sound: 74,242-250,251,368,370
Records (data): 33,263,266
Relevance (to learner): 66,131,135,143,336,337
Reprographics: 275,278-281
Review material: 105,258,331,363
Rhetorical questions: 209-210
Roget's Thesaurus: 214
Rub-down letters/symbols: 187,189,295,296
RUL-EG: 149-151
Russell, B.: 193

Sample pages: 91-117,121,123,126,135,298
SAQs: 115,121,128,129,248,302
Schedules for production: 26-30,79,361
Schwartz, J: 153
Selection tests: 39
Self-assessment: 77,302,332,364
Self assessment questions: 115,121,128,129,337
Self-help groups: 267,270
Sentences: 223-228
    length of, 223-224,225,227,228,230,231,364

Sequence of content: 39,61-71,80,138
    backward chaining, 65-66
    causal, 63
    chronological, 62
    concentric circles, 63
    learner's choice, 17,70,114,252
    logical v psychological, 66
    place-to-place: 62
    problem-centred, 64
    spiral, 64
    structural logic, 63
    topic-by-topic, 62
Sexism: 131,203-204,364
Side-headings: 172,284,367
Signposts:
    verbal, 173-174
    visual (graphic), 174-175,286
Simplification: 195,202,203,223-228,337
Simulation: 263,264
Situational exercises/tests: 312-314,332
Skills: 46,76,80,167,233,314
Source material: 244-245,256
Specification (for lesson): 25,78
Specimens: 74,143,182
Spiral sequence: 64
Spray diagrams: 50,128
Statement networks: 54
Stencil duplicating: 279-280
Stolurow, L.M.: 264
Stoppers: 93,95,97,99,101,103,105,109,132,133,135,188,293,298
Storyline: 61,251
Strip cartoon: 112-113,191,240,254
Strong v weak verbs: 218-220
Structural logic: 63
Structure (of lessons): 137-161,163-179,363
Study guides: 26,90,131,173,337
Study time: 80,83,84,131,173,250,261,314,337,365
Style of writing: 95,103,109,114,155-156,207-232,248
Subject-matter experts/specialists: 20,28,38,78,159,335,336
Summaries: 148,175-176,258,363
Summative assessment: 303

Tables: 185,187,197,203,204,228
Teaching points: 67-70,138,209,247
Teaching point outlines: 68-71,127,137-138
Telephone, use of: 266,326,354
Television: 72,250,257,258,260,371
Testing: 148,262,263,301-332,337,339
Textbooks: 66,82,86,87,93,207,223,333
Titles: 79,114,164
Topic-by-topic sequence: 62
Topics: 62,64,67,170,178
    v teaching points, 68-69
Transformers: 21,127

Tutorial-in-print: 82,91,119,120,127,150,151,179,245,247,251,
    257,297
Tutoring: 11,12,19,32,60,72,82,119,123,130,132,155,176,207,237,
        246,262,265,266,267,268,269-270,271,302,304,314,322,
        326-331
Tutor notes: 269,323,324,
Typefaces: 132,133,154,172,289-291,295,296,366
Typing: 275,289,291,363,365-367,373,374,378
Typography: 101,103,111,179,221,289-298

Underlining: 164,179,221,229.291

Variety: 75,97,118,132,152-161,276
Verbal signposts: 173-174
Verbs: 218-220
Visual signposts: 174-175,286
Video material: 86,101,122,128,250-257,258,370
        applications, 255-256
        interactive, 86,251,252,261
        presentation, 252-253
        production, 251-252
        television, 72,250,253,258
        types of, 250-251
        video segments, 251,253,257,258
Videotape, 240

Wainwright, A.: 291,292
Weak v strong verbs: 218-220
Weasel-words: 217
Wells, H.G.: 211
White, E.B.: 155
Woolfenden, P.J.: 56
Words: 212-223,226,364
Writing: 81-91,127,156,361-365
        practical tips, 361-363
        style, 95,103,109,114,155-156,207-232,248
        time needed, 85-86,361,362